Postcard History Series

Macon

in Vintage Postcards

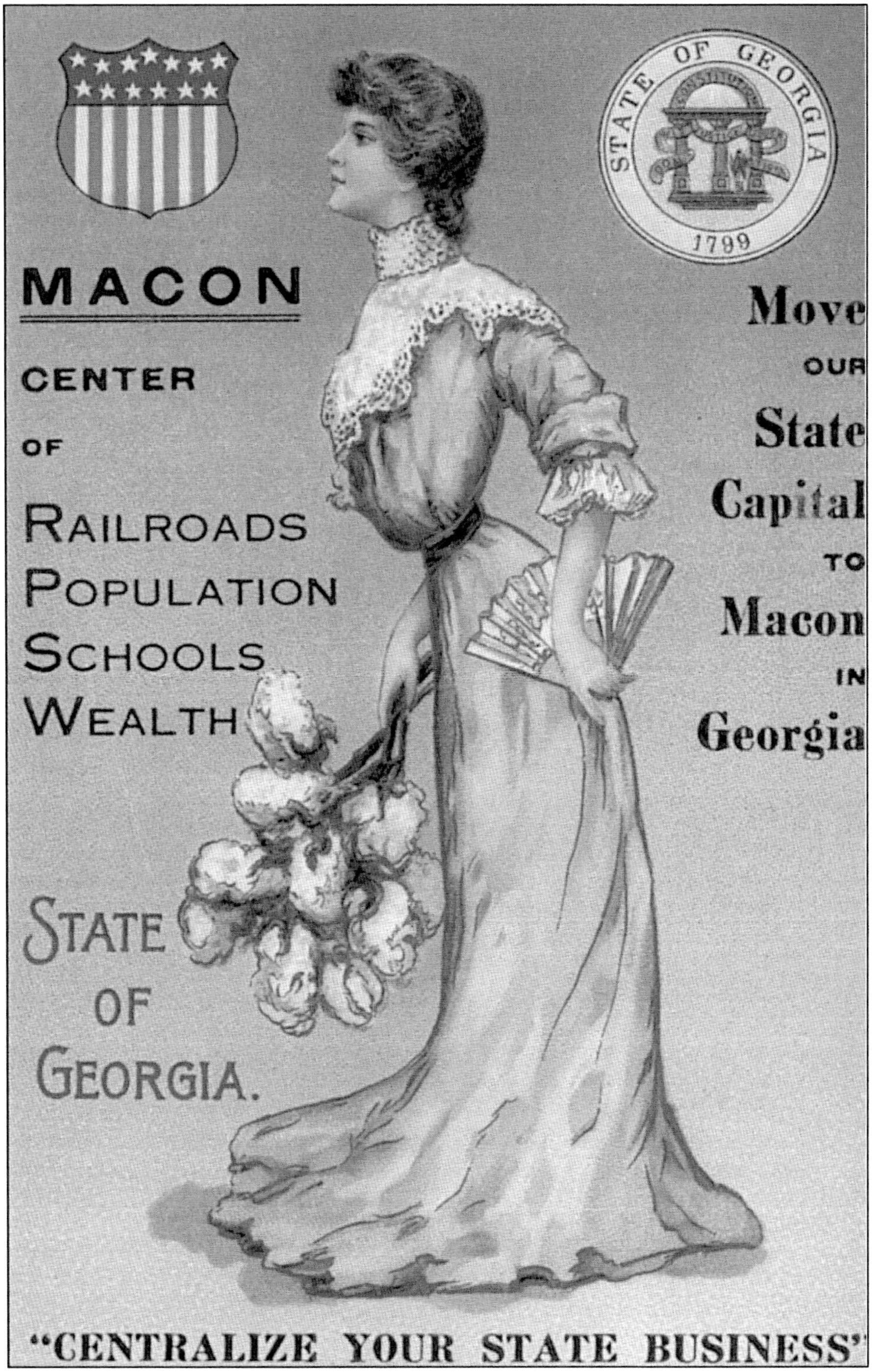

"Move our State Capital to Macon in Georgia," "Centralize Your State Business," "Macon, center of Railroads, Population, Schools, Wealth," This is a colorful embossed postcard showing a southern belle, holding a fan and a bundle of cotton, and the state shield and seal. The sender writes, "Macon is still teasing Atlanta about moving capitol." (Unidentified publisher, postmarked 1911, color.)

POSTCARD HISTORY SERIES

Macon

in Vintage Postcards

Vickie Leach Prater

ARCADIA
PUBLISHING

ISBN 978-0-7385-0200-7

Published by Arcadia Publishing
Charleston, South Carolina

Printed in the United States of America

For all general information contact Arcadia Publishing at:
Telephone 843-853-2070
Fax 843-853-0044
E-Mail sales@arcadiapublishing.com
For customer service and orders:
Toll-Free 1-888-313-2665

Visit us on the Internet at www.arcadiapublishing.com

Dedicated to my family,
George Prater, my beloved husband,
William Prater, my son and the light of my life,
Jack & Francine Leach, my loving parents.

Contents

Acknowledgments		6
Introduction		7
1.	Ocmulgee Indian Mounds	9
2.	Memories of the Confederacy	15
3.	Transportation	25
4.	Educational Opportunities	41
5.	Religious Diversity	57
6.	Good Times	63
7.	Southern Homes	77
8.	Wish You Were Here	89
9.	A Thriving Business Center	99
10.	Public Places	113
Index		127

Acknowledgments

First, I need to thank my family for bearing with me through the hours I have spent compiling the information within this book. Without their help, I never would have succeeded. George, my husband, provided the emotional support I needed and helped me with proof reading. I thank William, my son, who kept telling me I was doing "good," even when all I had around me was stacks of papers and postcards.

Next, I need to thank my father, Jack Leach, for introducing me to the world of postcard collecting and instilling in me a love of history. Together, we accumulated over 2,000 postcard images of Macon. Many hours were spent looking at the pictures and discussing the history of each. Jack knew of my desire to document the cards, make a checklist, and hopefully one day put together a book using the images. Thus, when I married and moved from Macon, Jack encouraged me to carry the collection with me to continue my work. Now 11 years later, the dream has come true thanks to our good friend and fellow collector, Gary Doster, who graciously submitted my name to Arcadia Publishing.

Acknowledgments would not be complete without a special thank you to my mother, Francine Leach. Francine has been an inspiration my entire life. She has never said never to any task at hand. When I first told her of my opportunity to write this book, she was the first to say, "You can do it."

Introduction

Over 40 million years ago, the first inhabitants of the Macon area were sea creatures. The fossilized-skeleton remains of a large whale were found in local kaolin pits. This is the only whale remains of its kind ever discovered in the U.S. It appears that even before man roamed these lands, Macon and its vicinity was destined to be unique.

The first human inhabitants of the area were Native Americans. The Earthlodge and Temple Mounds at the Ocmulgee National Monument appear to be among the earliest public buildings in North America. This is the site of the first settlements of the Creek Nation after their migration from west of the Mississippi. Here, they built their homes, hunted, farmed, and raised their families for many generations.

During his 1539 explorations through Georgia, De Soto came upon the Creek village situated upon the banks of a river at the head of a swamp with two Native-American mounds nearby. Historians have identified this place as the Ocmulgee Fields in Macon. Here, it is said, Franciscan friars, who accompanied the expedition, baptized two Native-American boys. Thus, Macon has the honor of being the first place in Georgia where a Christian sacrament was administered. Also during De Soto's stay at the Creek village, it is said that the explorers fired the first cannon in Georgia. The cannon was fired at a tree along the banks of the Ocmulgee River in a demonstration for the Creek Indians.

De Soto moved on, but the tales of the beauty of the area lived on. The famous botanist William Bartram, who came in 1774, mentioned in his *Travels* that he found "yet conspicuous very wonderful remains of the power and grandeur of the ancients in this part of America in the ruins of a capital Town and Settlement of vast artificial hills and terraces."

In 1804, Benjamin Hawkins, Native-American Agent, negotiated a treaty with the Creeks whereby they ceded all of their lands between the Oconee and Ocmulgee Rivers to the government. The Creeks reserved one strip of 100 acres, because Hopoie Micco, spokesman for the Creeks, insisted that "the tract of land at Oakmulgee old field is ours; we have reserved it to meet and trade with our white friends." The Creeks did allow the building of a trading post on the lands and, in 1806, Fort Hawkins was built. During the Creek War of 1812–14, Capt. Phil Cook was in command of the fort; on October 8, 1813, his daughter, Martha Pearson Cook, was the first white child born in the section. Martha Cook continued to live in Macon and was eventually the first president of the Ladies of the Memorial Society, founded after the Civil War.

After the War of 1812, the Native Americans were forced to give up all of their lands in the southern part of the state. Still not satisfied, President Monroe requested funds to purchase all claims of Native-American land in 1820. In the Treaty of Indian Springs in 1821, all land between the Ocmulgee and the Flint Rivers was ceded to the state. The fertility of the area became known when settlers came to live. On December 9, 1822, the lawmakers opened up the lands to the west of the Ocmulgee River for settlement. For a brief period, this outpost settlement was called Newtown. In 1823, the land was surveyed, and town plans were laid out. Trees were soon felled, and construction began. On December 8, 1823, the town was incorporated and commissioners appointed. The new county was named for William Wyatt Bibb, U.S. Senator from Georgia, while the county seat was called Macon for the North Carolina statesman Nathaniel Macon.

By 1827, residences, commercial buildings, a school, and a church were constructed. The *North Carolina* became the first steamboat to come up the river, reaching Macon in 1829. Industry and trade thrived as merchants used the river to transport cotton and other commodities to the seaport towns of Savannah and Darien. Wharves and warehouses lined the river's bank from First to Sixth Streets. It was not uncommon for Macon to receive and handle 100,000 bales of cotton. When river transportation became too slow, Macon looked to the railroads to improve trade transport. In 1833, Macon became the first city in the state to charter a railway, under the name of the Monroe Railroad and Banking Company. In 1838, construction began on the Monroe Railroad, and the first train in the state of Georgia, the *Ocmulgee*, arrived by boat from Savannah.

After the War Between the States, railroads became increasingly important to the Macon economy, and of more than 2,200 miles of track in Georgia, over 1,600 miles of it centered in Macon. By the turn of the century, Macon was proving herself to be the center of the state geographically and the center of transportation, trade, industry, agriculture, education, wealth, and society.

Visitors to Macon today will find the city beautiful and vibrate. The old southern houses were spared during the Civil War, and most have been lovingly taken care of. Downtown is being constantly renovated. J. Russell Kennedy wrote in 1898, "in after years the street parks of Macon will be its greatest blessing, as they are now its greatest luxury." Truer words were never spoken. Parks filled with gorgeous trees and flowers divide the wide streets of Macon. Thousands now flock to Macon each spring to see the awesome Cherry Blossom trees in bloom. At the Cherry Blossom Festival, the streets come alive with art shows, international food tasting events, street dances, and parades.

In the following pages are images that show Macon from the turn of the century until around 1940. Almost exclusively, these images are postcards; publication information is given in parentheses after the caption. Postcards during this era were a large part of social life, as people exchanged cards all over the world. Because of their popularity, postcards were carefully saved and stored for generations. These cards offer us a look at the people, events, and places of another time. We can, through reading the messages and looking at the images, get a feel for life as it was in Macon in the early 1900s.

One

Ocmulgee Indian Mounds

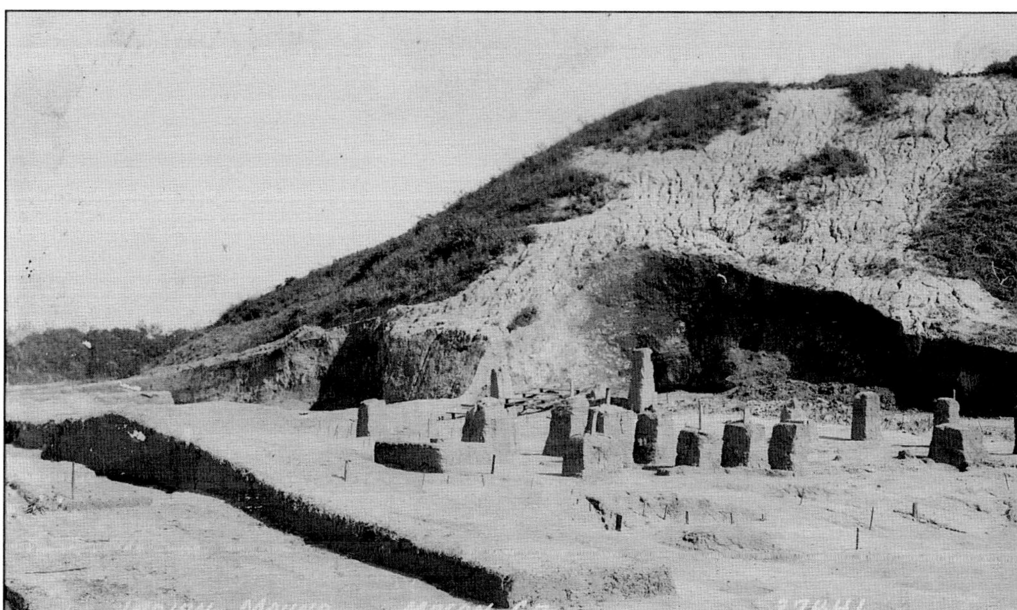

The Ocmulgee National Monument in Macon is the site of prehistoric Native-American Mounds. Workers, under the direction of Dr. A.R. Kelly, a representative of the Smithsonian Institute, have found hundreds of skeletons and thousands of artifacts. Excavation has uncovered the arts and customs of the Native Americans who lived here, built the mounds, and even farmed long before Columbus sailed for the this continent. Excavation of the mounds is shown in this real photograph postcard. (L.L. Cook, *c.* 1935, B/W.)

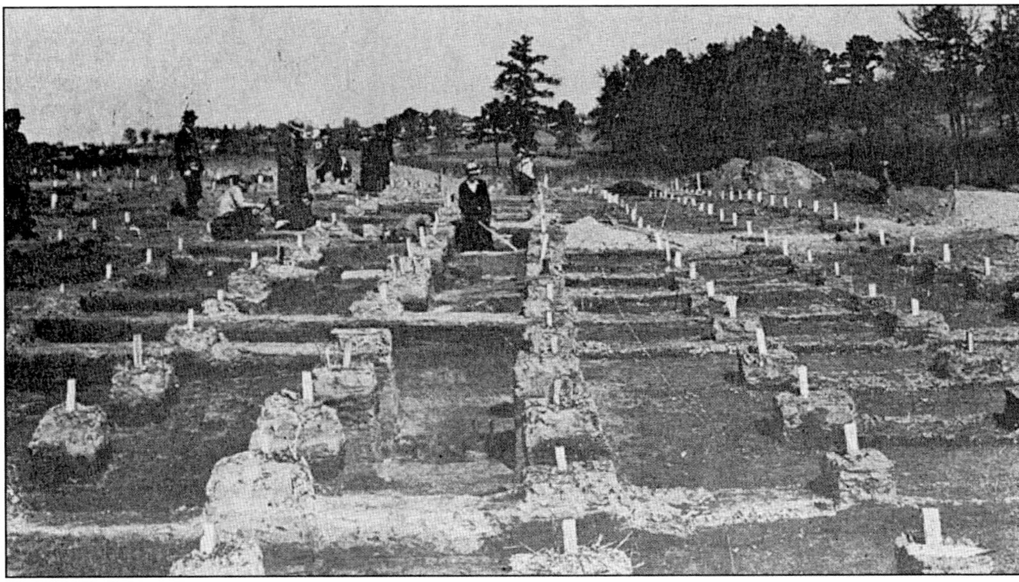

This is the site of the Round Winter Council House on top of Mound "D" on the Dunlap Estate. The council chamber has been reconstructed in its original form from evidence found during excavation. (Unidentified publisher, *c.* 1933, B/W.)

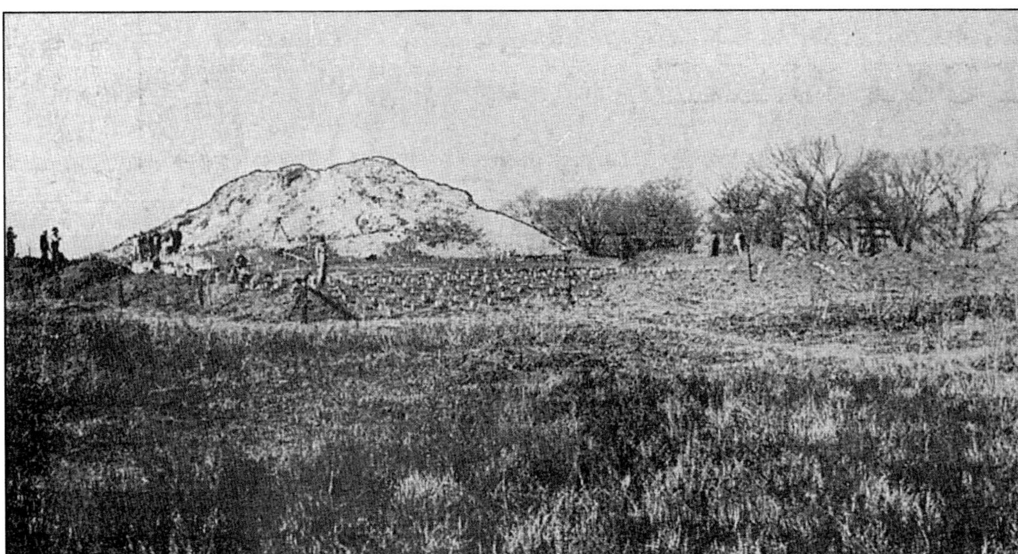

The western face of Mound "C" can be seen here before excavations commenced. It has been established that this was not merely one mound but actually five mounds built on top of one another and constructed in different stages during different occupations. Construction of this type is rare in Native-American architecture. Tombs were also found in each of the different mound levels, along with many artifacts. Found in the slopes of the outer, most recent mound layer were European artifacts that were obviously traded with early, European explorers. Thus, the mound provides a rich resource of information from prehistoric to historic eras. (Unidentified publisher, *c.* 1933, B/W.)

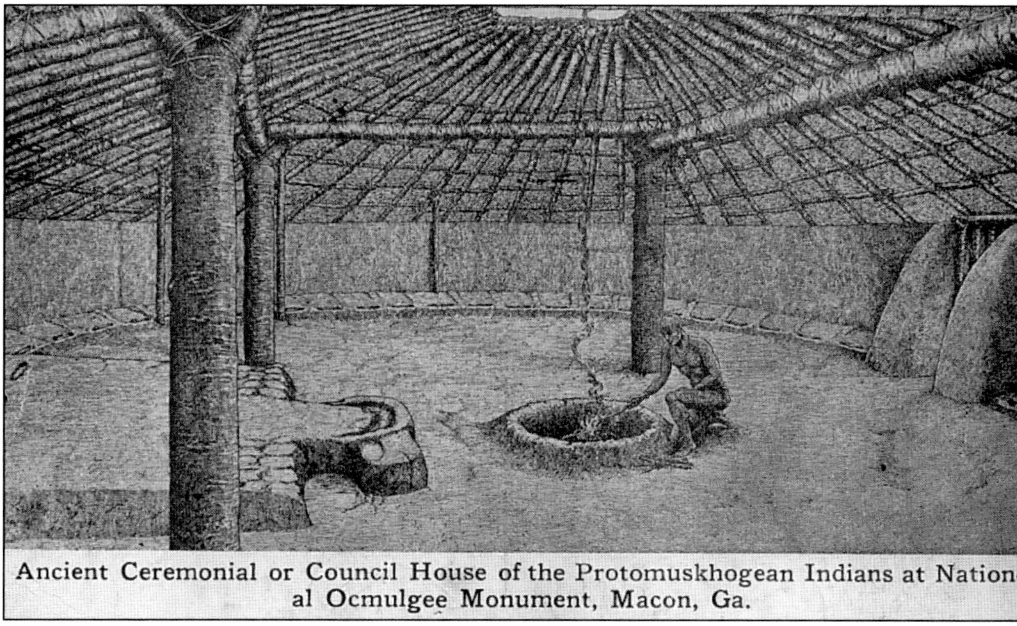

This artist rendition shows the ancient Ceremonial Earth Lodge or Council House of the Protomuskhogean Indians at Ocmulgee National Monument. The council chamber, unearthed in the Mound "D" area of the plateau, has been reconstructed in its original form from evidence discovered. In this chamber room, Native-American leaders held conferences or religious ceremonies. Around the wall, extending from both sides of the platform, are raised seats molded of yellow clay. In front of each seat is a dish-shaped depression, which was probably used during ceremonies. These seats and receptacles are unique in the U.S. (Unidentified publisher, postmarked 1937, B/W.)

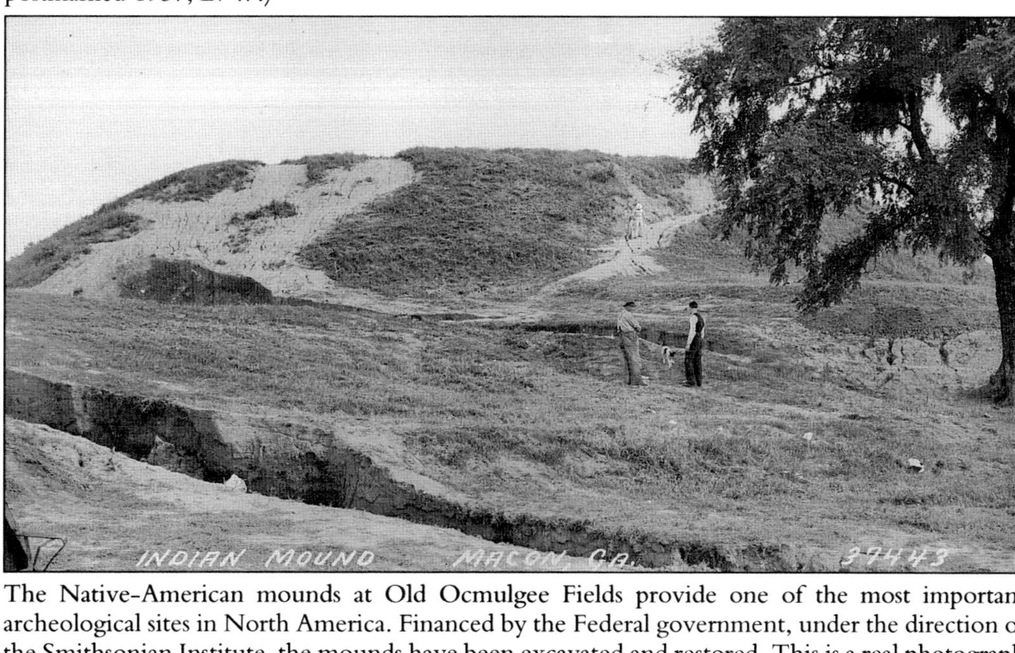

The Native-American mounds at Old Ocmulgee Fields provide one of the most important archeological sites in North America. Financed by the Federal government, under the direction of the Smithsonian Institute, the mounds have been excavated and restored. This is a real photograph card showing the Native-American Mounds. (EKC back, *c.* 1930, B/W.)

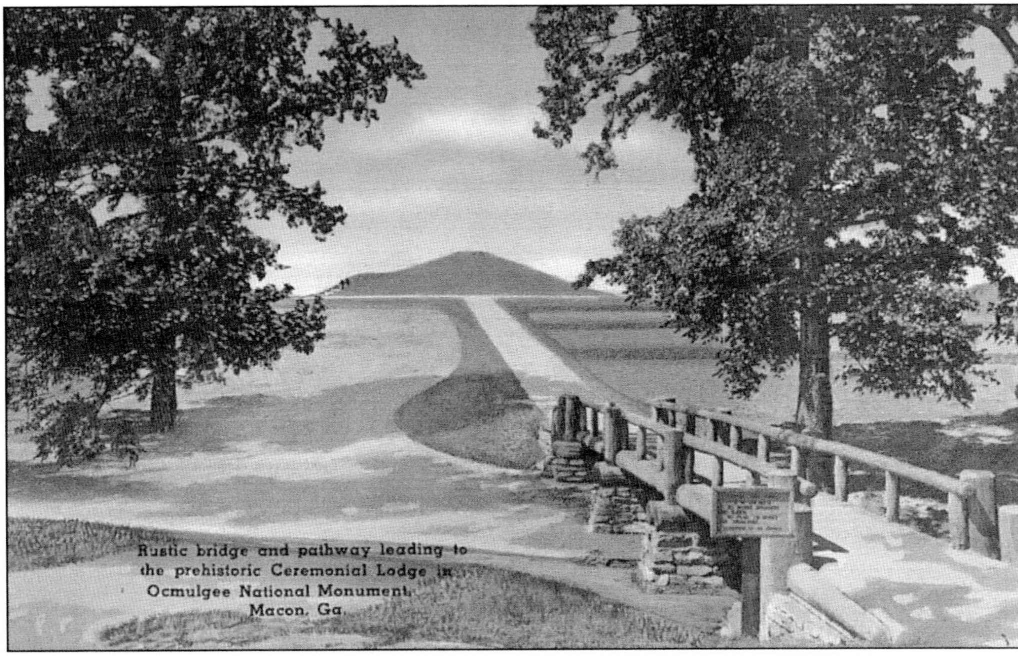

Shown here are a rustic bridge and pathway leading to the prehistoric Ceremonial Lodge in Ocmulgee National Monument. There are many such pathways around the Mounds and along the river. (Tichnor Quality Views #65389, *c.* 1940, color.)

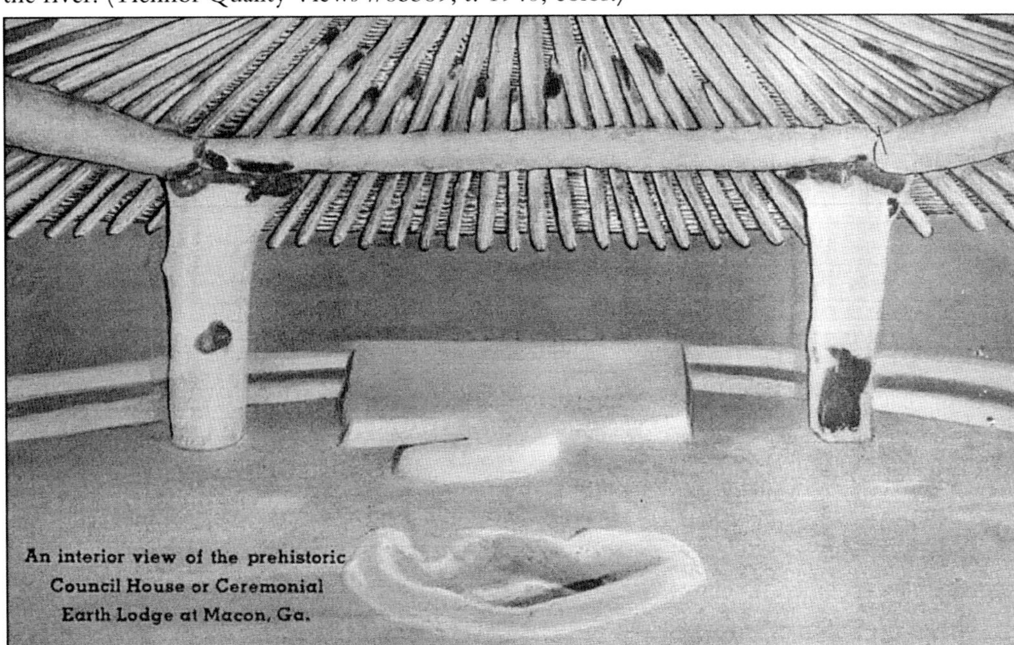

Here is an interior view of the prehistoric Council House or Ceremonial Earth Lodge. This structure has been restored to its original condition. The throne, made in the form of an eagle, is shown with a ceremonial fire pit in the foreground. Forty-eight seats encircle the building. The underground entrance faces east, and the structure is an almost exact circle. (Tichnor Quality Views #65392 , *c.* 1940, color.)

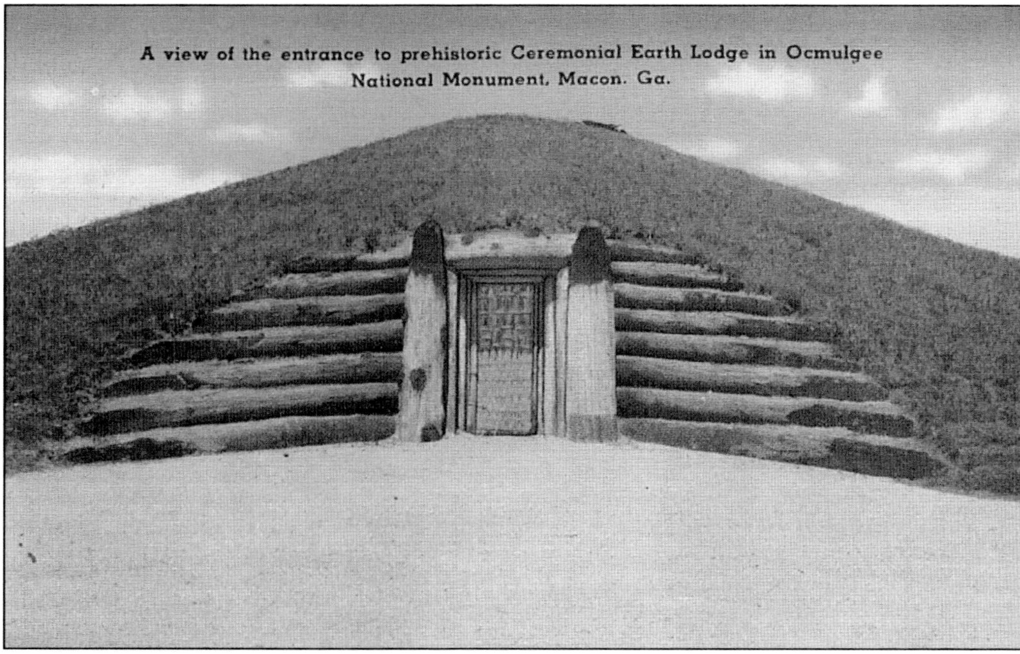

The entrance to the inner chamber of the prehistoric Ceremonial Earth Lodge leads through a narrow passageway, permitting single-file entry. The mound is a small, round, grass-covered hill of earth that is a perfect symmetrical pyramid except for the shoulder projection, housing the entrance. (Tichnor Quality Views #65393, *c.* 1940, color.)

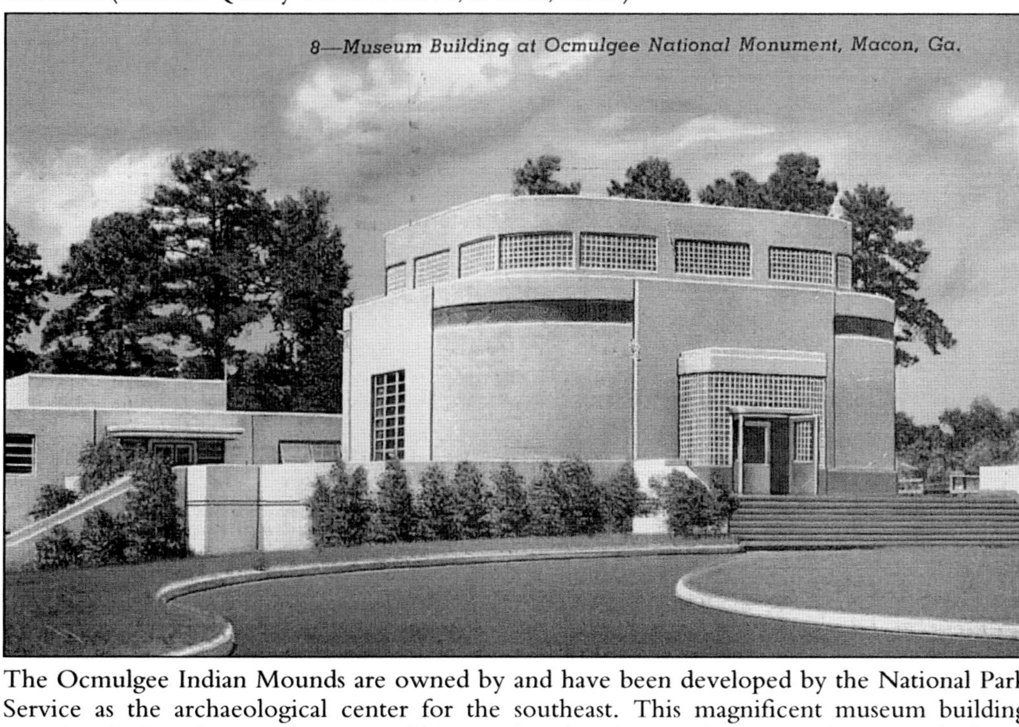

The Ocmulgee Indian Mounds are owned by and have been developed by the National Park Service as the archaeological center for the southeast. This magnificent museum building contains displays from excavations of historical and prehistorical interest. (Curt-Teich #8, *c.* 1940, color.)

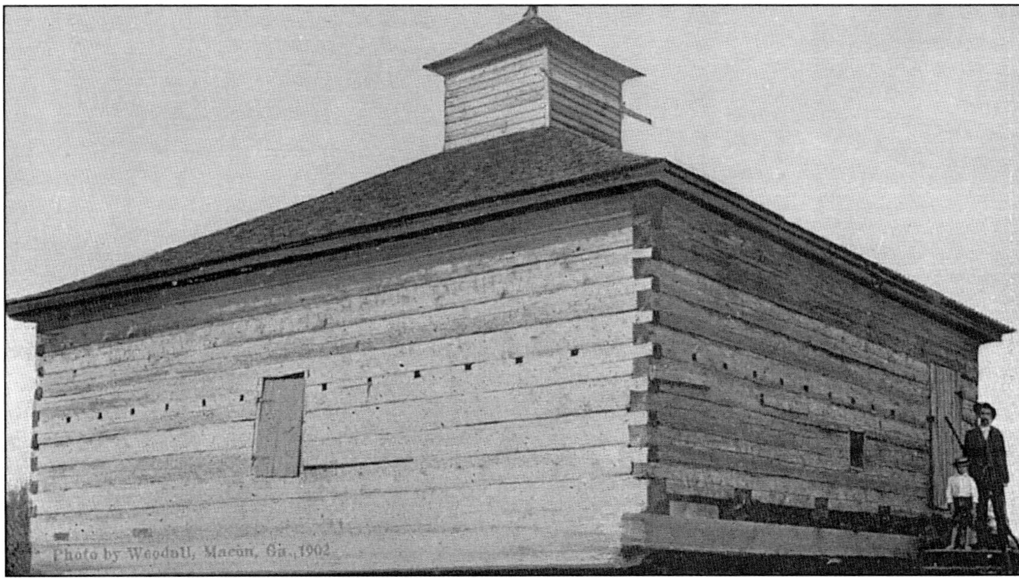

In 1804, Benjamin Hawkins, a Native-American agent, negotiated a treaty with the Creek Indians for all of their lands between the Oconee and Ocmulgee Rivers, except for a strip of 100 acres on the east side of the Ocmulgee, known as the Old Ocmulgee Fields. The government was permitted to build a trading post on this "reserved" land. In 1806, the trading and military post named Fort Hawkins was built. In 1812, Fort Hawkins was made a central point for the concentration of troops as the threat of war loomed close. A replica of Block House No. 2 was built and is shown in this photograph by Woodall in 1902. (Unidentified publisher #540-5, *c.* 1910, color.)

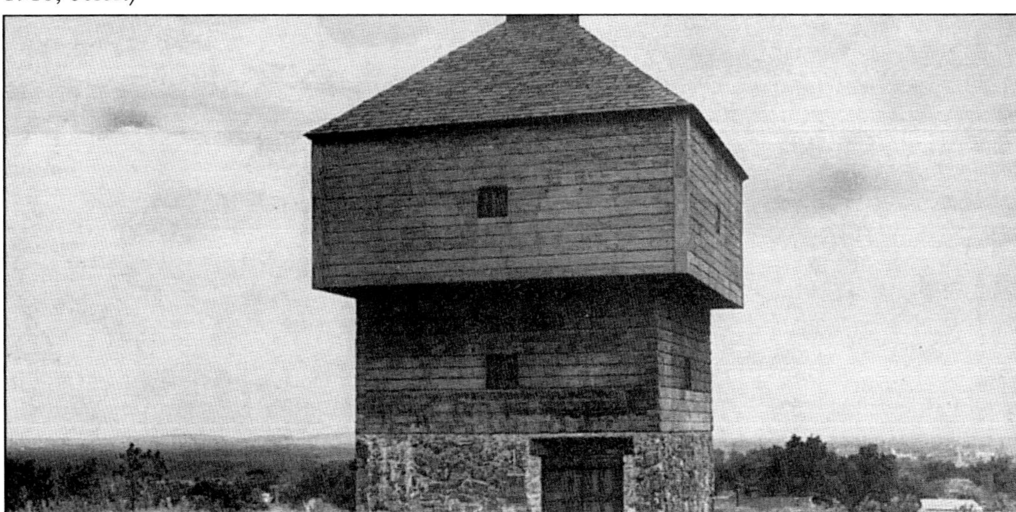

Macon's first celebration of Independence Day was held at Fort Hawkins on July 4, 1823. After the reading of the Declaration of Independence, the assembly ferried across the river to Macon, where a feast was laid. There, 13 toasts were drank in successive response to salutes from the "old four-pounder," the cannon that was left behind when Fort Hawkins was abandoned. This replica of the original fort was built through the efforts of the Nathaniel Macon Chapter of the Daughters of the American Revolution in 1939. This replica still stands today. (Graycraft Card Co. #M-236, *c.* 1940, B/W.)

Two

Memories of the Confederacy

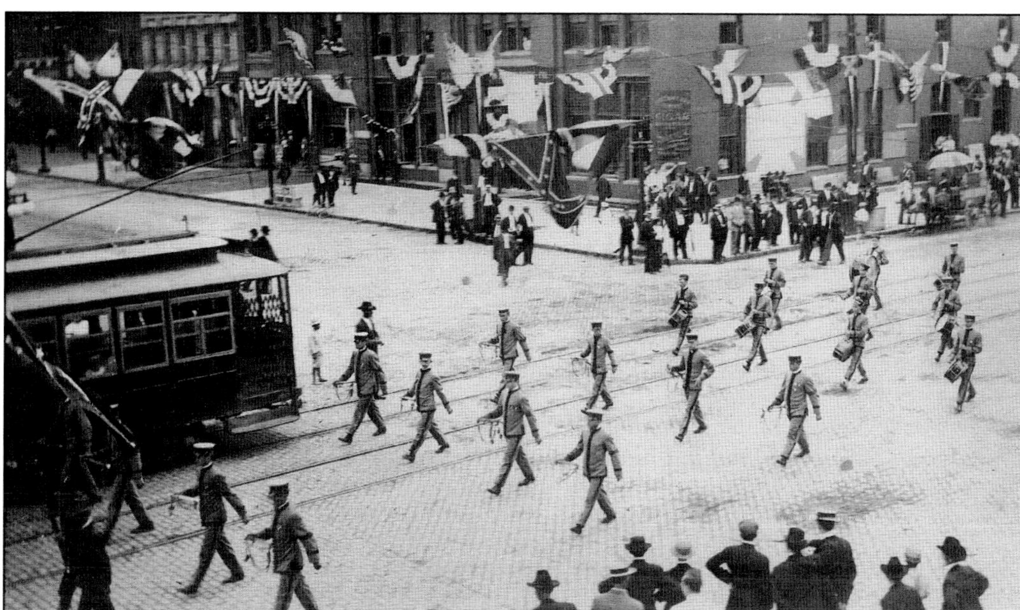

In 1887, Jefferson Davis came to Macon for the Georgia State Fair, which was to be held in conjunction with the Confederate Veterans Reunion. This reunion was to be Davis's last chance to review his troops. High atop Coleman Hill, Davis's troops watched as he fervently kissed the battle torn Confederate flag of his battery. Macon has since hosted many Confederate Veteran Reunions; the last was in 1912. In this picture, the Cadet Band leads the parade of Veterans during the 1912 Confederate Veterans Reunion. (Real photograph postcard, *c.* 1912, B/W.)

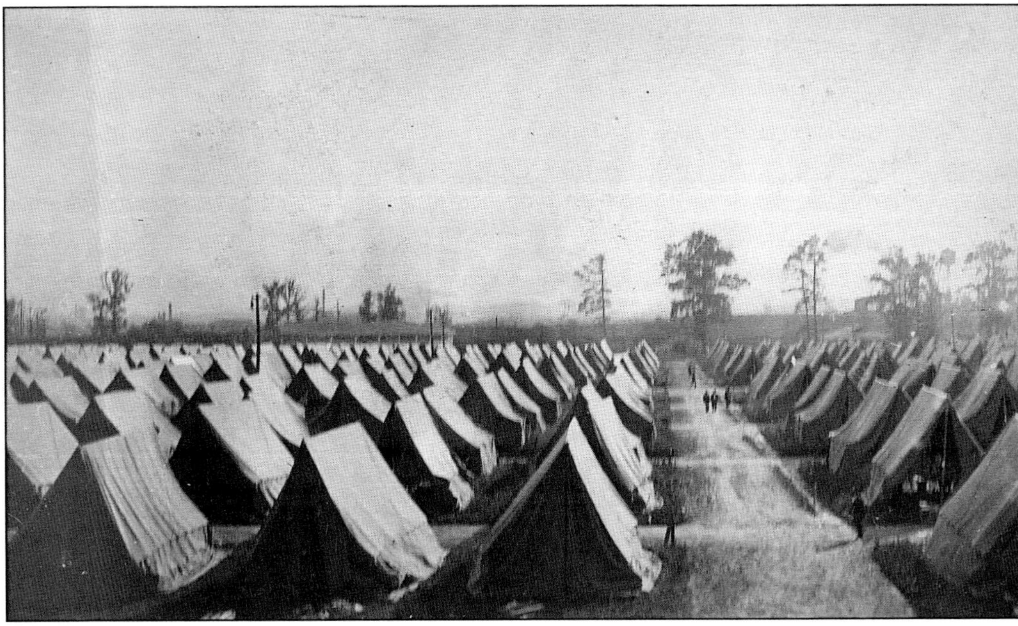

This Confederate Veteran's Tent City was located at Central City Park in 1912. The tent city was named the "John B. Gordon Camp." Confederate Brigadier General and Georgia Governor John Brown Gordon (1832–1905) was one of Georgia's dominant figures of the late nineteenth century. (Real photograph, *c.* 1912, B/W.)

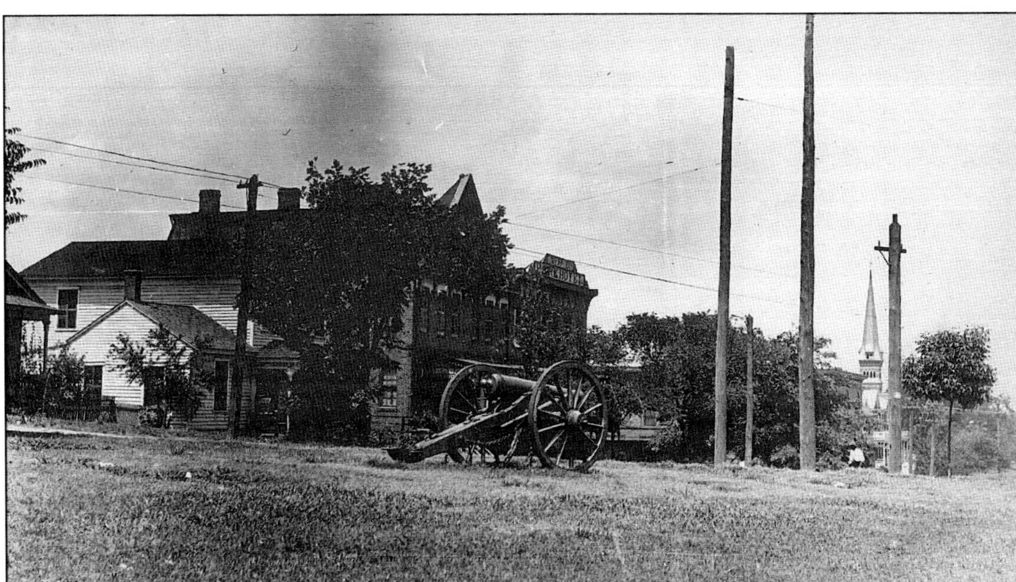

The Confederate cannon was once located in front of the Park Hotel. A few years after this picture was taken, the cannon was removed, the park area was planted with flowers, and the YMCA building was built. (Real photograph, *c.* 1902, B/W.)

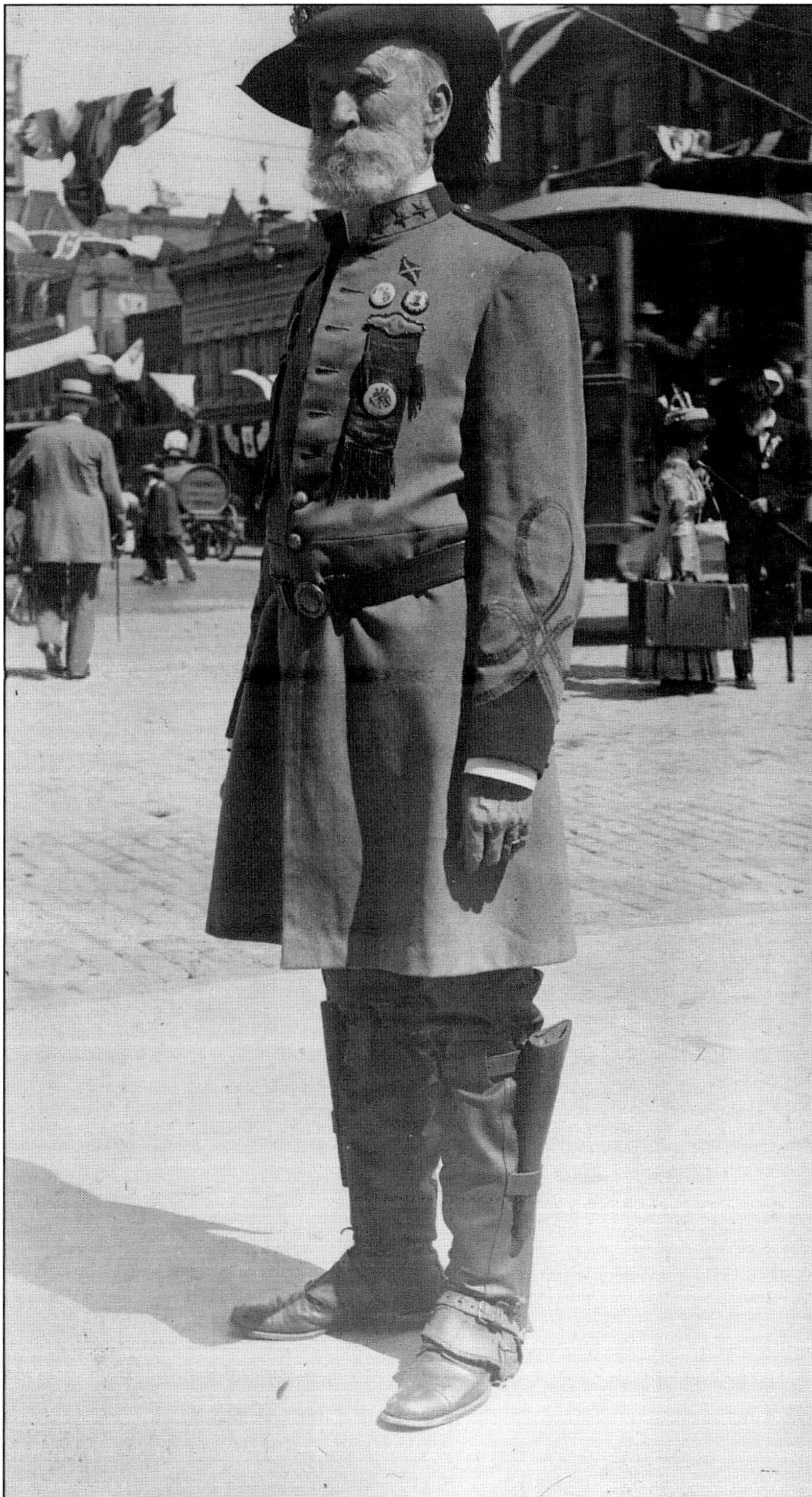

Here, Warren A. Moseley portrays "Johnnie Reb" at the Confederate Veterans Reunion in Macon in 1912. Moseley served in Company H, 4th Regiment of the Georgia Volunteer Infantry. Moseley was a member of the Macon Police Department for over 30 years. (Real photograph, *c.* 1912, B/W.)

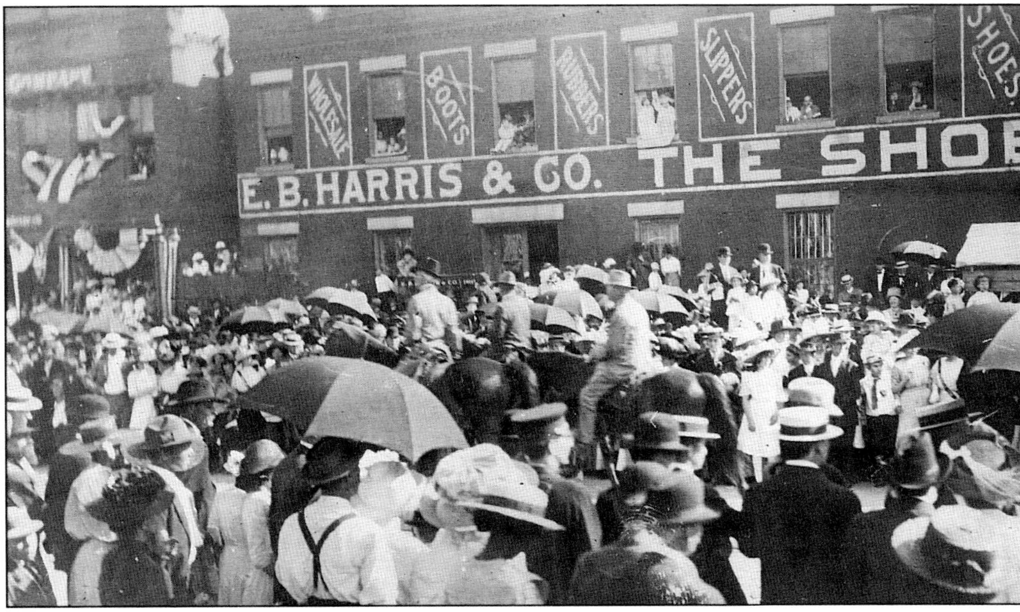

This crowd gathered on Cherry Street in front of the Harris & Co. Shoe Store in order to view the 1912 Parade of Veterans. Many in the crowd are using umbrellas to shade them from the hot Georgia sun. (real photograph postcard, *c.* 1912, B/W.)

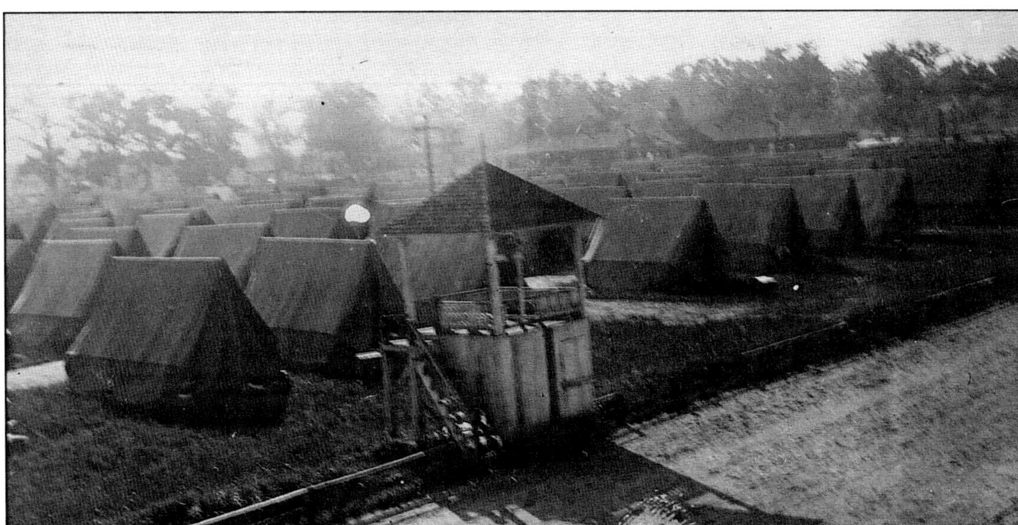

This view of the Confederate Veteran's Tent City shows the judge's review stand on the racetrack in Central City Park. This location for the camp was perfect as the ground was level, in close proximity to the city, and located near the railroad tracks. (Real photograph, *c.* 1912, B/W.)

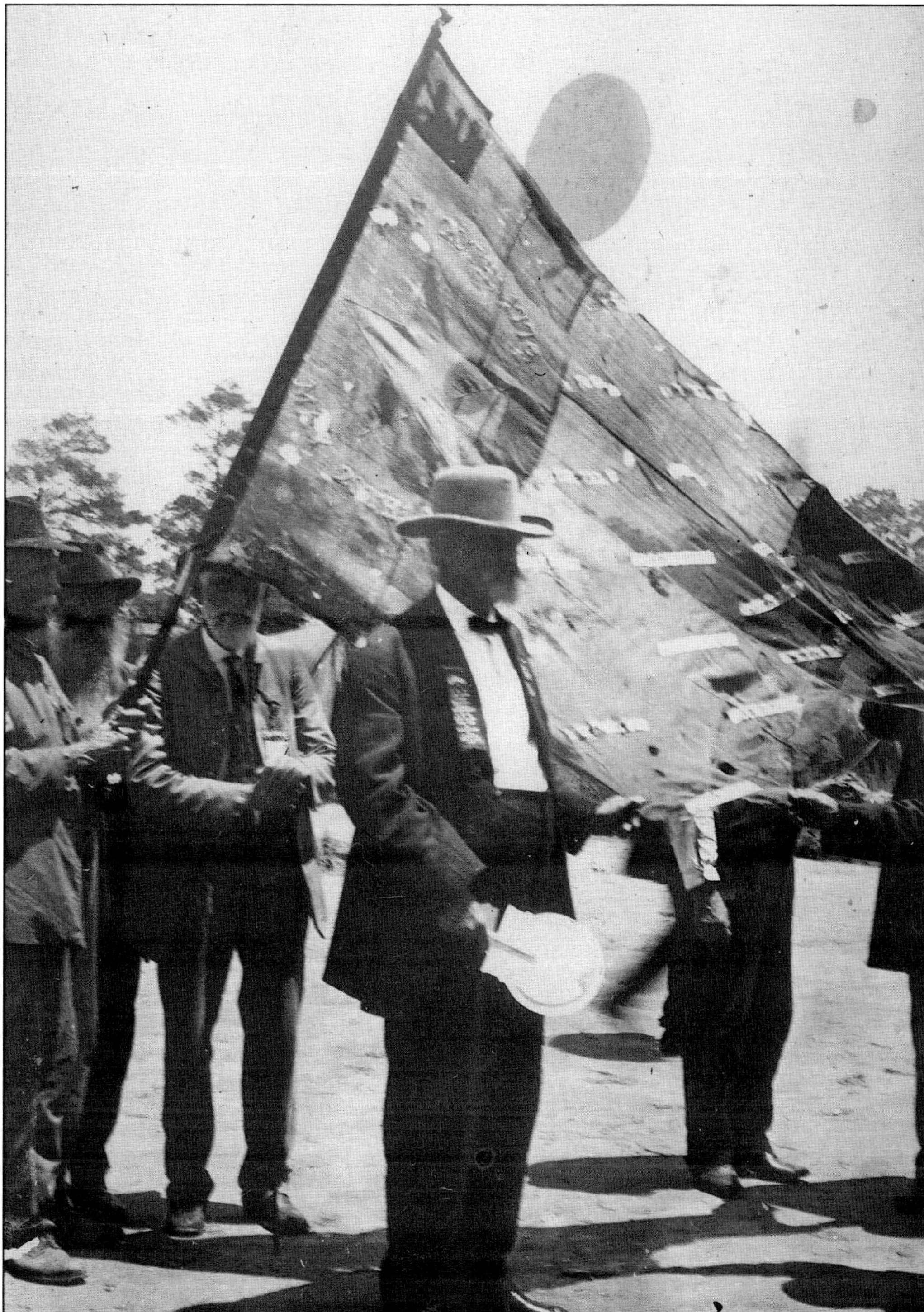

This battle-scarred flag was carefully carried by Confederate veterans during their reunion in 1912. (Real photograph, *c.* 1912, B/W.)

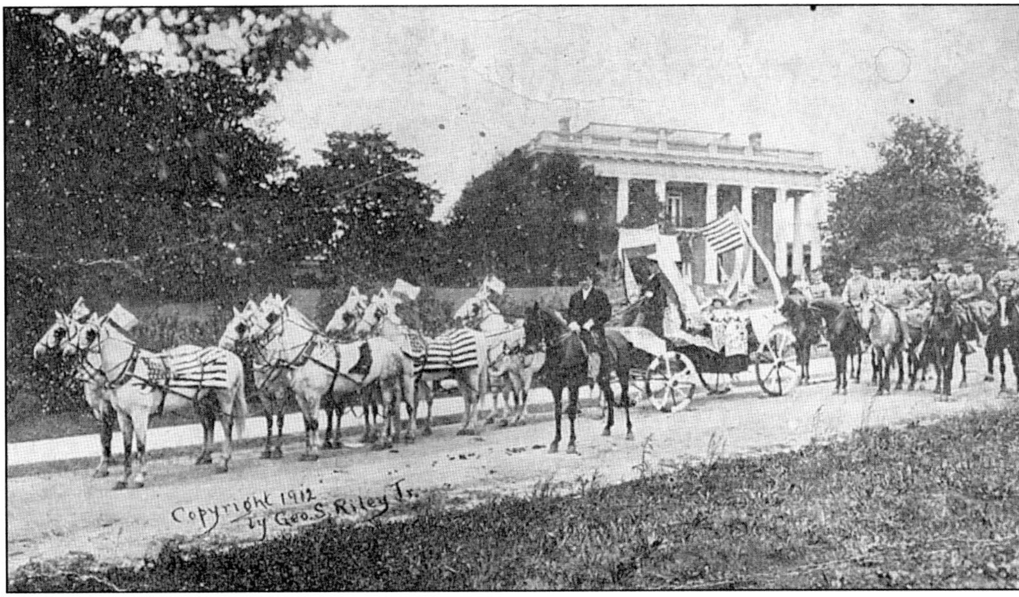

The Queen and her maids of the Confederate Veteran's Reunion, May 7–9, 1912, are shown here in a full view picture of the eight-horse team in front of the Johnson residence. Even the horses were decorated with flags for the parade (Geo. S. Riley Jr., postmarked 1912, B/W.)

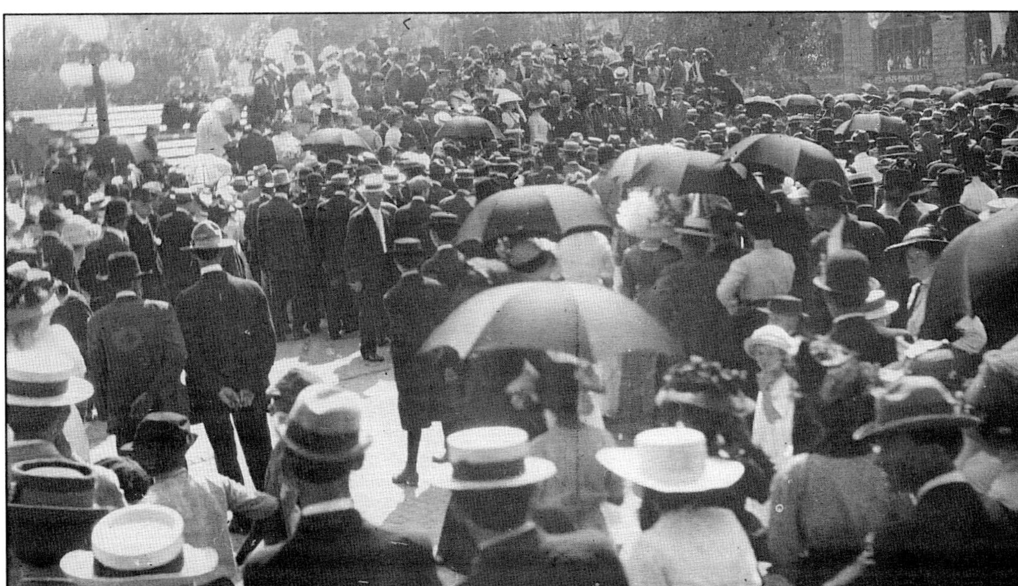

Over $70,000 was raised to spend on entertaining the veterans, and a record number if 46,000 people attended the 1912 event. Shown here is a large crowd gathered to watch the crowning of the queen of the reunion. (Real photograph, *c.* 1912, B/W.)

The Confederate Monument is located on Courthouse Square facing Mulberry and Second Streets. The marble statue of a Confederate private was sculpted in Italy. The soldier's hat is turned slightly to one side, the front pointing symbolically toward the south. The Ladies' Memorial Association erected the statue in 1879. On April 26, 1866, this organization sponsored Macon's first Confederate Memorial Day. Since the city was then under military rule, several Federal officers were present. (McEvoy Book & Stationary, *c.* 1905, B/W.)

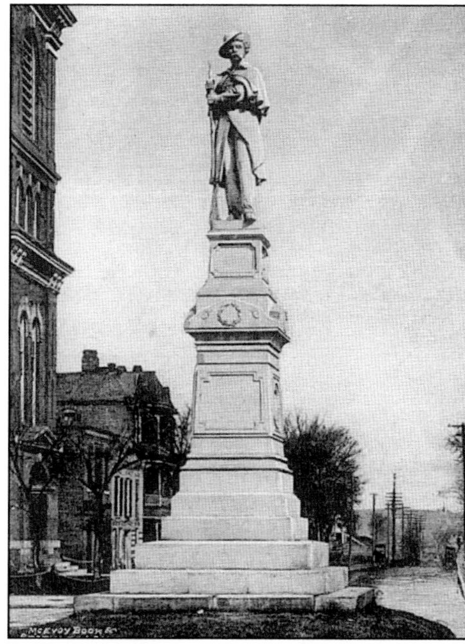

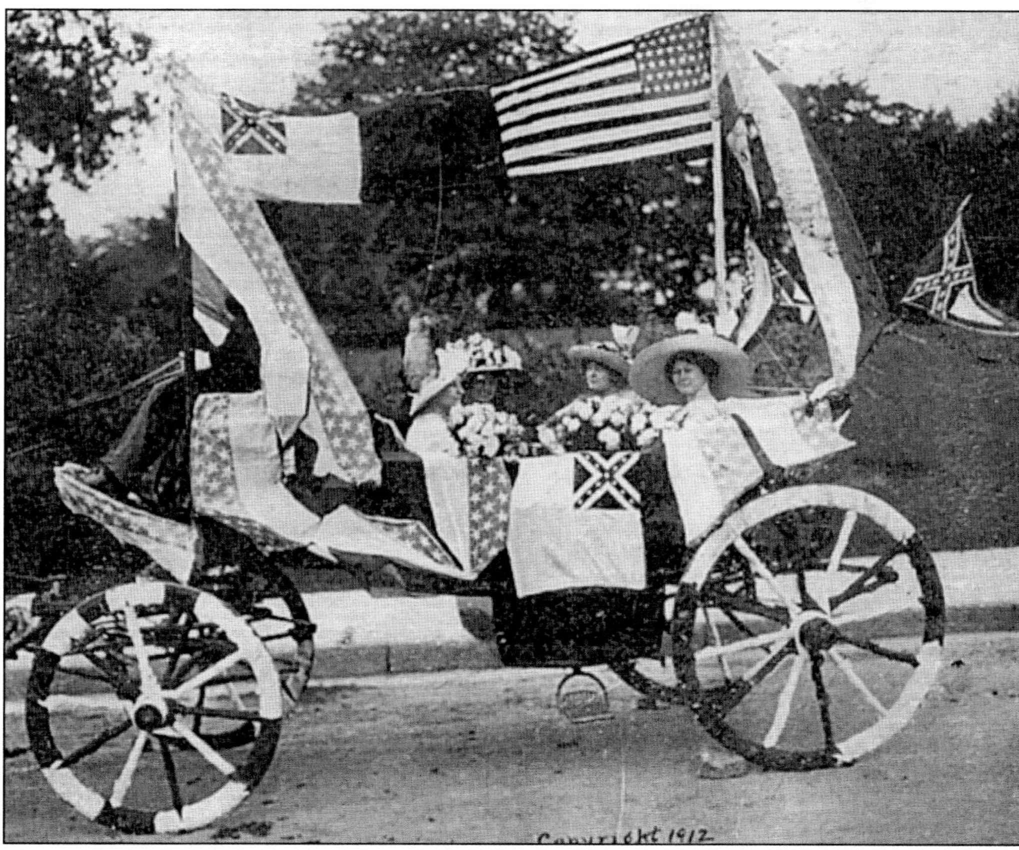

This 1912 close-up shows the patriotically decorated coach carrying the queen of the Confederate Veteran's Reunion and her maids . (Geo. S. Riley Jr., *c.* 1912, B/W.)

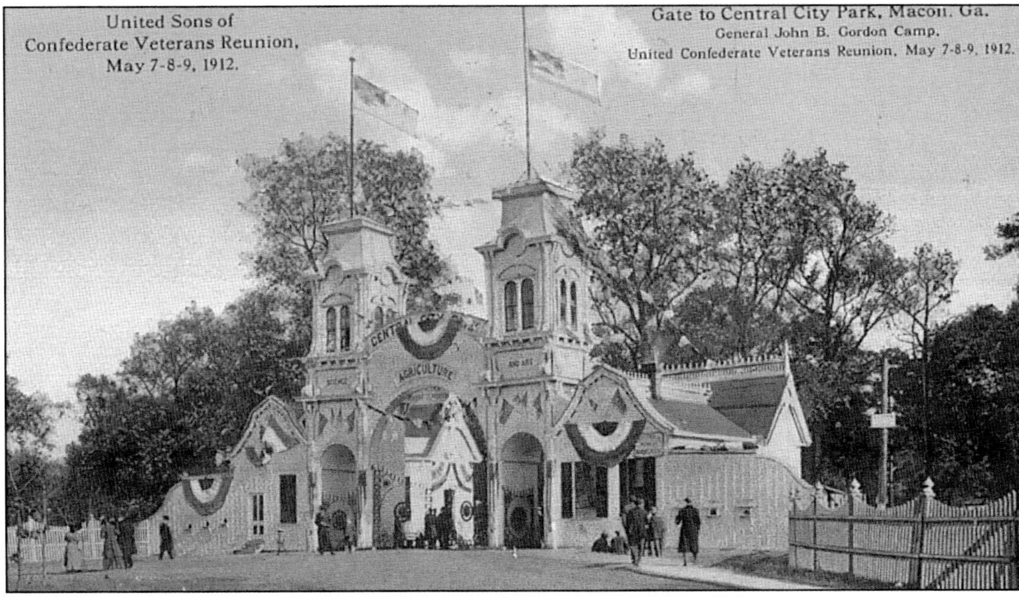

The gate to the Central City Park was decorated for the Confederate Veteran's Reunion, *c.* 1912. During the Civil War, a Federal prison was located in the park, and many Federalist prisoners died there. (Power's Curiosity #A-27772, postmarked 1912, color.)

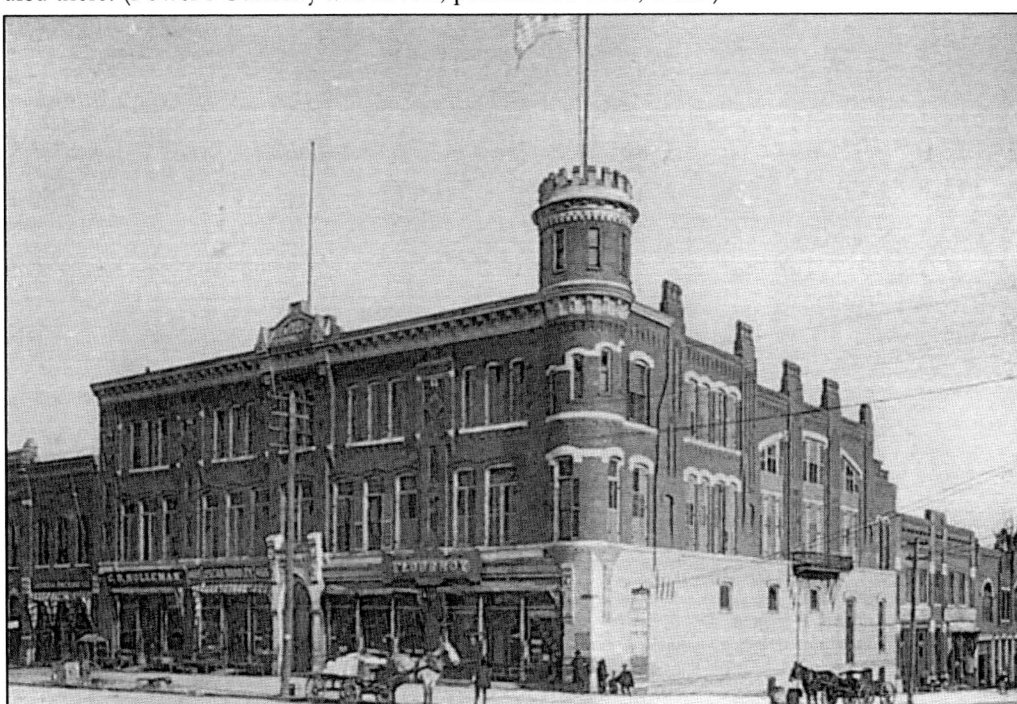

The Volunteer's Armory Building was built in 1884. The carved heads on either side of the center door depict Robert E. Lee and Stonewall Jackson. The bottom floors of the building were used as storefronts while the upper floors were used for social events. This outstanding building is still standing on the corner of First and Poplar Streets. (McEvoy Book & Stationary, *c.* 1907, B/W.)

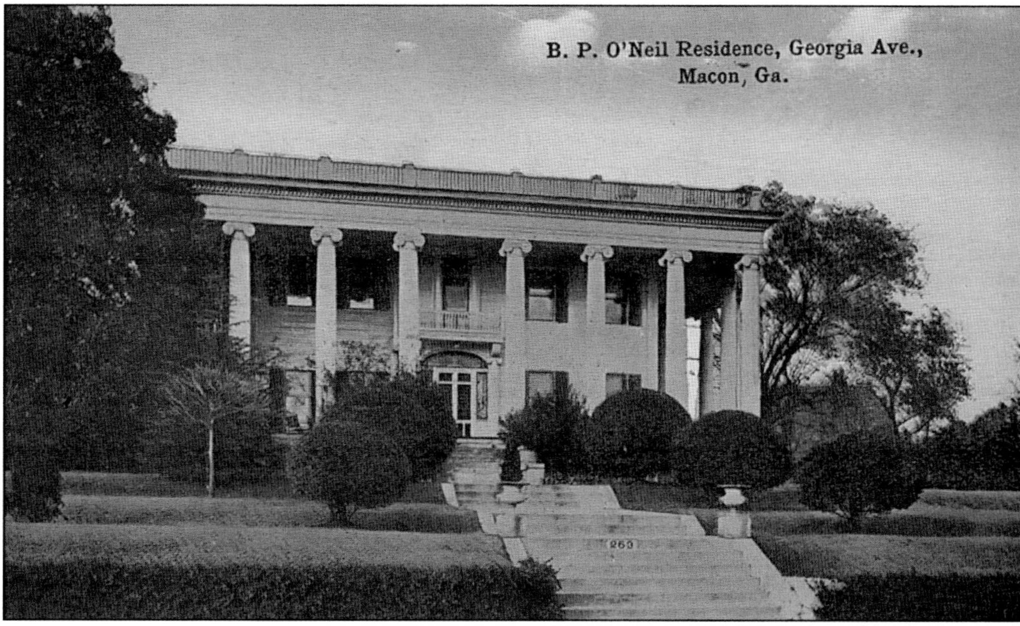

Built in 1836 and located on Bond Street, the Cowles-Bond-O'Neil residence is a Greek Revival-style dwelling. It is said that General Wilson used this house as his living quarters after the capture of Macon during the Civil War. Once known as "Overlook," the house, located on Coleman Hill, became Stratford Academy in 1960. It was later purchased by Mercer University and given to the city. It is now known as the Woodruff House. (Real photograph postcard, *c.* 1920, B/W.)

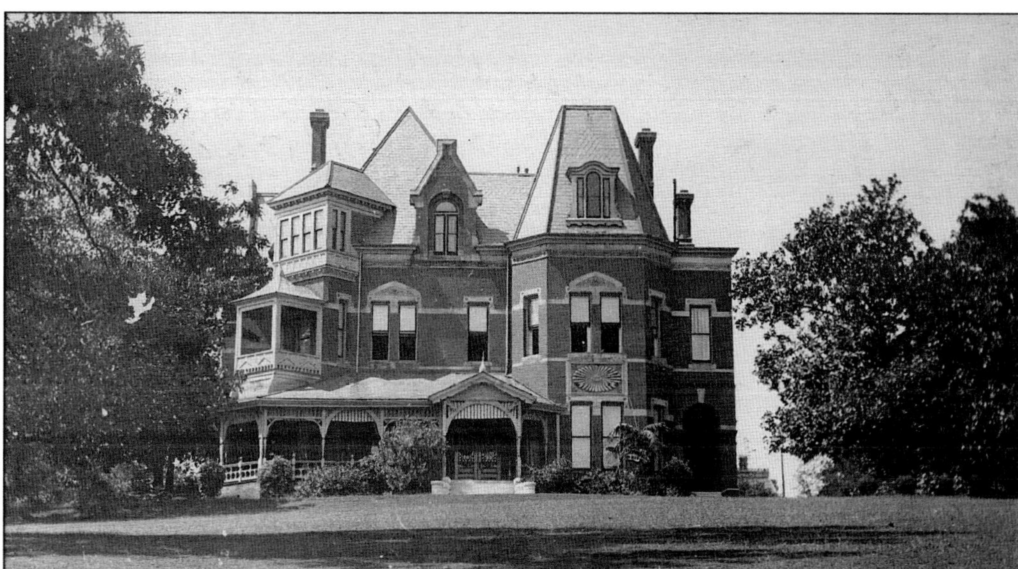

Jefferson Davis and his family stayed at this home of Mrs. J. Marsh Johnson in 1887, as Davis attended a Confederate Veteran's Reunion and the Georgia State Fair. The house was converted to the Mansion Hotel by Mr. Beall, who later sold it to the North American Insurance Company. It is now the home of the Mercer Law School. (Real photograph, *c.* 1902, B/W.)

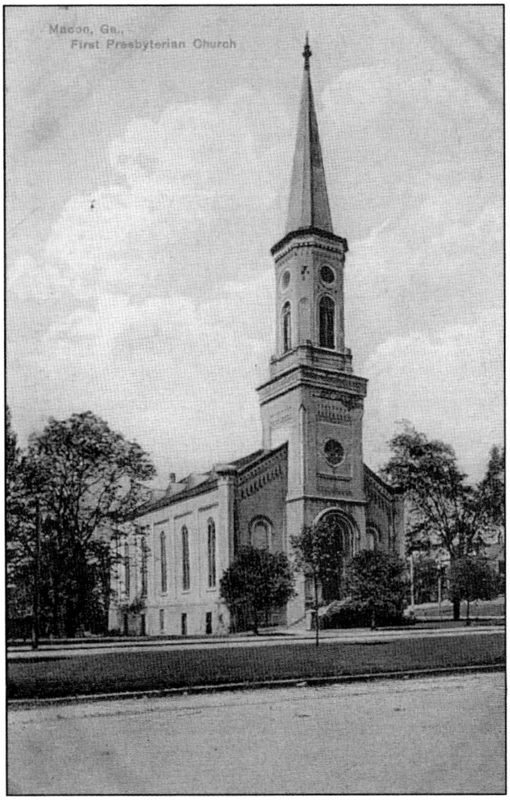

The First Presbyterian Church, located on the southeast corner of Mulberry and First Streets, is a brick building with a stucco finish scored to simulate blocks. The church has a 183-foot tower, an entrance with a deeply recessed arch, and carved double doors. In 1826, the church was organized by Rev. Benjamin Gildersleeve; the building was dedicated in 1858. During the Civil War, the church bell was saved from the arsenal because it was connected with the town clock. (Peacock Series #8714, *c.* 1910, hand tinted.)

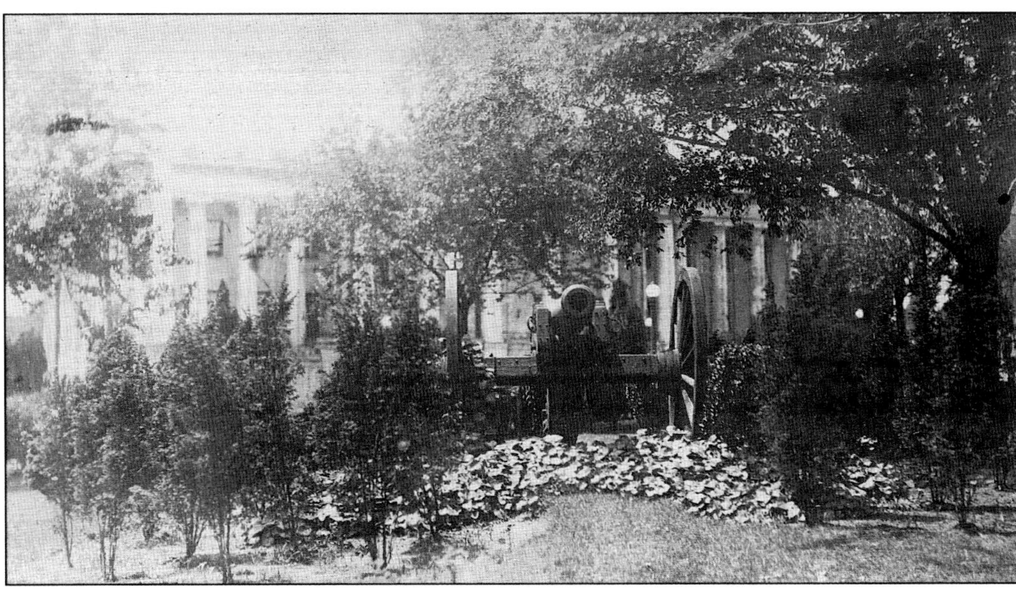

A cannon sits in the park foliage in front of the town's city hall. This building was purchased in 1860 by the city and was used as a hospital during the Civil War. (Real photograph, *c.* 1920, B/W.)

Three

TRANSPORTATION

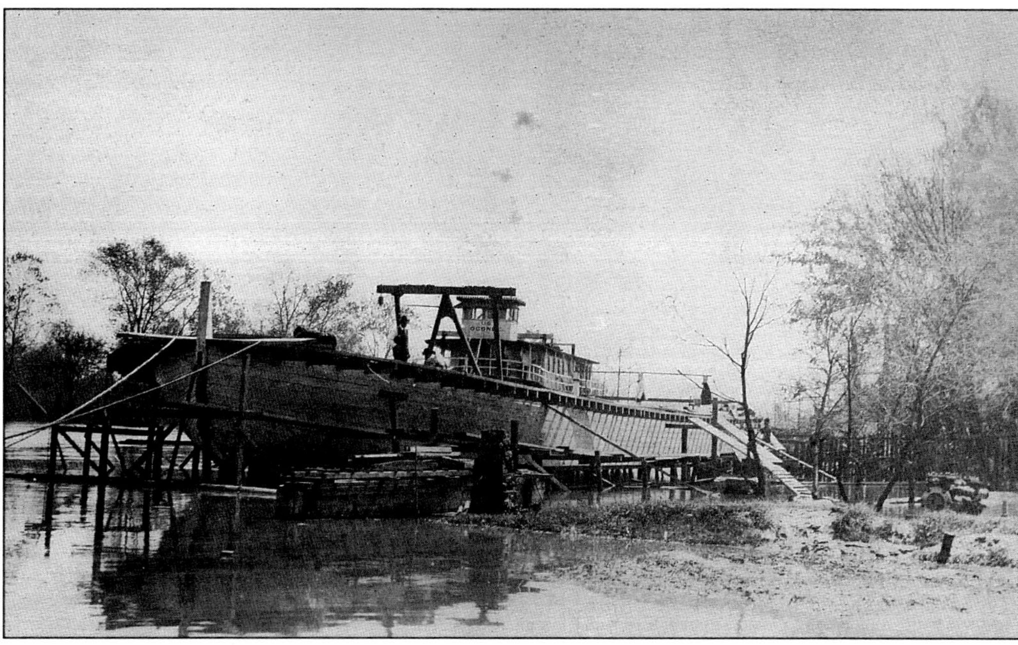

As early as the 16th century, the area had become a center of industry and trade for Native-American tribes. In 1829, the first steamboat reached Macon. By the early 19th century, white settlers used the Ocmulgee to transport cotton to the seaport towns of Savannah and Darien. Wharves and warehouses lined the river's bank from First to Sixth Streets. It was not uncommon for Macon to receive and handle 100,000 bales of cotton. A boat is being built for river transportation on the Ocmulgee River from Macon to Brunswick. (Real photograph postcard, *c.* 1905, B/W.)

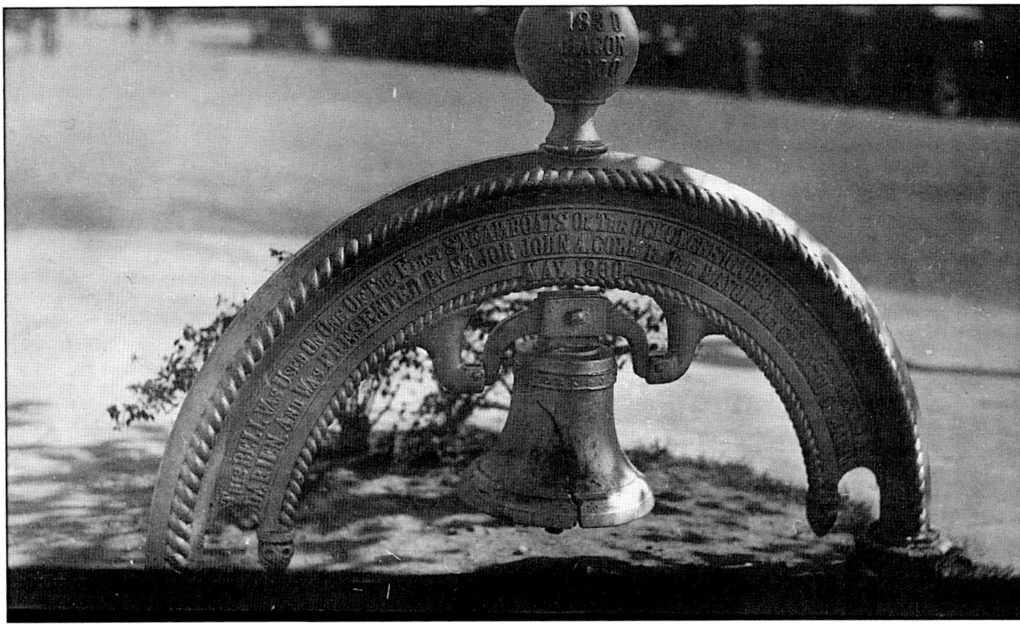

This riverboat bell was on the first boat to run from Macon to Darien in 1830. Maj. John A. Cobb presented it to the mayor of Macon in 1900. The bell sat for years in front of Commercial Bank Building before being moved to Central City Park. (Real photograph postcard, *c.* 1921, B/W.)

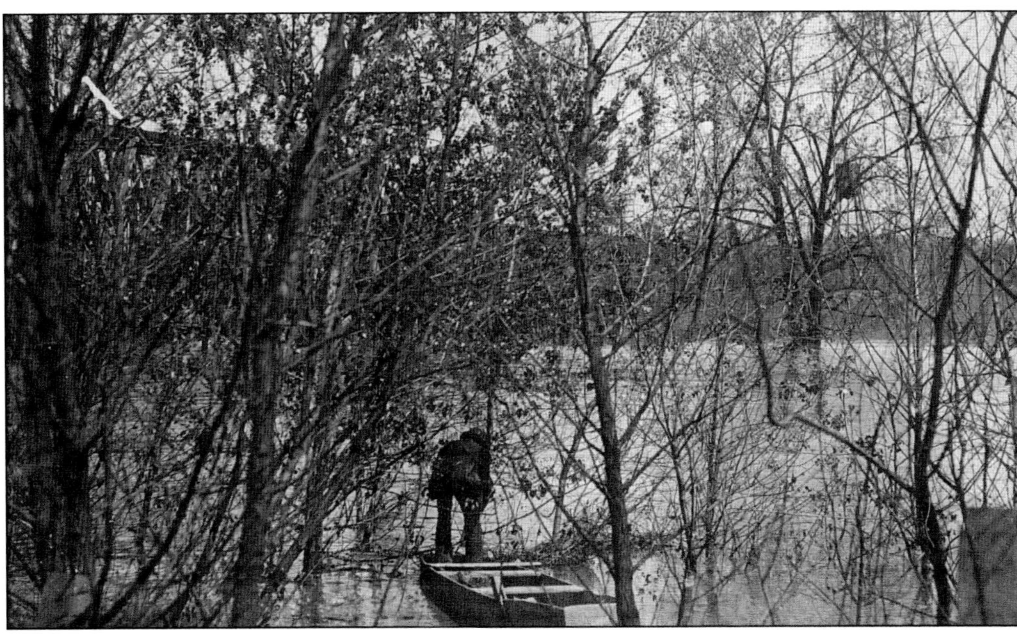

The Ocmulgee not only provided commercial transportation, but it was also used by fishermen as can be seen in this photograph of a man in a row boat on the banks of the river. (Real photograph, *c.* 1902, B/W.)

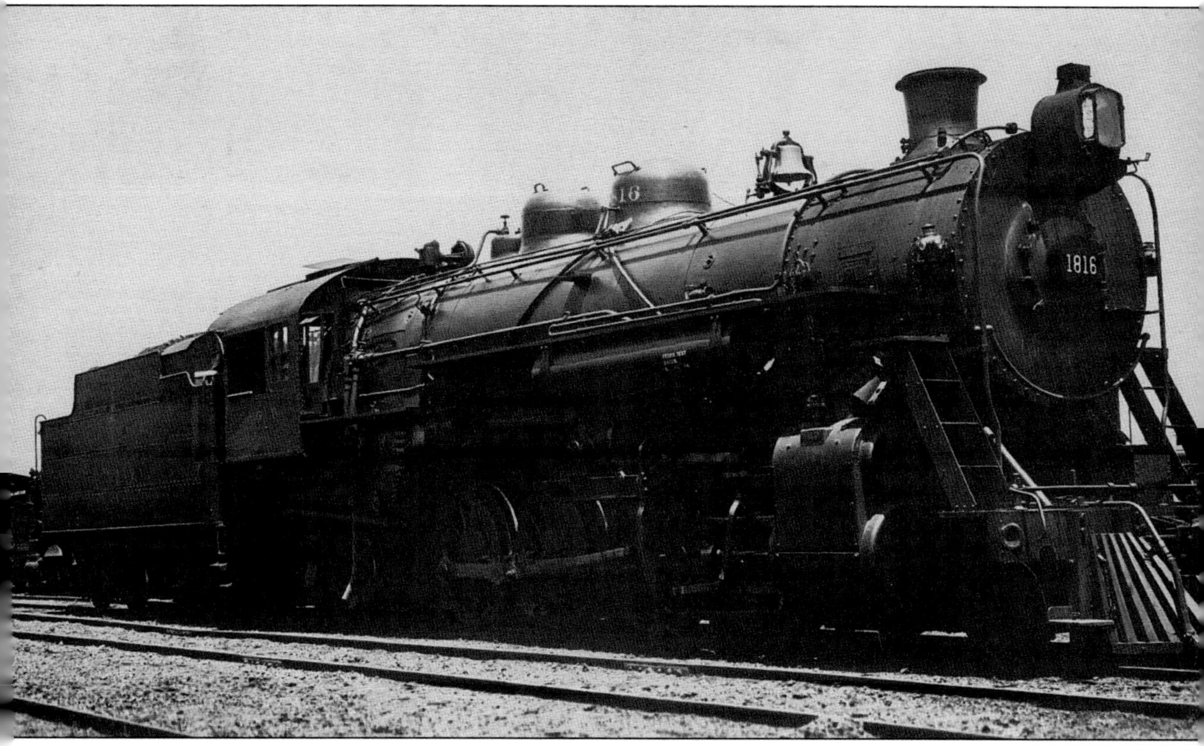

As trade increased, Macon looked to the railroads to improve trade transport. In 1838, construction began on the Monroe Railroad; in 1839, the first train of the Macon & Monroe Railroad made a trip to Forsyth, Georgia. In 1845, the railroad became the Macon and Western, and then, in 1872, it merged with the Central Railroad. By 1898, Macon was the center of eleven railroad lines: the Central to Savannah, Georgia; the Macon, Dublin, and Savannah to Savannah, Georgia; the Southern to Brunswick, Georgia; the Georgia Southern and Florida to Palatka, Florida; the Southwestern to Montgomery, Alabama; the Macon and Columbus th Columbus, Georgia; the Macon and Birmingham to LaGrange, Georgia; the Central to Chattanooga, Tennessee; the Southern to Atlanta, Georgia, Chattanooga, Tennessee, and Knoxville, Tennessee; the Central to Athens, Georgia; and the Georgia to Augusta, Georgia. Shown in the picture above, this powerful Central of Georgia Baldwin Engine #1816 was an impressive sight coming down the tracks. (AZO real photograph postcard, *c.* 1913, B/W.)

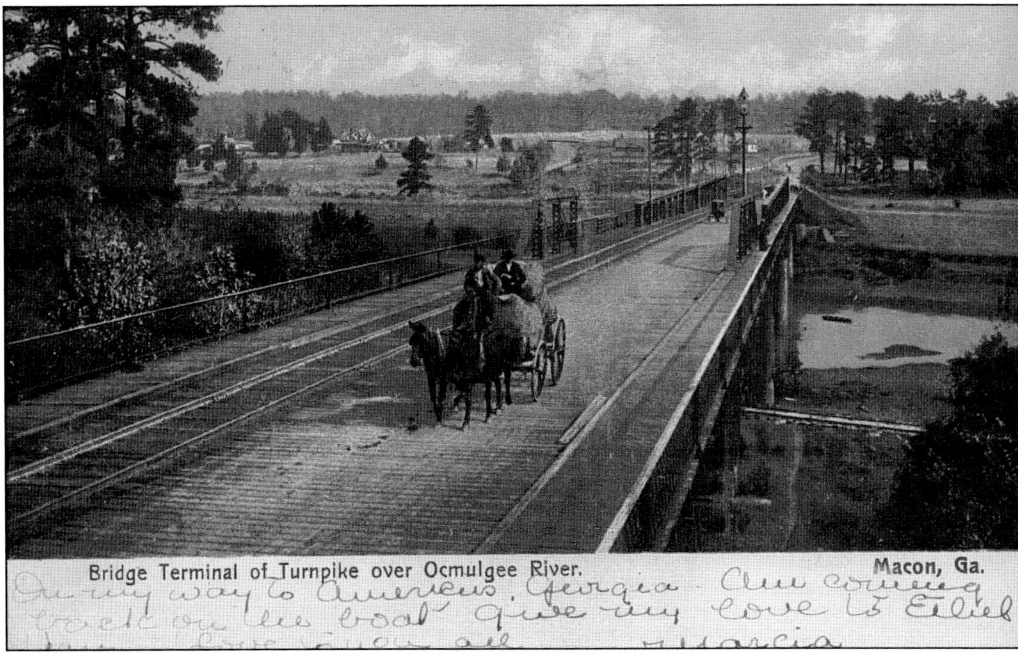

In this image, a horse-drawn wagon crosses the bridge built to provide pedestrian, animal, and rail passage across the Ocmulgee River. The sender of this card writes, "On my way to Americus, Georgia. Am coming back on the boat." (American News Co. #7452, postmarked 1909, color.)

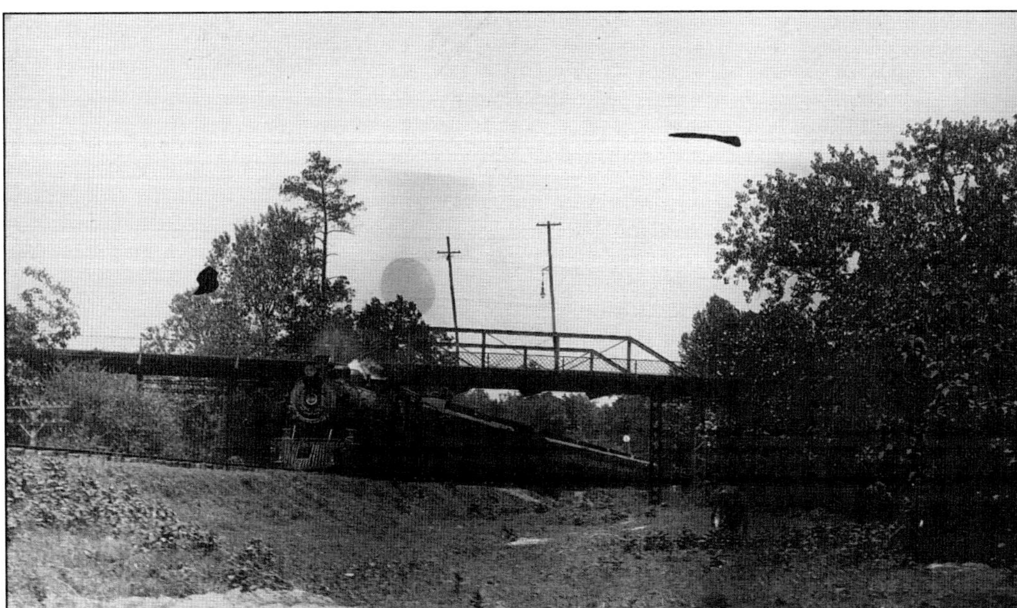

Shown here is a view of Southern Railroad train going under the Spring Street Bridge along the side of the Ocmulgee River. Train traffic along this track was heavy in the early 1900s since 75% of Georgia's railroads centered in Macon. Macon's business needs alone required over 5,000 cars per month. (Real photograph, *c.* 1922, B/W.)

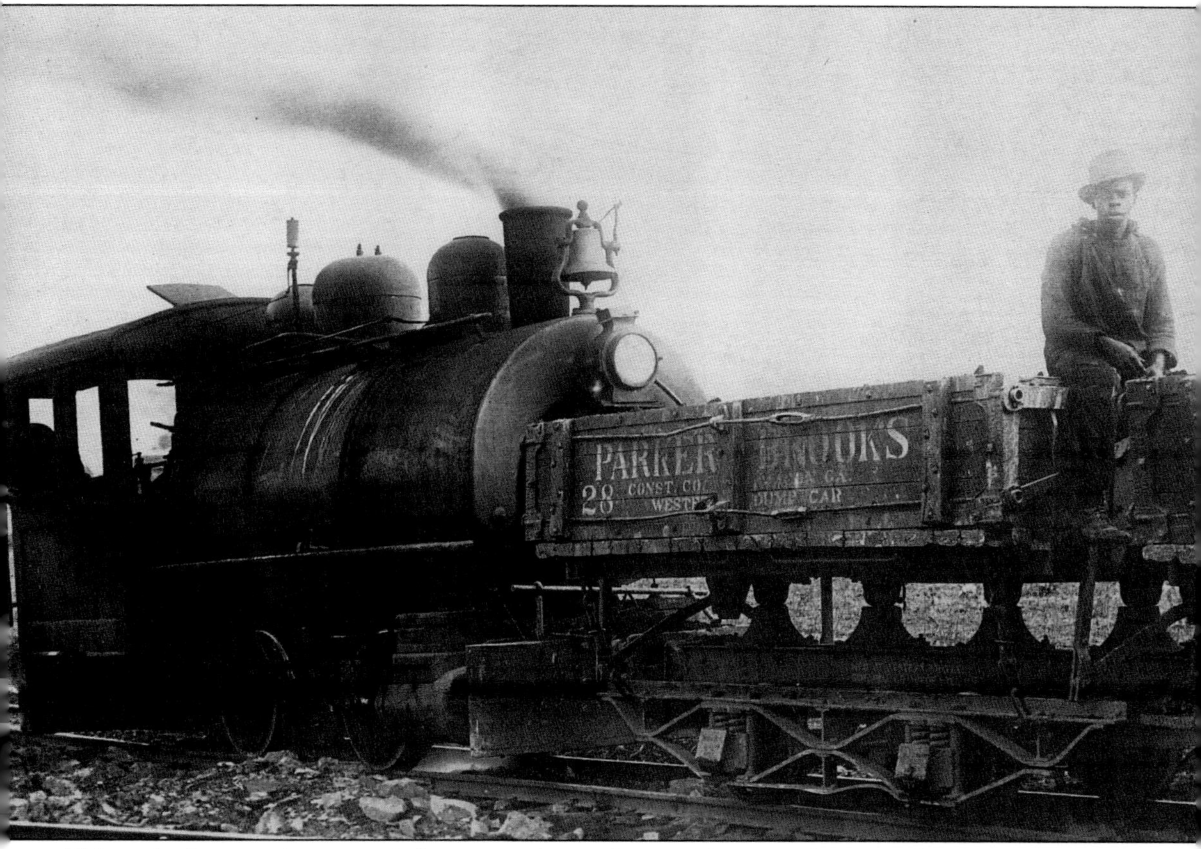

This real photograph postcard shows a train engine pushing a Parker Brooks Construction Company dump car. A colored laborer sits between the cars, as the engineer looks out from the engine's cab. (Unidentified publisher, postmarked 1914, B/W.)

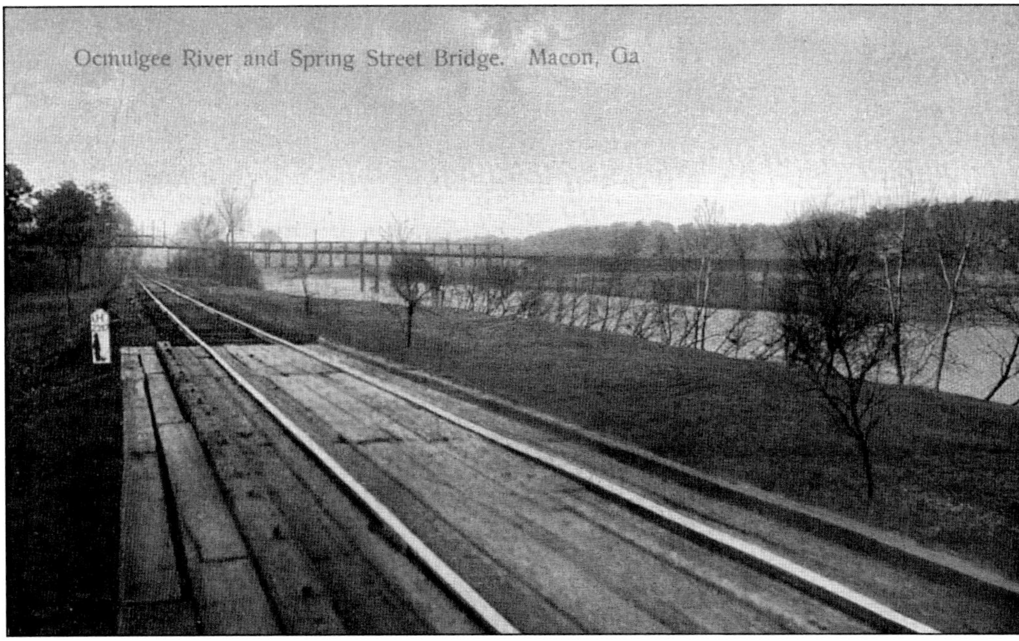

A post marker can be seen along the railroad tracks, which run parallel to the Ocmulgee River. In the background, you can see the Spring Street Bridge. It was said that the train tracks were placed on the east side of the river so as not to disturb the livestock on the west side near town. (International Postcard Co. #1808, *c.* 1910, color.)

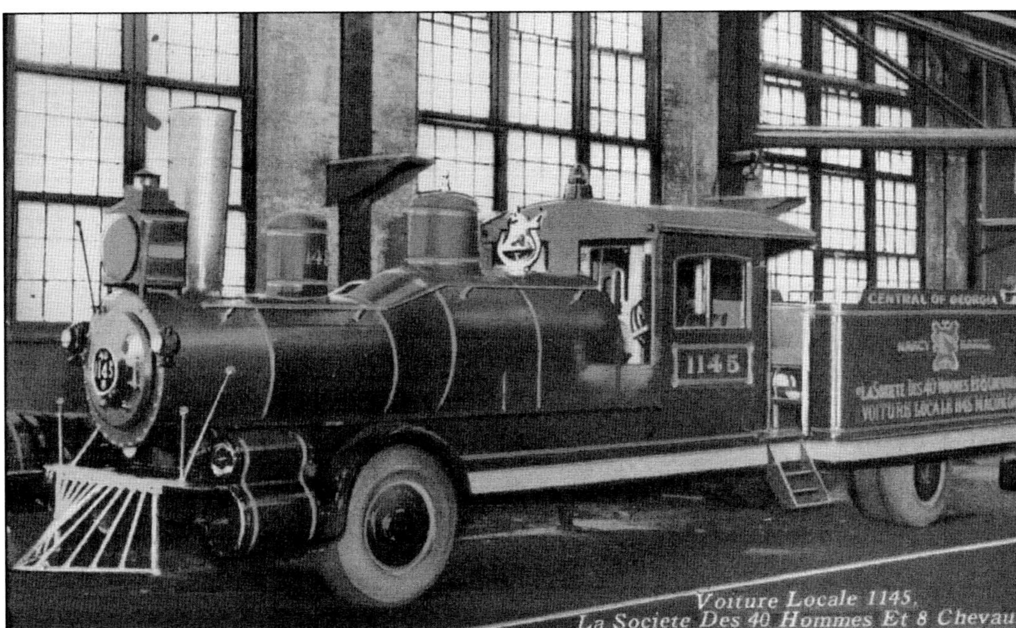

This engine is an exact two-thirds replica of the *Nancy Hanks* passenger train engine, which was operated between Savannah and Atlanta by the Central of Georgia Railroad in the 1880s. This card bears the French inscription, "Voiture Locale 1145, La Societe Des 40 Hommes Et 8 Chevaux, Macon." (Nationwide Advertising Co. #F9387, *c.* 1940, color.)

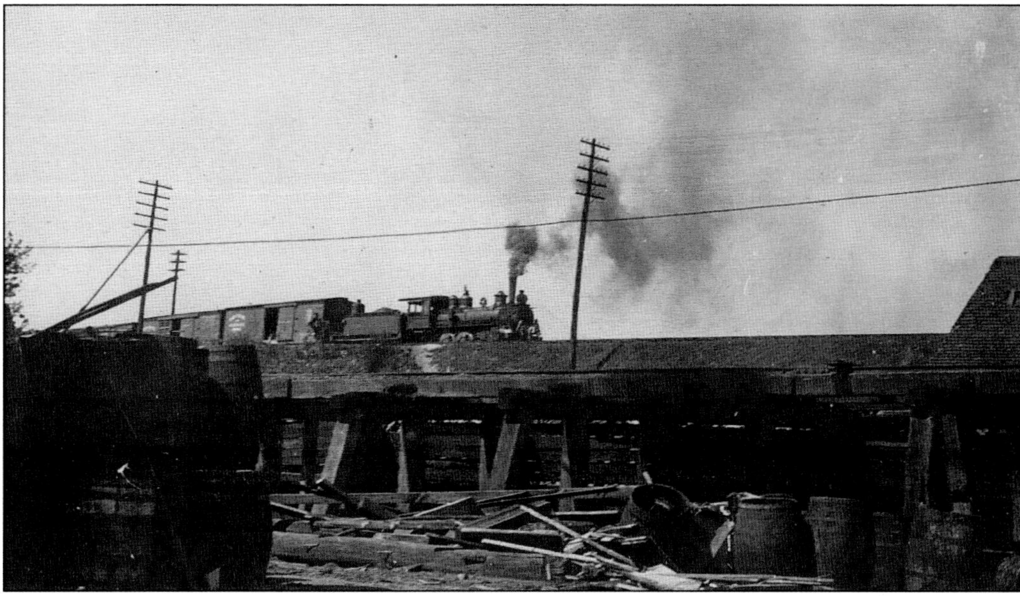

Here, you can see a Central of Georgia Railroad train at the CRR Fill Southern Division. The Central of Georgia was considered Macon's outlet to the sea, with railroad lines running to Savannah. (Real photograph, *c.* 1910, B/W.)

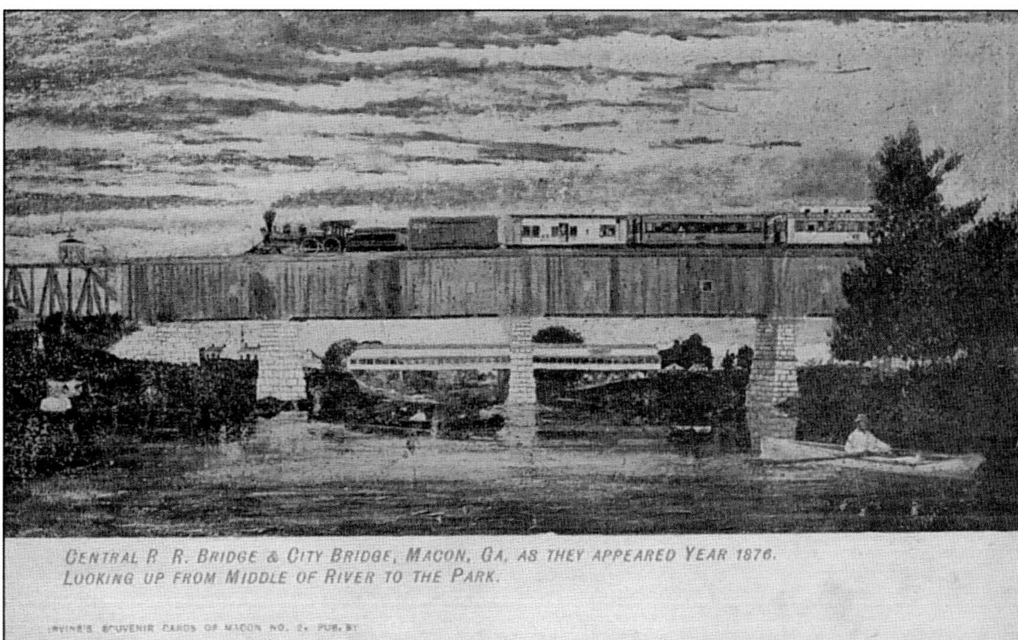

The Central of Georgia Railroad Bridge and the City Bridge appeared this way when looking up from the middle of the river to the park, *c.* 1876. The City Bridge was a covered toll bridge, built in 1826 by Daniel Pratt and Alexander McGregor. The bridge was built at the state's expense and sold to the city in 1829. (Irvine's Souvenir Cards, #2, *c.* 1905, B/W.)

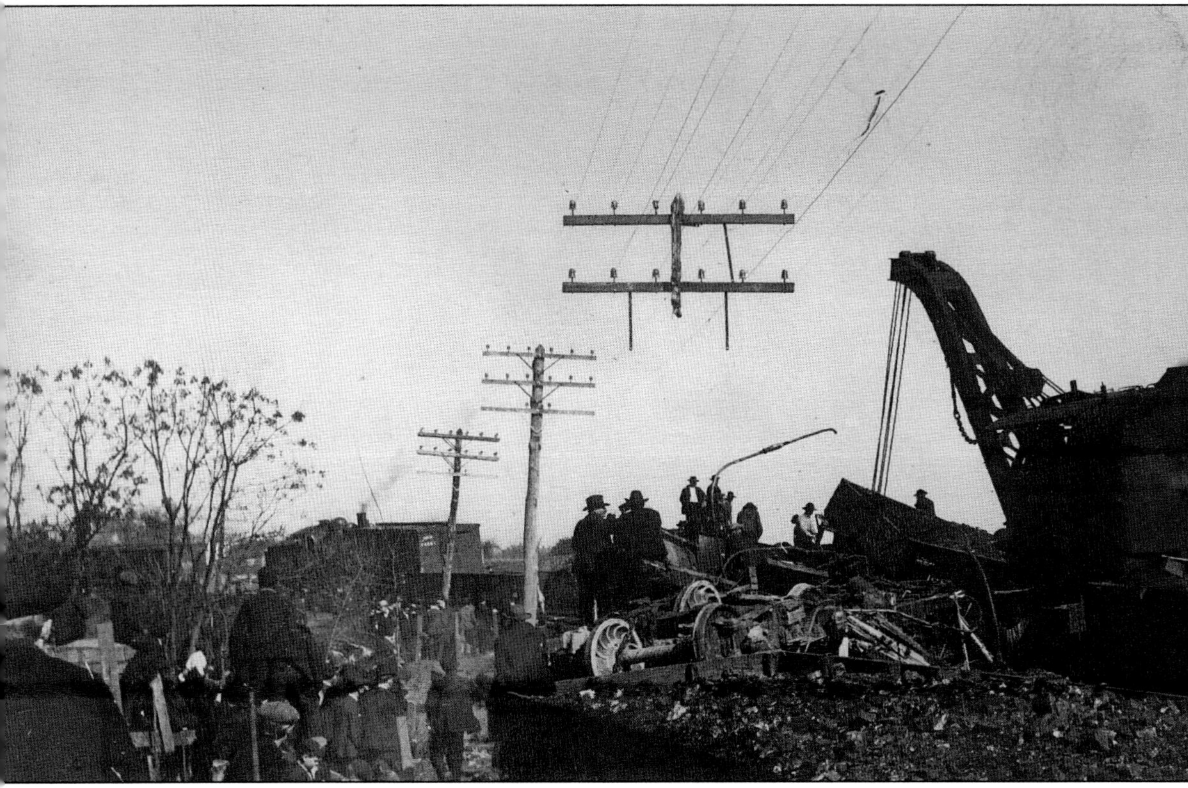

Here, we see a freight train wreck at Macon, showing a "strange freak telegraph pole snapped off between the cross arms and ground." A crane car was brought in to remove the wreckage. (Real photograph postcard, *c.* 1905, B/W.)

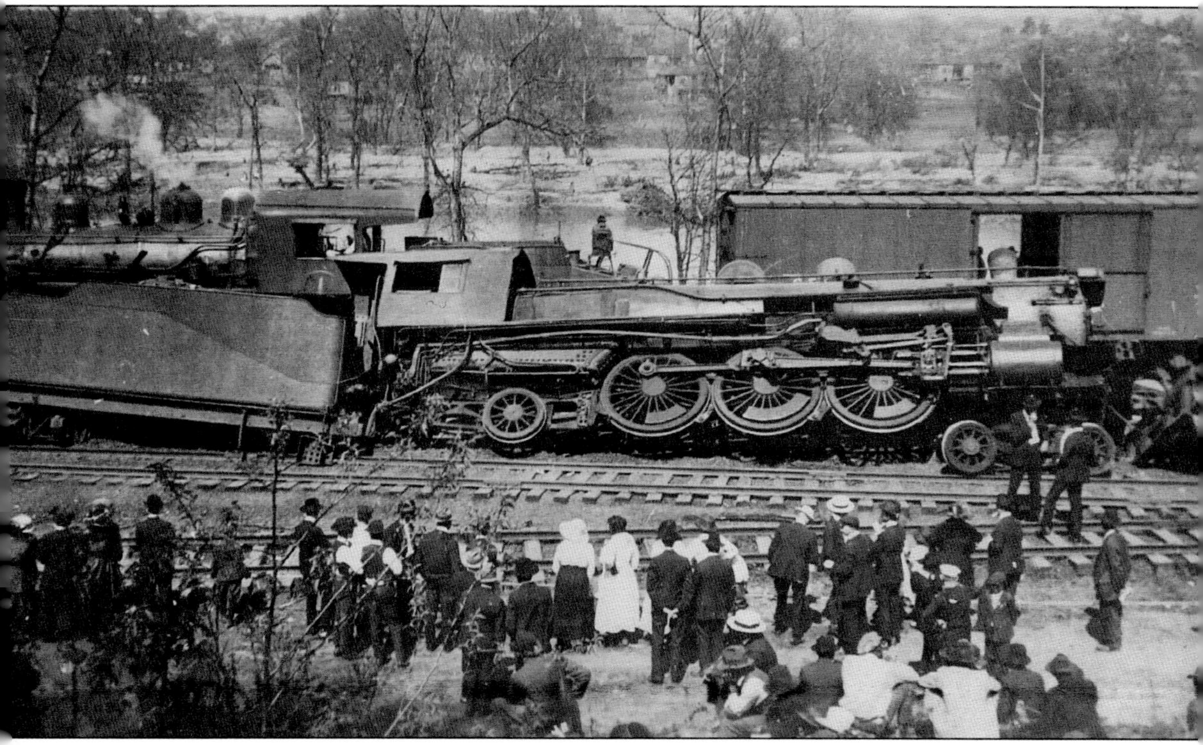

In the early 1900s, train accidents were not uncommon, and Macon had her share of them. Here, we see the *Engine of Royal Palms*, "a Southern R.R. Crack Tourist Train," turned over in the yards at Macon, *c.* 1921. (Real photograph postcard, *c.* 1921, B/W.)

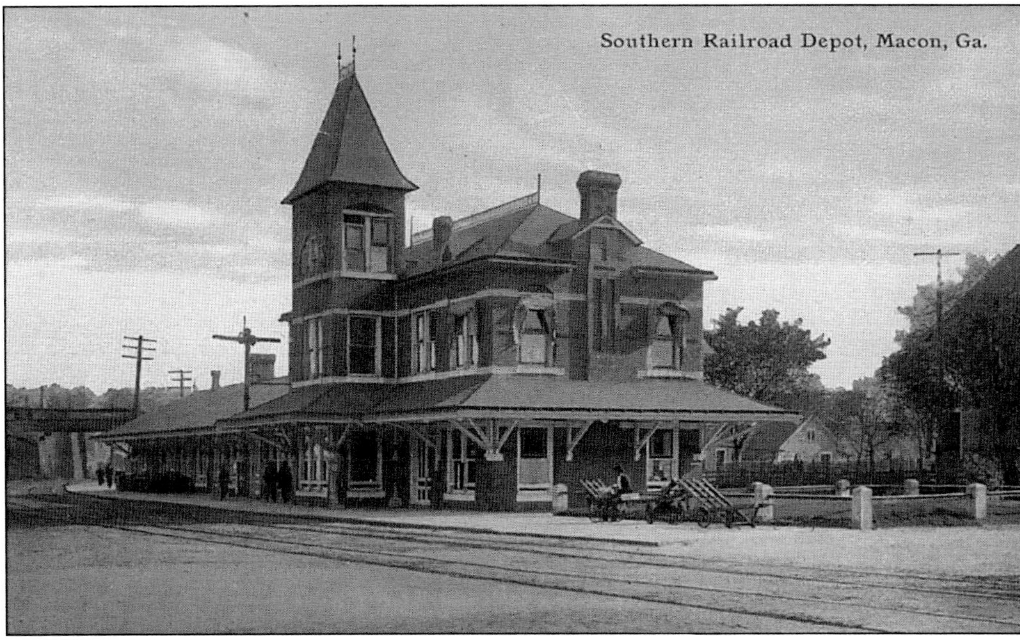

The Southern Railroad Depot is shown here during the early part of the century. One unhappy traveler wrote of their experience, "We were told we had only 15 minutes to get to the other depot, got there in 10 minutes and had 35 minutes to wait." (Curt-Teich #A-13846, *c.* 1910, color.)

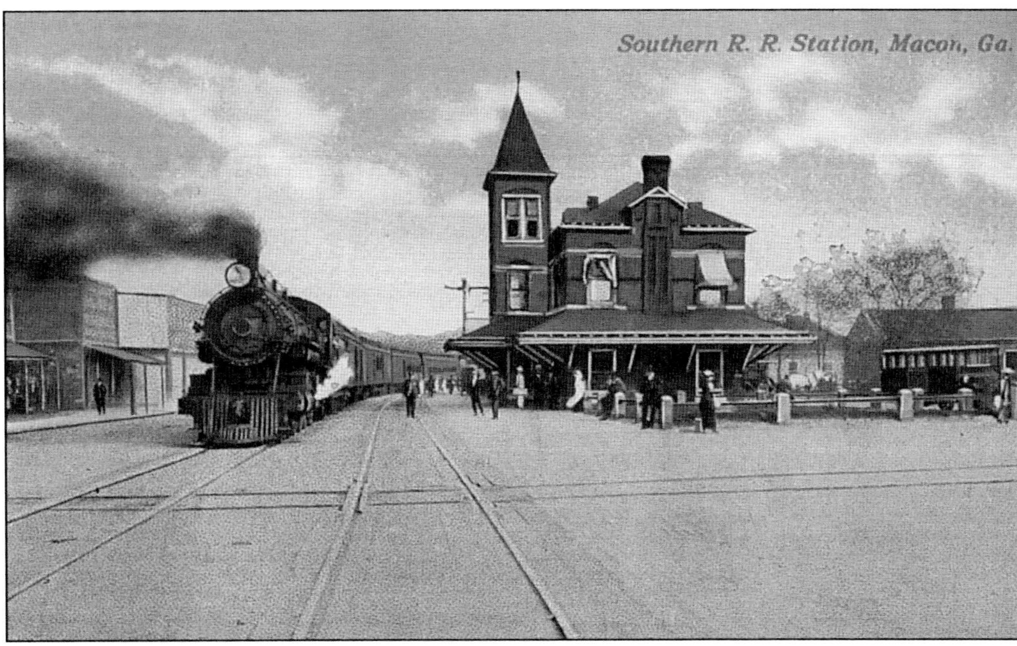

This view of the Southern Railroad Station features a train pulling in and a bus waiting in the parking lot. Another traveler writes, "Do hope our mad rush to the station didn't get on your nerves. We just did make it. I was fairly blowing when I got on." (Octochrome, Power's Curiosity Shop #38649, *c.* 1910, color.)

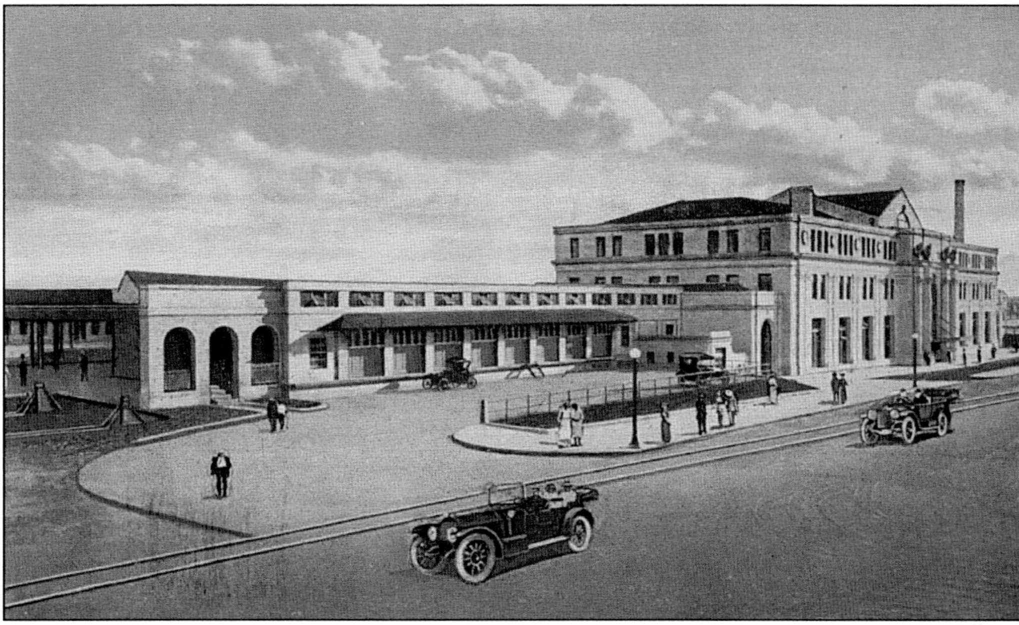

The new Union Station (Terminal Station) building, located on Fifth Street at the head of Cherry Street, is a massive building erected in 1916. This station served the Georgia Railroad, the Central of Georgia Railroad, the Southern Railroad, the Georgia-Southern Railroad, and the Macon, Dublin, & Savannah Railroad. (Curt-Teich #A71206, *c.* 1916, color.)

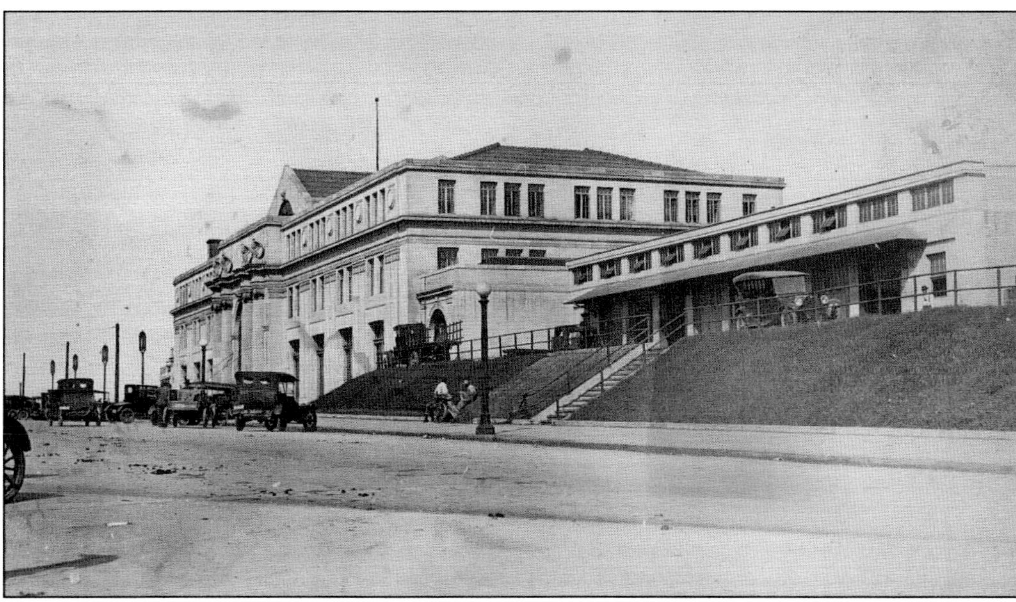

The Terminal Station is made of Indiana limestone and has beautiful columns. Because of its size and location, it is a good landmark for city visitors. (Real photograph postcard, *c.* 1915, B/W.)

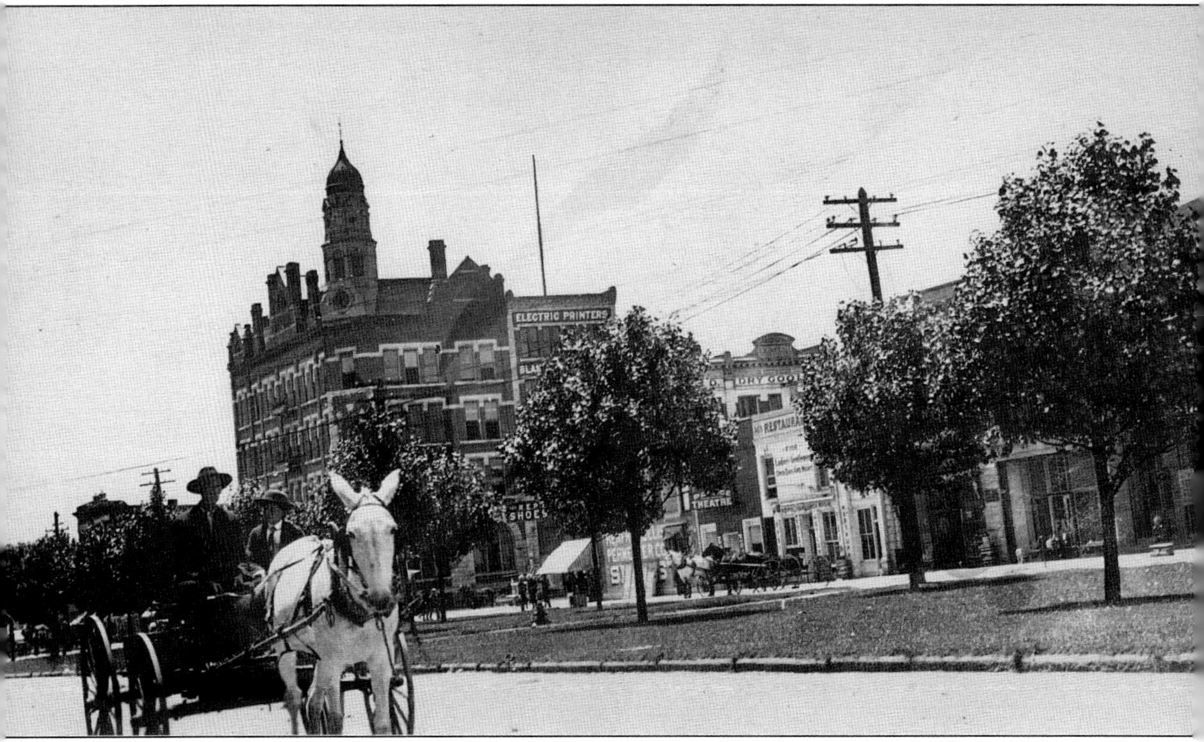

James Webb made the survey and drew up plans for the city of Macon, which was supposedly in the pattern of the ancient city of Babylon. A valley at the crook in the Ocmulgee River was selected as the sight for the rectangular city. Streets parallel to the river were named "for the trees of the forest though which they were laid," Walnut, Mulberry, Cherry, Poplar, Plumb, and Pine. Cross streets were numbered from First through Seventh. The plan's symmetry was only broken by Cotton Avenue, the old Federal road already in place when the plans were drawn. Macon's streets were designed to be unusually wide, alternating from 120 feet to 180 feet across. From her beginning, Macon's streets have been the first feature to inspire comment from visitors. The downtown business district is softened by the parks, flower beds, and trees that offer not only beauty, but also shade from the heat. Visitors and residents alike were often found resting beneath the sheltering leaves of the trees or quietly admiring the colorful displays of the flowers in bloom. Horse-drawn buggies, as seen in this typical scene along Third Street, were the mode of transportation in the early 1900s. (Real photograph, *c.* 1900, B/W.)

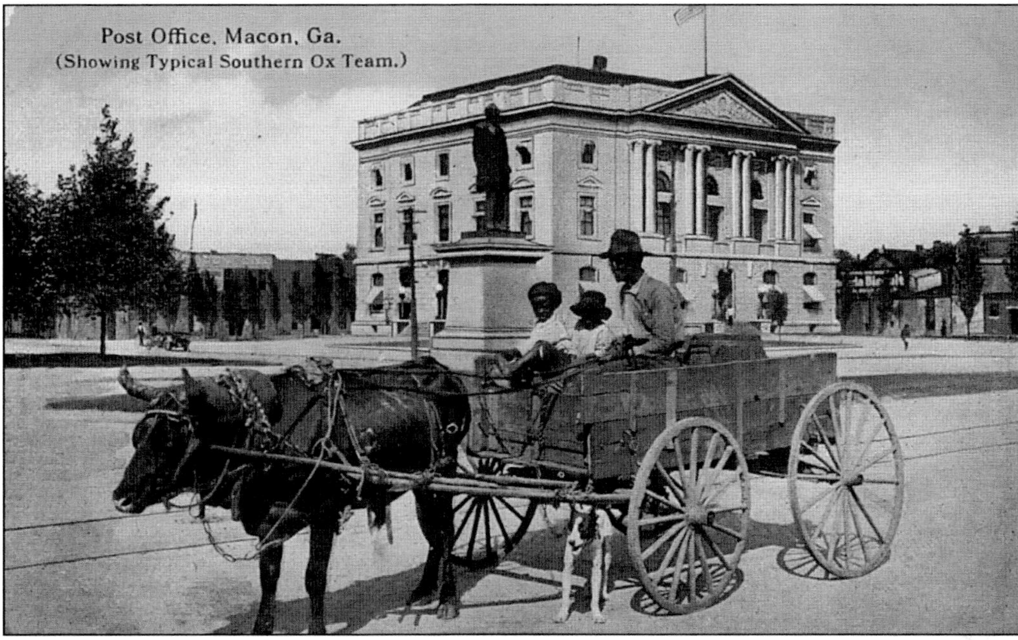

Here, a typical southern ox team can be seen in front of the post office building. The message on the back of the postcard reads, "How does this look to you? This is only conveyance of its kind in our city. You could hardly call it an automobile, so I suppose you would have to call it an oxo-mobile. How would you like to take a ride in an oxo-mobile?" (Powers Curiosity Store #A-216990, *c.* 1910, color.)

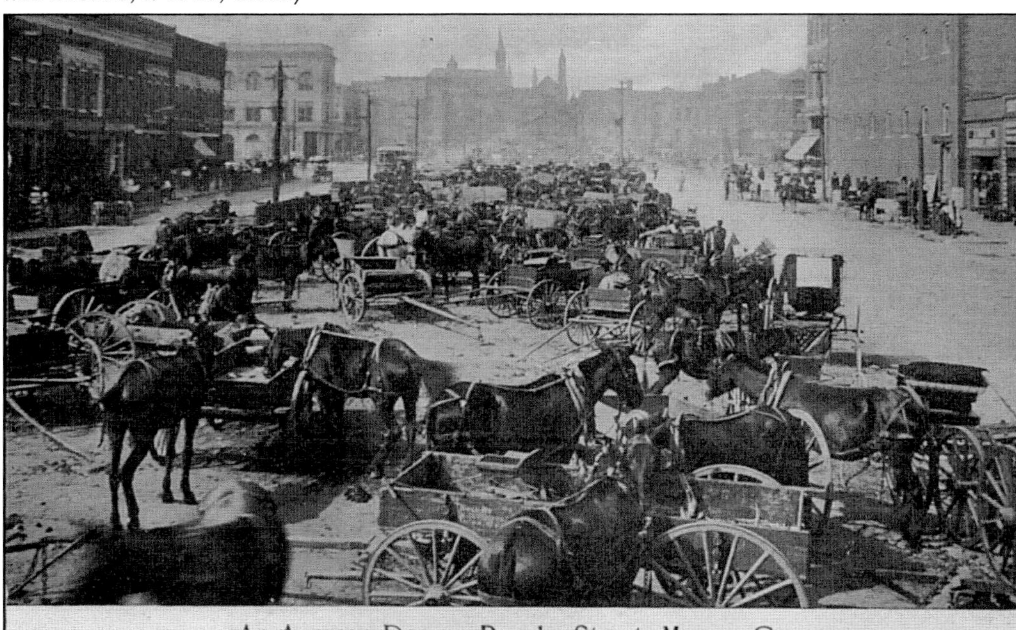

This postcard shows an average day on Poplar Street as horses, buggies, and wagons are parked in the middle of the extra wide street. Even with the visible parking congestion, there was still ample room on either side of the street for normal traffic to proceed. (Unidentified publisher, postmarked 1912, B/W.)

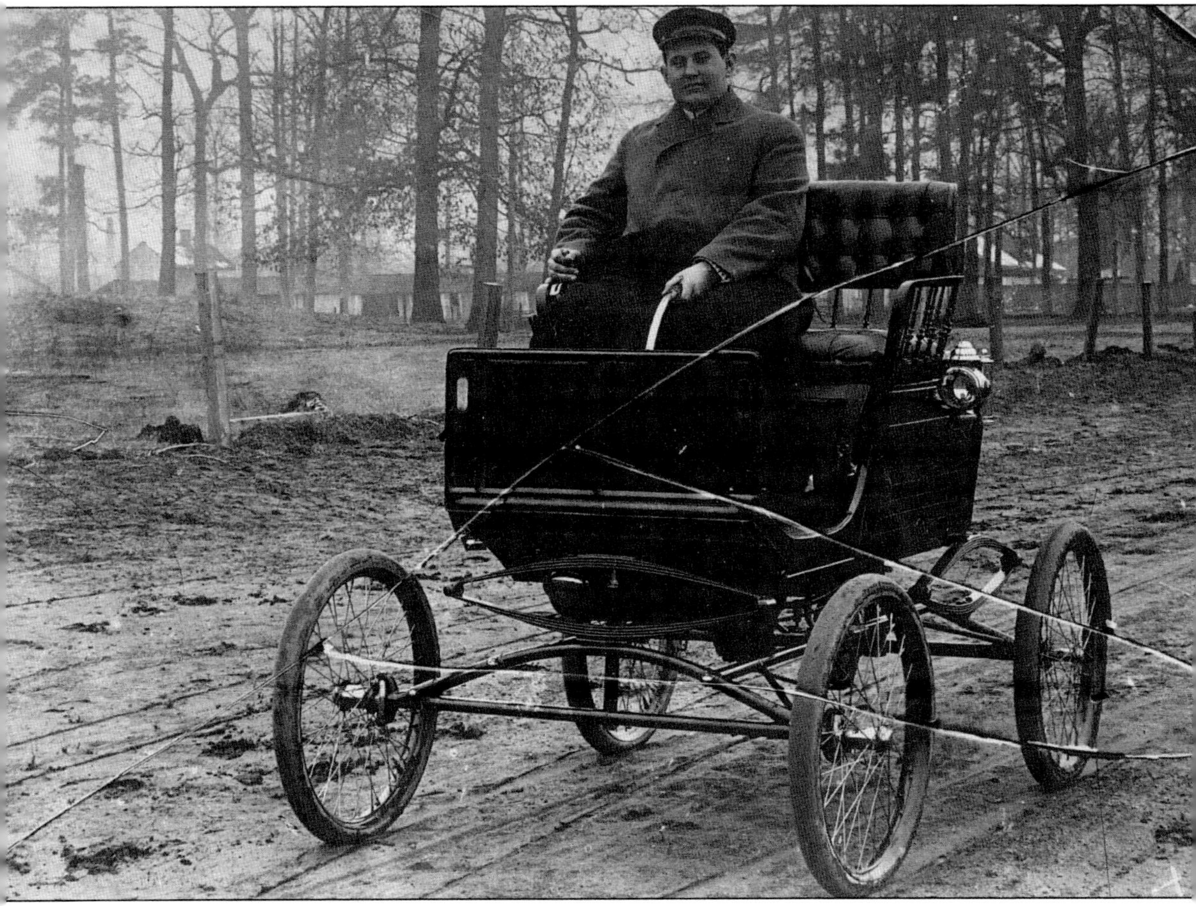

For most of the nation's history, the power that pulled wagons and carriages had hooves. During the 1890s, America began manufacturing and selling their first automobiles. From steam, to electric, to gasoline power, inventors and entrepreneurs were busy trying to meet the demand for reliable hoof-less transportation. In 1901, manufactures saw two major developments that paved the way for the growth of the automobile industry. The first was the discovery of rich oil fields in Texas, and the other was the introduction of mass production. With the discovery of oil, gasoline prices dropped, which, of course, lowered the cost of operating a vehicle. Mass production was first introduced at the Olds Motor Works. Then the Cadillac Automobile Company introduced the idea of interchangeable parts. Both of these ideas were incorporated into Henry Ford's production plant, where he installed his famous moving assembly line. The automobile and the 20th century roared in together. The 1900s saw automobiles coming off the assembly lines at affordable prices, and Americans bought them. Seen here is a picture of Macon's first automobile, brought to town in 1899 and sold to Granville Connor. (Real photograph, *c.* 1899, B/W.)

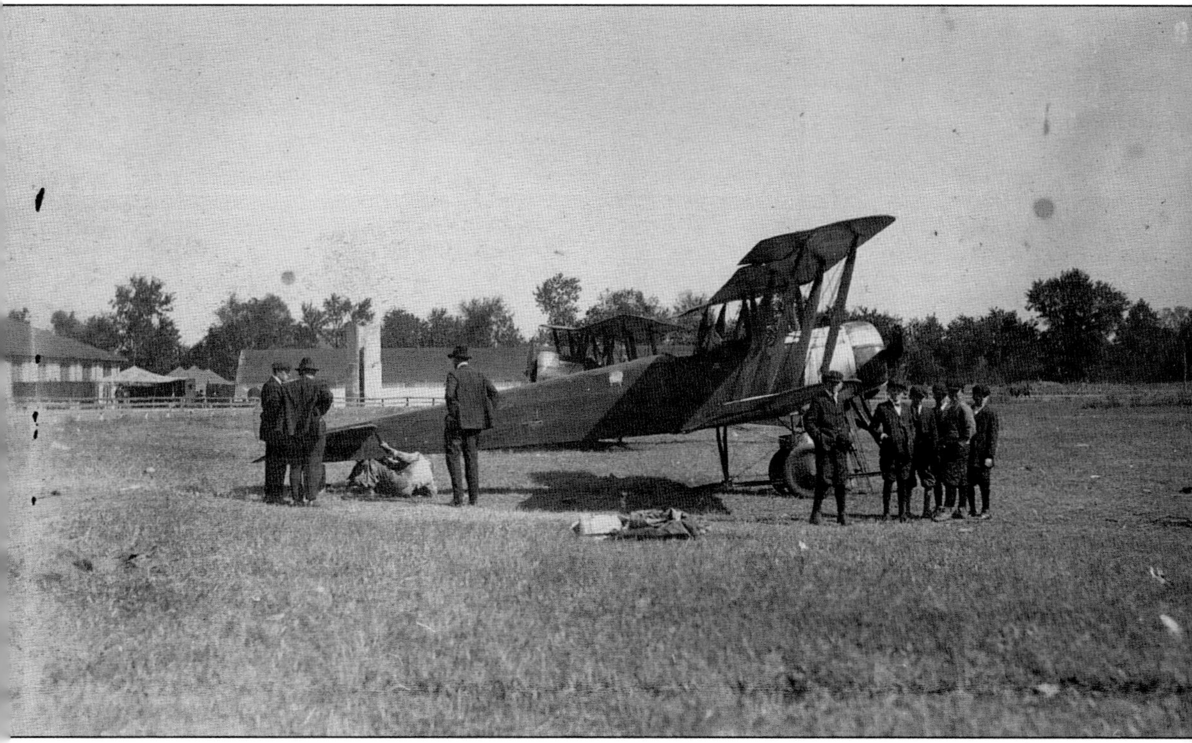

Man had long dreamed of flying above the earth like the birds of the air. In 1903, the Wright brothers made the first sustained, man-carrying, heavier-than-air flight in history. Within just a few years of the brief but successful flight, men and women were flying all over the world in ever-improving types of aircrafts. At the 1911 Georgia State Fair, in Macon, aviator Richard Ely crashed his stunt plane and died. The disaster did not end Macon's interest in aviation. In 1919, the Southeastern Aeronautical Congress was held in Macon. During the air show, a local newspaperman, Mark Etheridge, ventured high into the sky to provide a firsthand glimpse at flying for his readers. Shown here, a mechanic is working on an airplane's tail section, making last minute checks prior to a flight from Central City Park. (Real photograph postcard, *c.* 1920, B/W.)

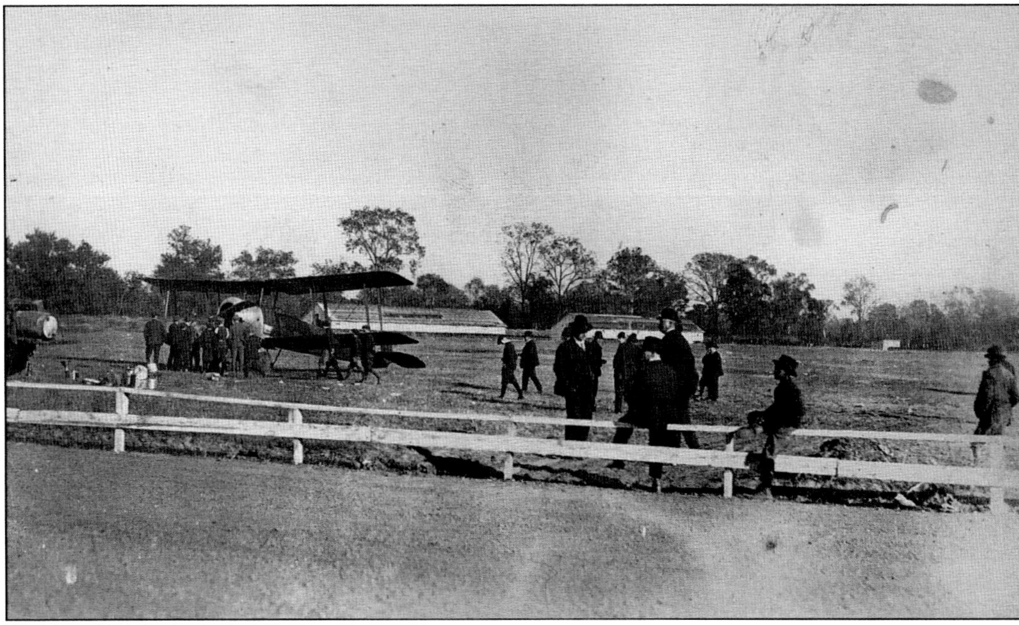

Macon was a progressive city that eagerly embraced early aviation. Central City Park was home to Aviation Field, where early aircrafts were flown. Here, citizens inspects a plane before takeoff. (Real photograph postcard, *c.* 1920, B/W.)

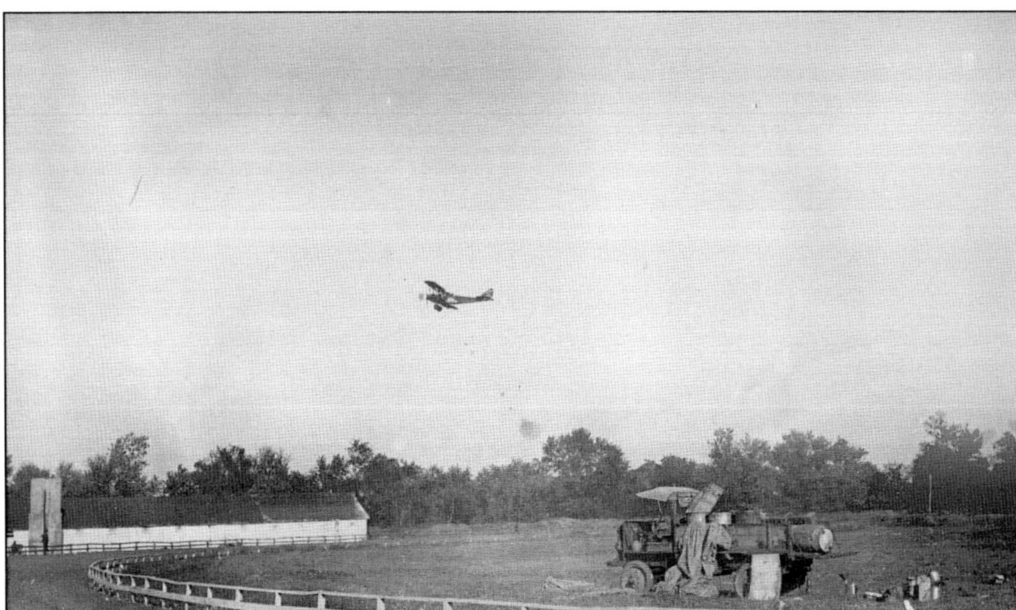

A beautiful sight is the airplane in flight over Central City Park. In 1925, the city prepared landing strips at Camp Wheeler, and in the 1930s, the Herbert Smart Airport was built. (Real photograph postcard, *c.* 1920, B/W.)

Four

Educational Opportunities

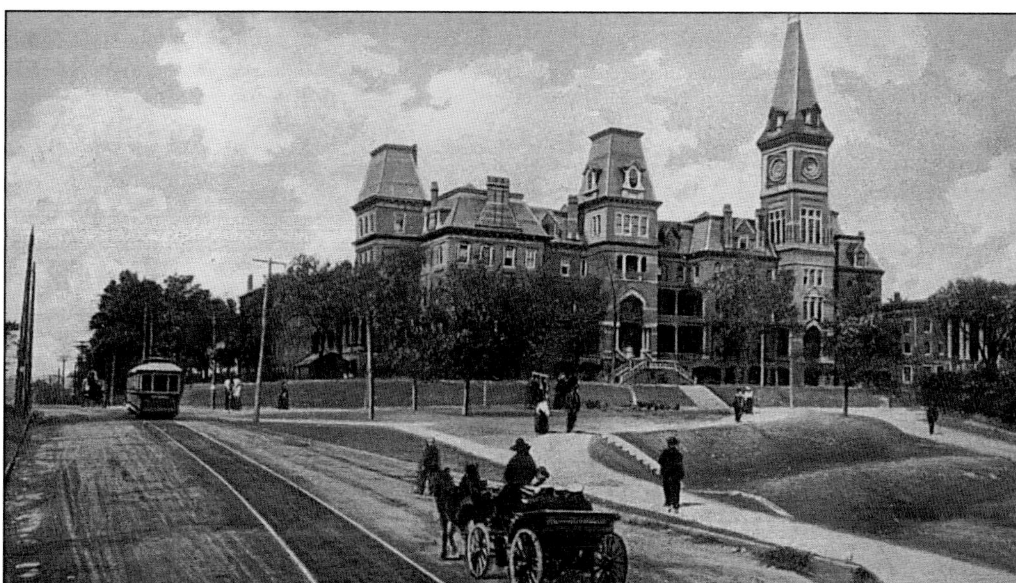

Education has always been important to the citizens of Macon. Located here is the mother of female colleges, Wesleyan. Also here is the famous, old Mercer University. Add to that St. Stanislaus, Mt. De Sales, the Academy for the Blind, numerous business institutes, and a fine group of public elementary and high schools, and Macon has an educationally progressive city. The Wesleyan College building, located on Encampment Hill, can be seen in this photograph. In 1836, the Georgia Female College became the first college in the world chartered to grant degrees exclusively to women. In 1843, the name was changed to Wesleyan Female College. (Raphael Tuck #2074, *c.* 1905, color.)

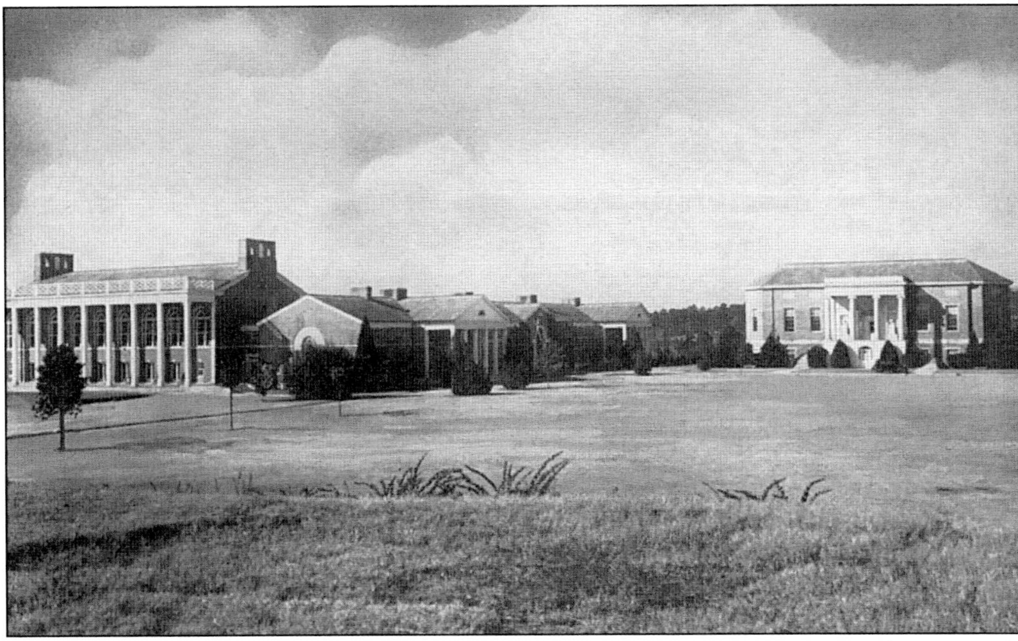

In 1928, Wesleyan students moved to their new campus in Rivoli, 5 miles north of Macon. The campus included 13 buildings finished in brick and marble on 132 acres of land. Shown here is a campus view of Wesleyan College. (Graycraft Card Co. # M-225, *c.* 1930, B/W.)

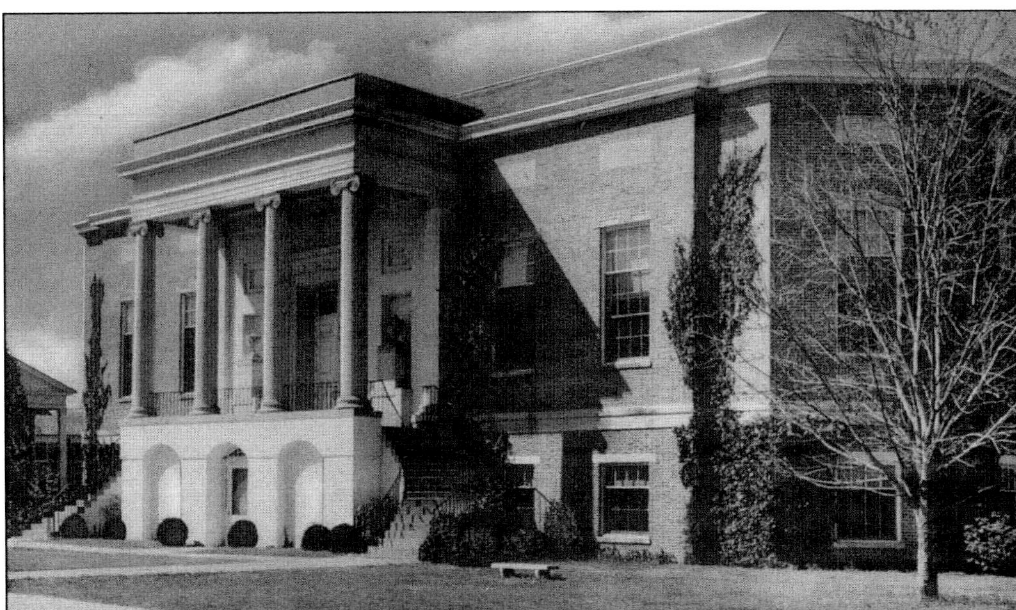

Many students spend hours reading and doing research at the Candler Memorial Library on the Wesleyan College campus. This building is an architectural adaptation of the famous Savannah plantation house, the Hermitage. (Albertype Co., *c.* 1930, B/W.)

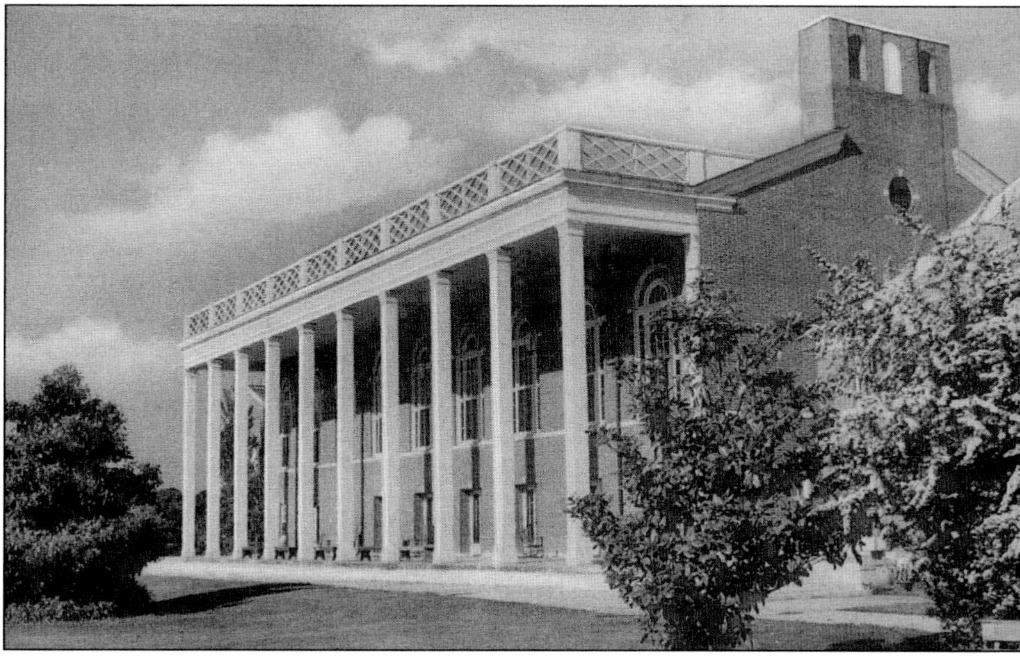

Complete with a beautiful facade, benches, and rocking chairs, the Mount Vernon Porch at Wesleyan is a peaceful spot to sit, study, or visit with friends. (Albertype Co., *c.* 1930, B/W.)

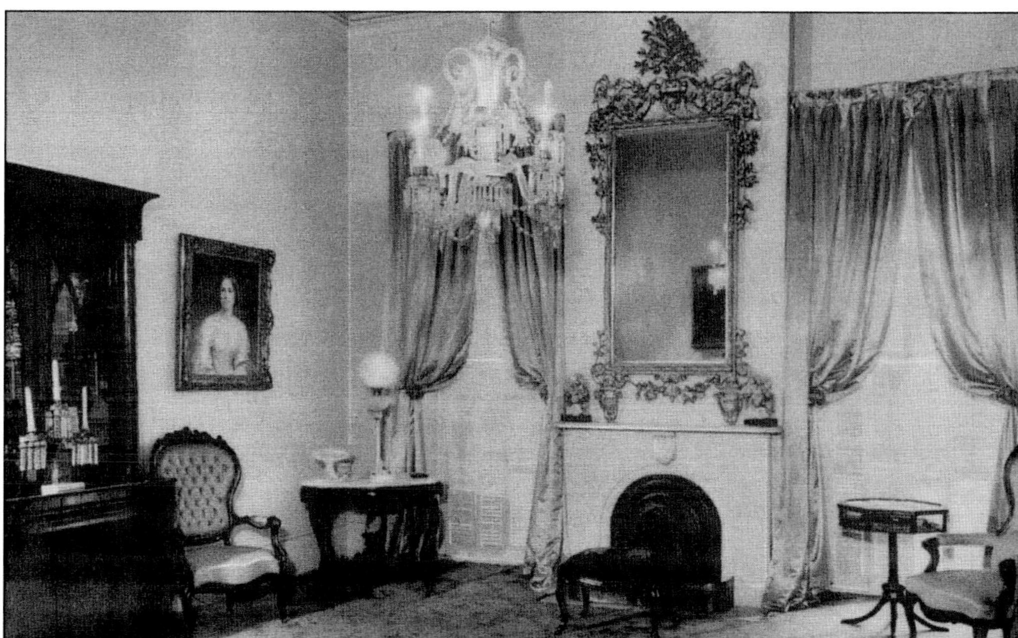

This elegantly appointed room is the Memorial Room of the Phi Mu Fraternity, founded at Wesleyan College. (Albertype Co., *c.* 1930, B/W.)

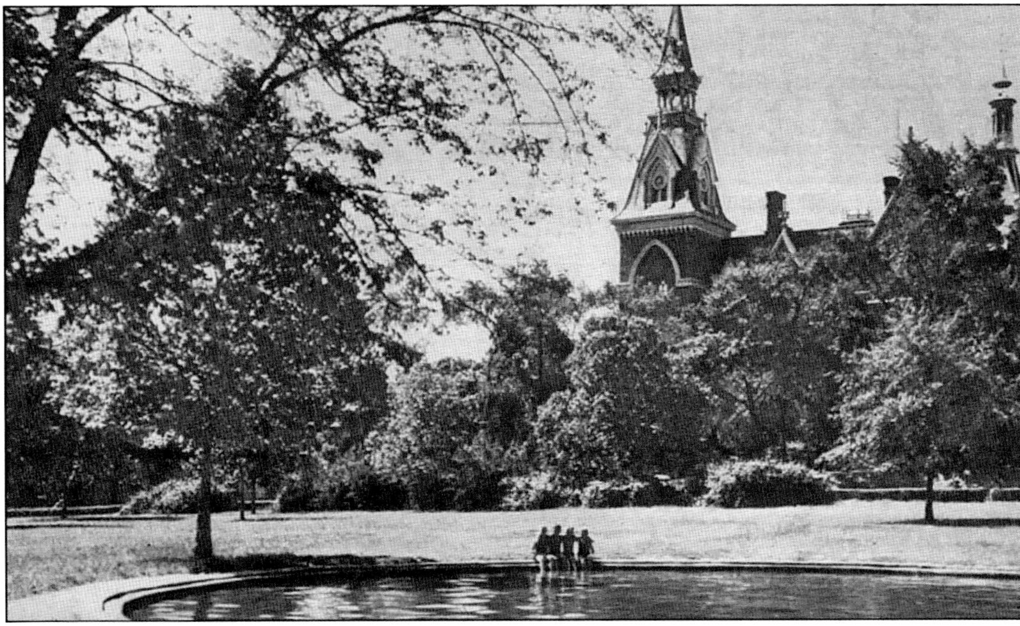

The President of Mercer sent this message to graduating high school seniors, "True to the high standard of her founders, Mercer offers those who are capable and worthy superior advantages amid healthful surroundings and the influence of high ideals." Shown here are four students dipping their feet into the reflecting pool in front of the administration building. (Everett Waddey Co., *c.* 1936, B/W.)

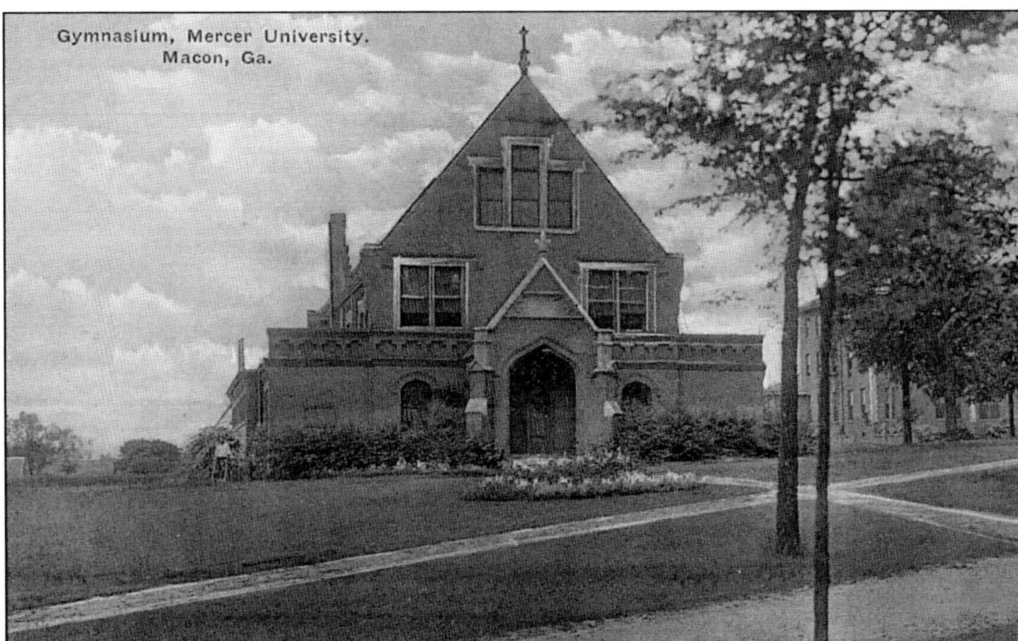

Sports have always played an important part in Mercer's overall educational setting. Shown here is Mercer University's Gymnasium building. (Albertype Co., *c.* 1930, B/W.)

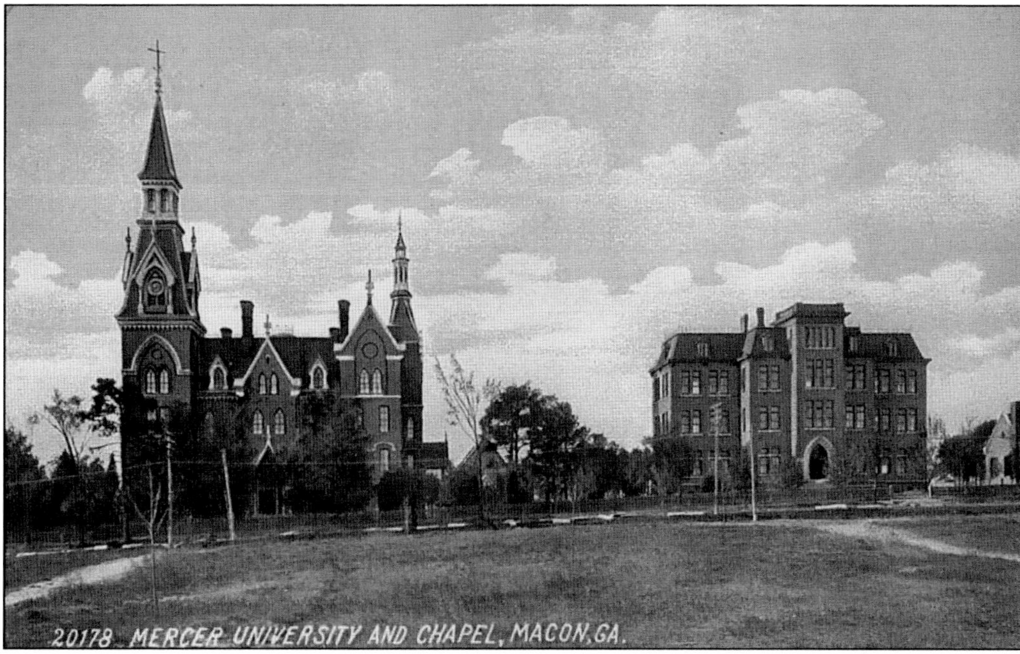

Mercer was founded in 1831 under the auspices of the Georgia Baptist Convention. First called Mercer Institute, the school was named in honor of Rev. Jesse Mercer, a Baptist divine and early advocate of a thorough educational system. Originally located at Penfield, the school was moved to Macon in 1870. Shown here are the administrative and chapel buildings. (Souvenir Postcard Co. #20178, *c.* 1910, color.)

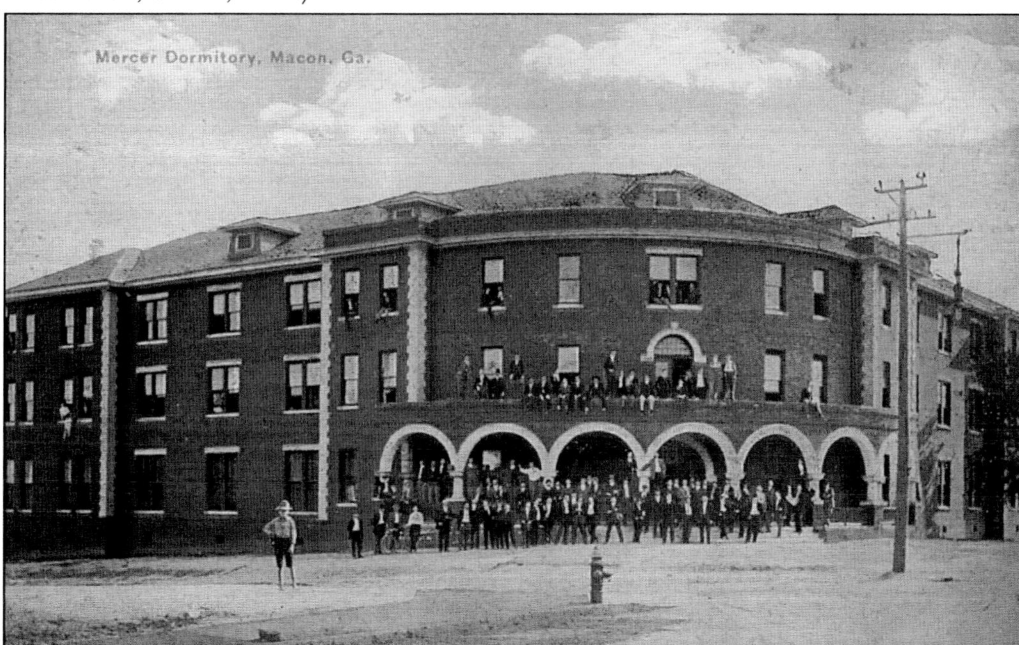

College students generally enjoy their experience of living away from home. These students look like they are having fun as they pose for a picture in front of the dormitory building at Mercer University. (Unidentified publisher, *c.* 1910, color.)

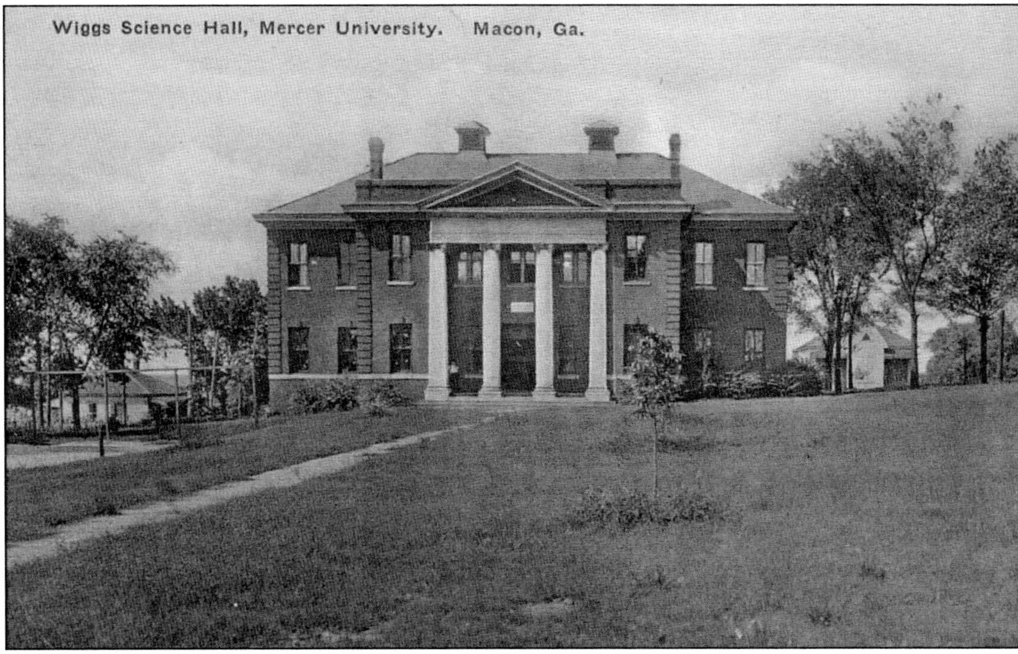

This impressive structure with the four large white columns is the Wiggs Science Hall at Mercer University. (Albertype Co., *c.* 1930, B/W.)

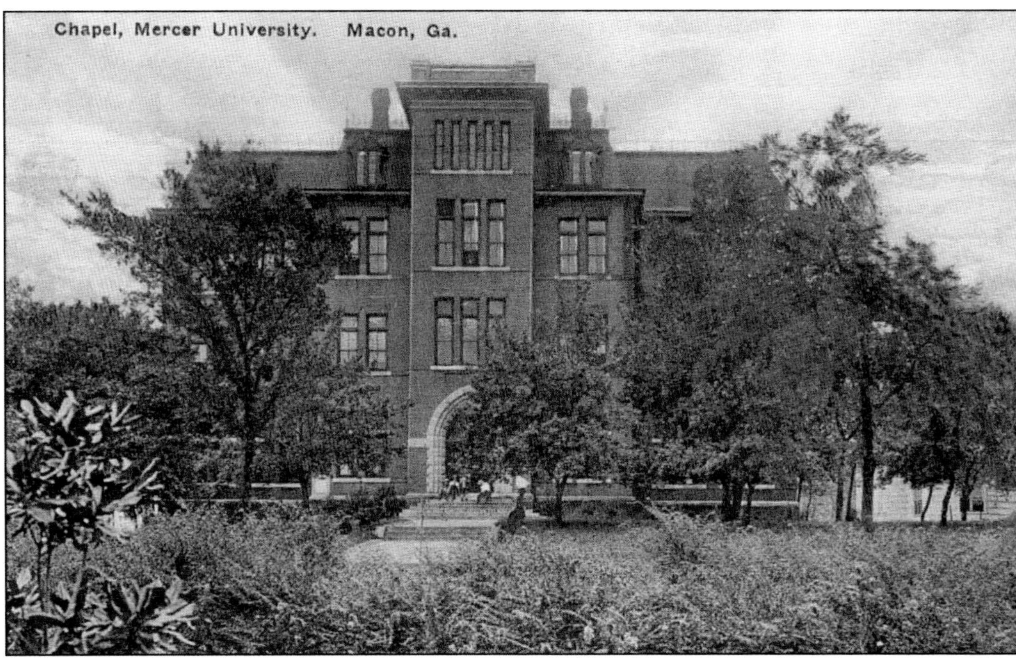

As a Baptist educational institution, Mercer's Chapel played an important role within the school. Many students graduated from Mercer and went on to become clergymen. (Albertype Co., *c.* 1930, B/W.)

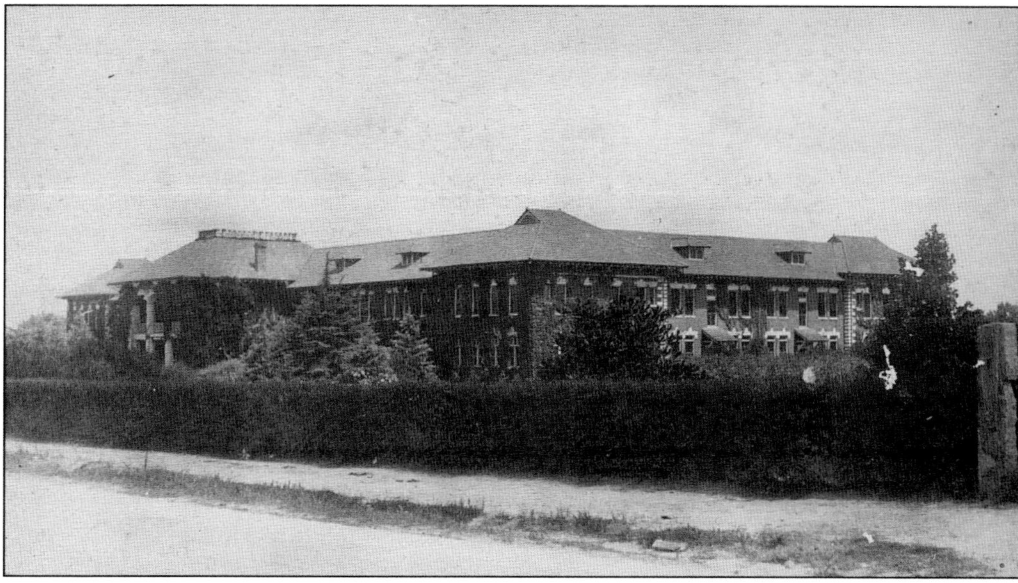

In 1851, W.S. Fortescue came to Macon from Philadelphia to establish a school for the blind in Georgia. At that time, there were 220 blind people in the state without benefit of educational facilities. Fortescue found Maconites supportive of his cause, and they helped fund the school until 1852, when the Georgia State Legislature formally took over and chartered the Georgia Academy for the Blind. (Real photograph , *c.* 1922, B/W.)

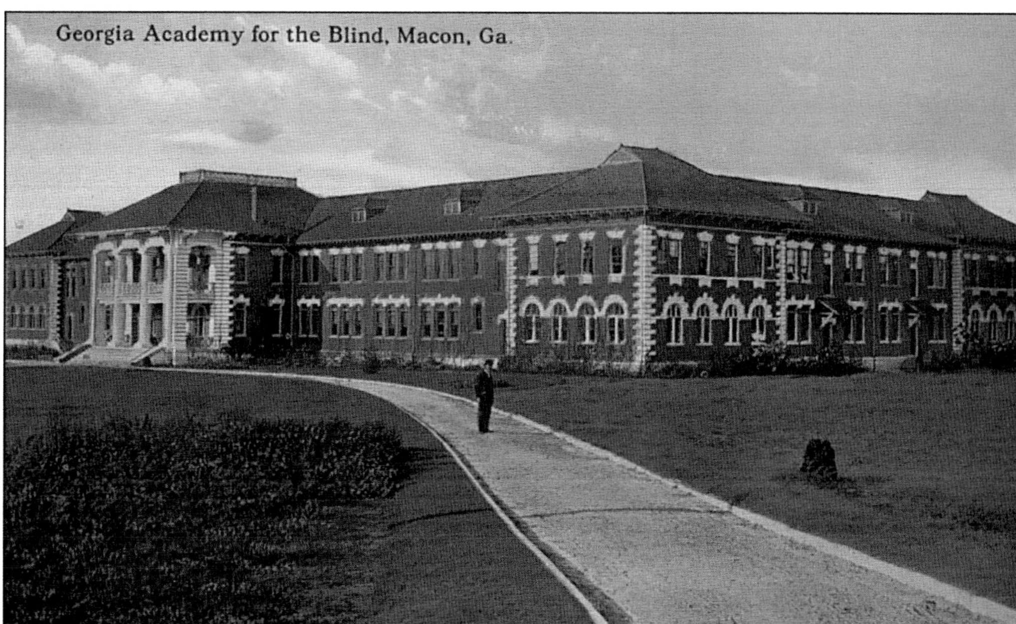

In 1905, the Georgia Academy for the Blind opened on Vineville Avenue. At this point in time, the Vineville area was still mostly rural, although it was growing constantly. The Academy building is shown in this picture as it appeared *c.* 1910. The picture above, *c.* 1922, shows the building after the trees and shrubs had grown so as to almost hide the building from the street's view (S.H. Kress #A-27001, *c.* 1910, color.)

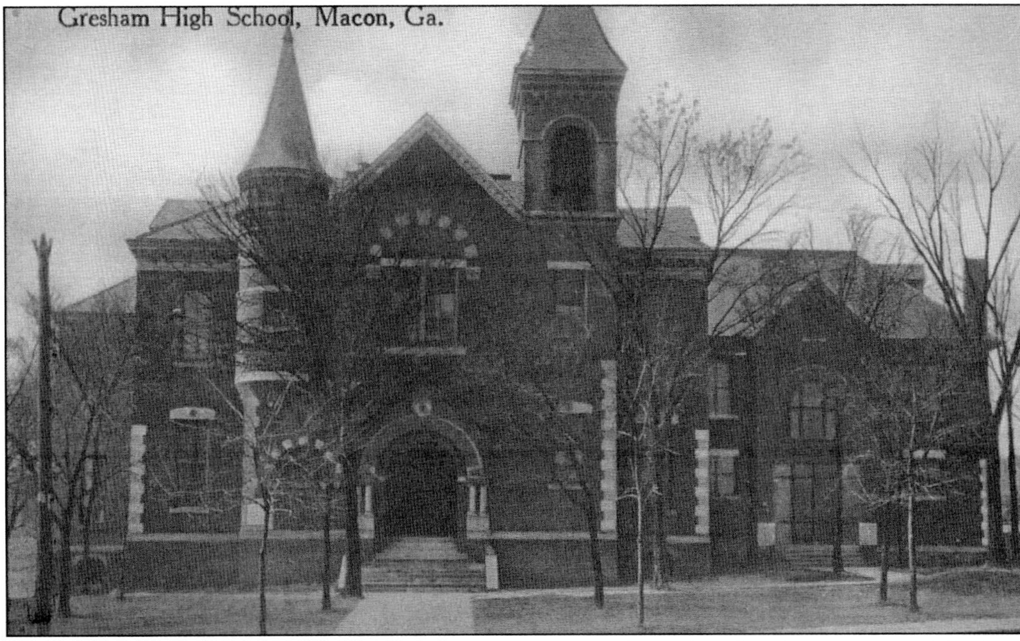

The Gresham High School, originally known as Central High School, was opened in 1873 and became the city's principal secondary school. Both boys and girls used the school until 1908, when the board of education asked that the sexes be separated. (Unidentified publisher, *c.* 1910, sepia.)

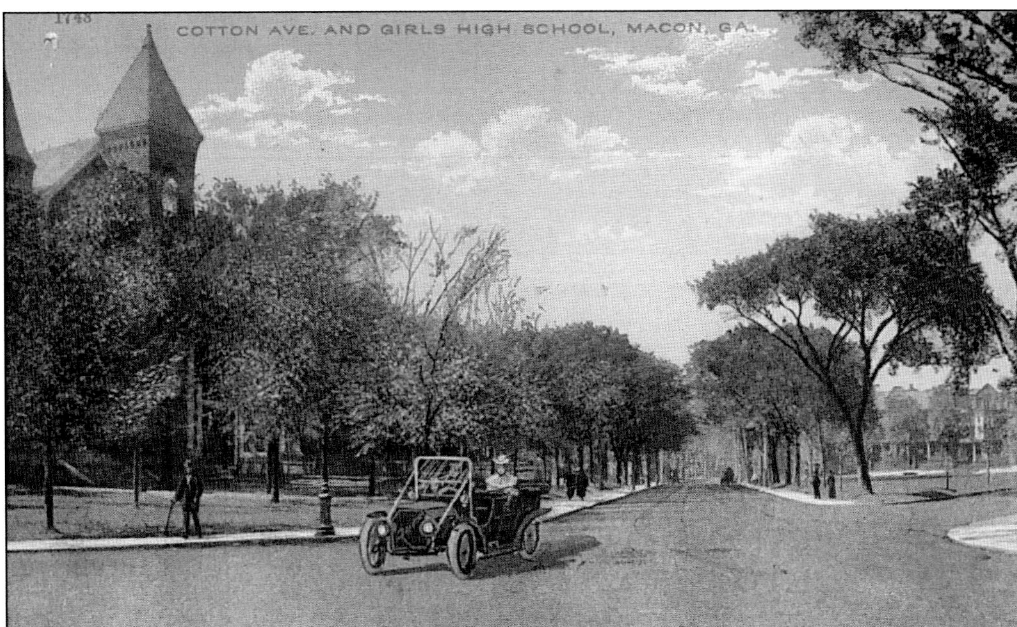

This image shows a glimpse of the Gresham High School from Cotton Avenue. Girls were taught here alone for several years after the boys had moved into remodeled buildings on Forsyth and Orange Streets. Once a new high school had been built, the girls rejoined the boys until another separate facility could be built. (S.H. Kress #1748, postmarked 1912, color.)

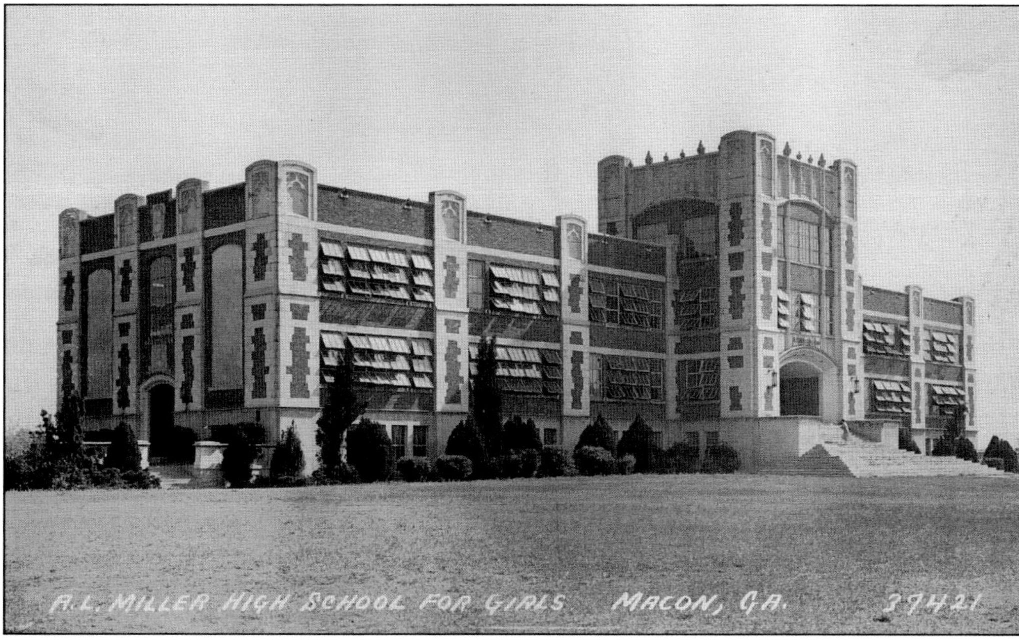

The A.L. Miller High School for girls was named for Bibb County Board of Education president A.L. Miller. Miller was a proponent of teaching high school boys to shoot guns, march, wear uniforms, and obey rules. (L.L. Cook real photograph postcard #37421, *c.* 1940, B/W.)

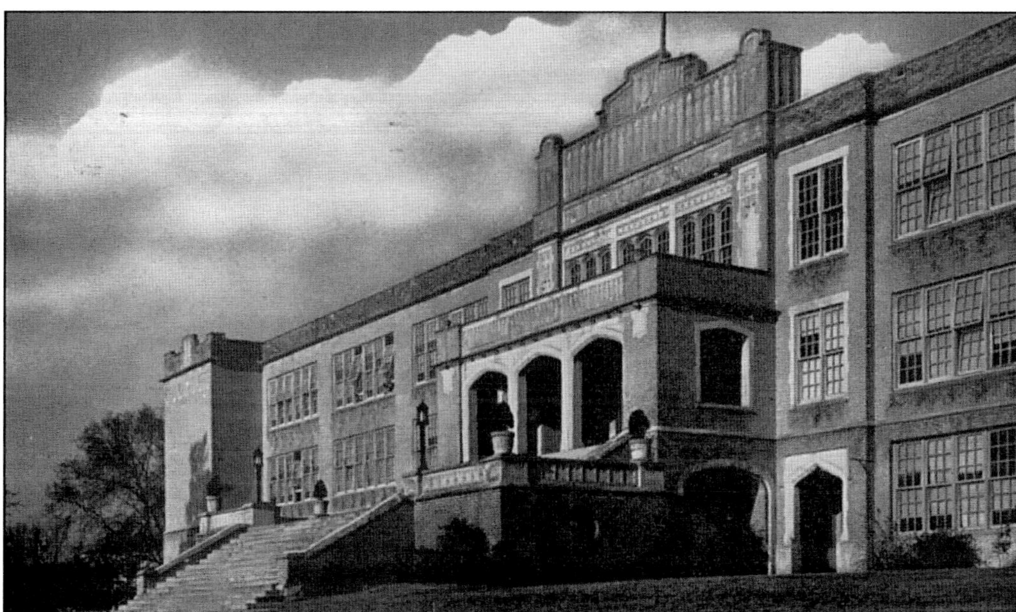

Lanier High School for boys consists of two cream-brick structures, completed in the fall of 1924. The armory and gymnasium were separate from the main building. (Graycraft Card Co. #M-235, postmarked 1943, B/W.)

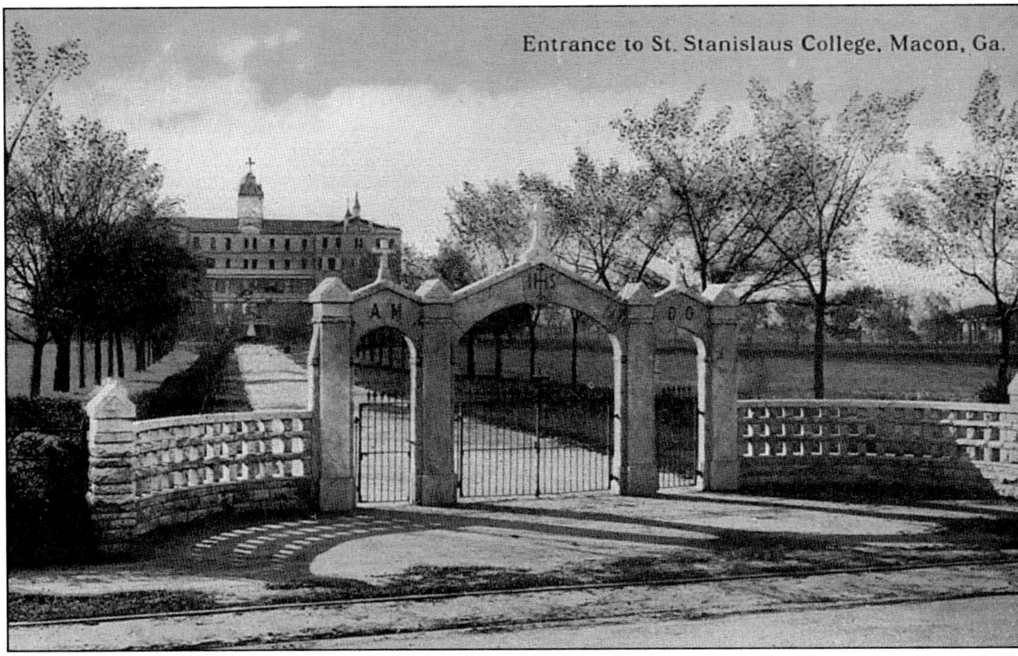

Shown here is the entrance gate to St. Stanislaus College. The sender of this card writes, "This is the entrance to college for Catholic Priests. They have very pretty grounds." (Power's Curiosity # A26988, *c.* 1910, color.)

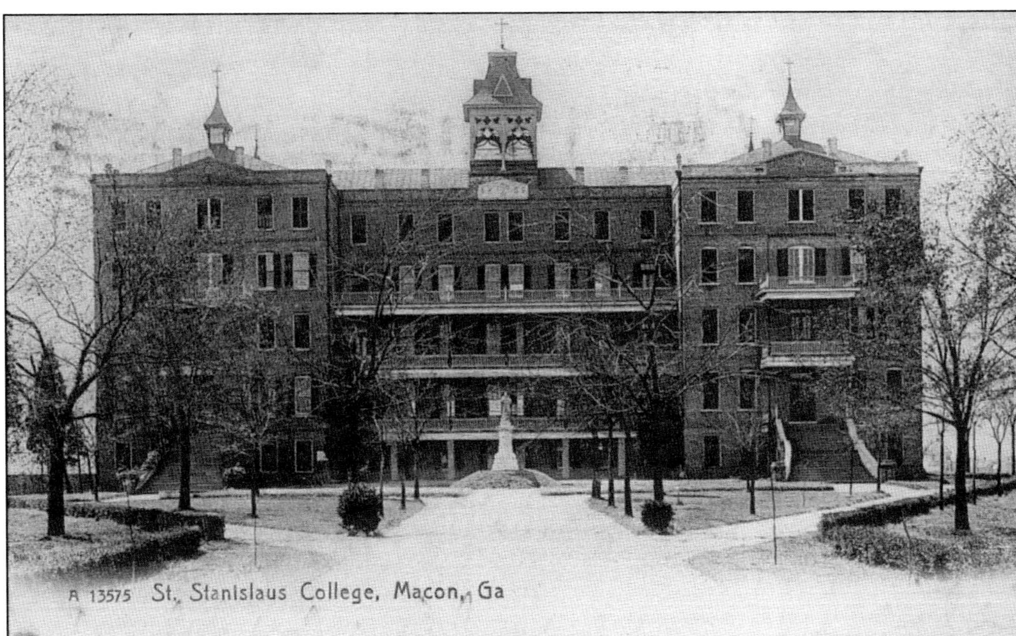

In 1921, St. Stanislaus College was destroyed by fire. Originally, the school was founded by the Roman Catholic Church in 1874 as the Pio Nono College. In 1887, the Society of Jesus took over the college as a training school for Jesuit priests and the school's name was changed. (Rotograph Co. #A-13575, postmarked 1906, B/W.)

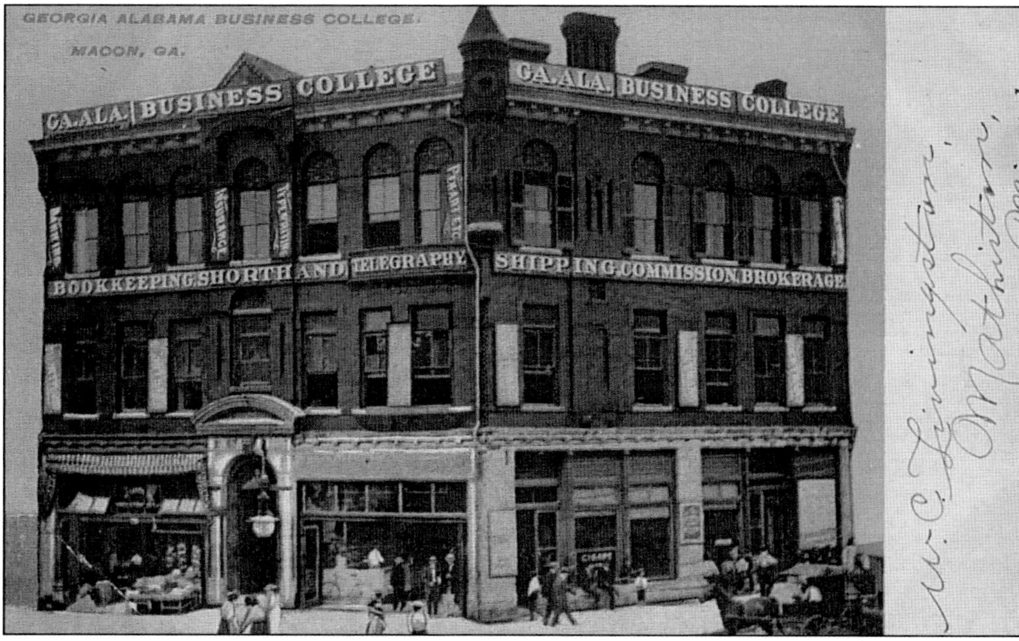

The Georgia-Alabama Business College was opened in 1889. Signs on the building cited subjects taught that included bookkeeping, shorthand, telegraphy, shipping, commission, brokerage, banking, insurance, typewriting, pen-art, etc. (McEvoy Book & Stationary Co., *c.* 1910, color.)

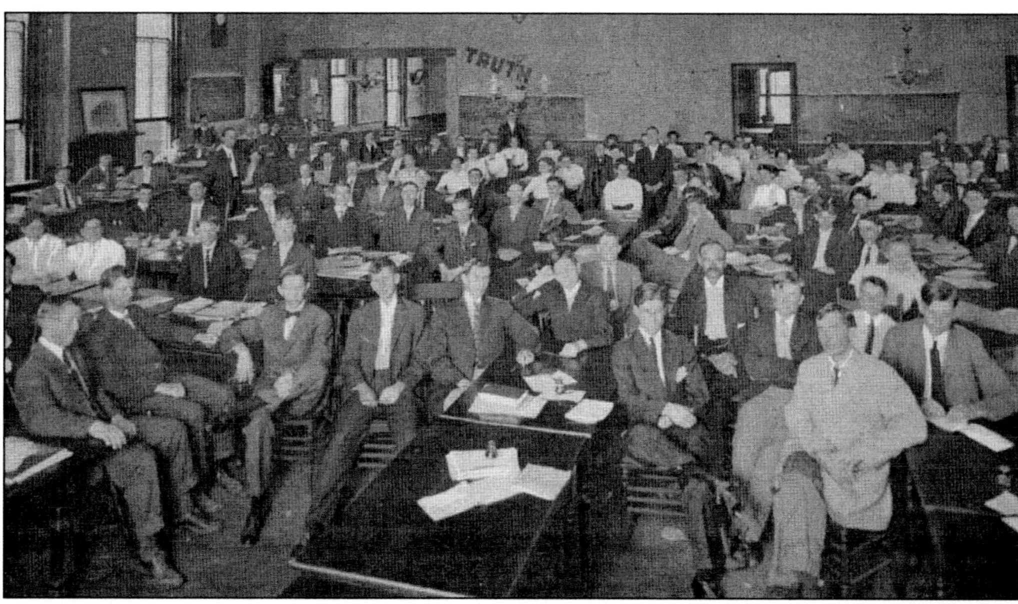

Approximately 100 male and female students can be seen in the bookkeeping department of the Georgia-Alabama Business College in this September 1, 1910 photograph. (McEvoy Book & Stationary Co., *c.* 1910, color.)

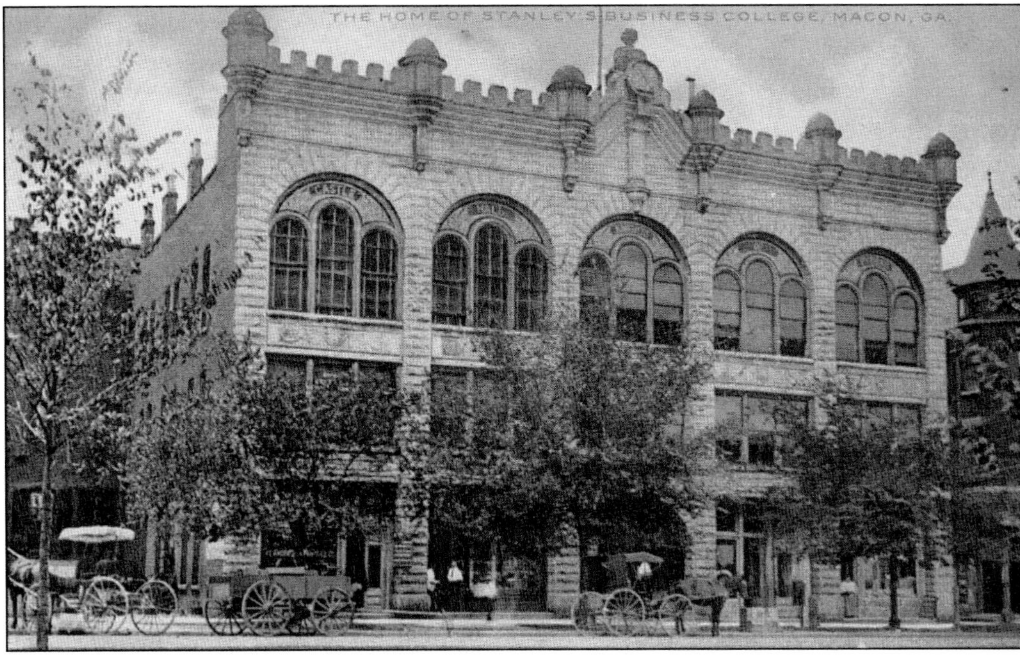

Stanley's Business College, located in the Castle Hall, Knights of Pythas, was a school for shorthand and telegraphy. (McEvoy Book & Stationary, *c.* 1910, color.)

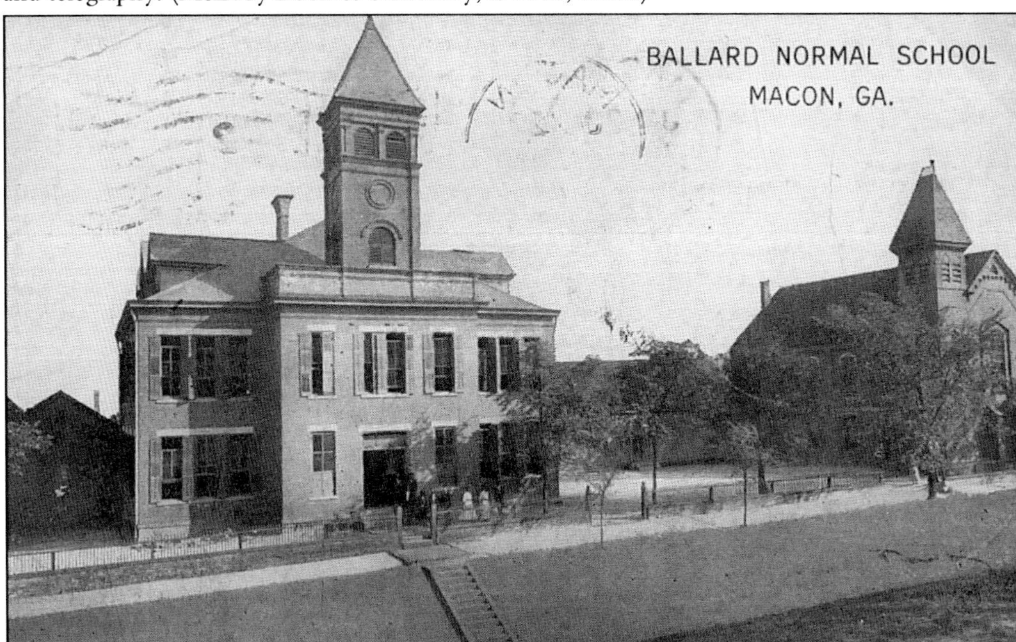

Ballard Normal School began as the Lewis High School; it was named for Gen. John Lewis, an active member of the Freedmen's Bureau. In 1876, the school was expanded into a teacher's training school. Its name changed in honor of Stephen Ballard, who donated funds for the new building. One person writes of the Ballard School saying, "I am enjoying my work at Ballard School, also like Macon, it is very hilly... We have a pleasant home, fine teachers. The principal has an auto." (Unidentified publisher, *c.* 1910, B/W.)

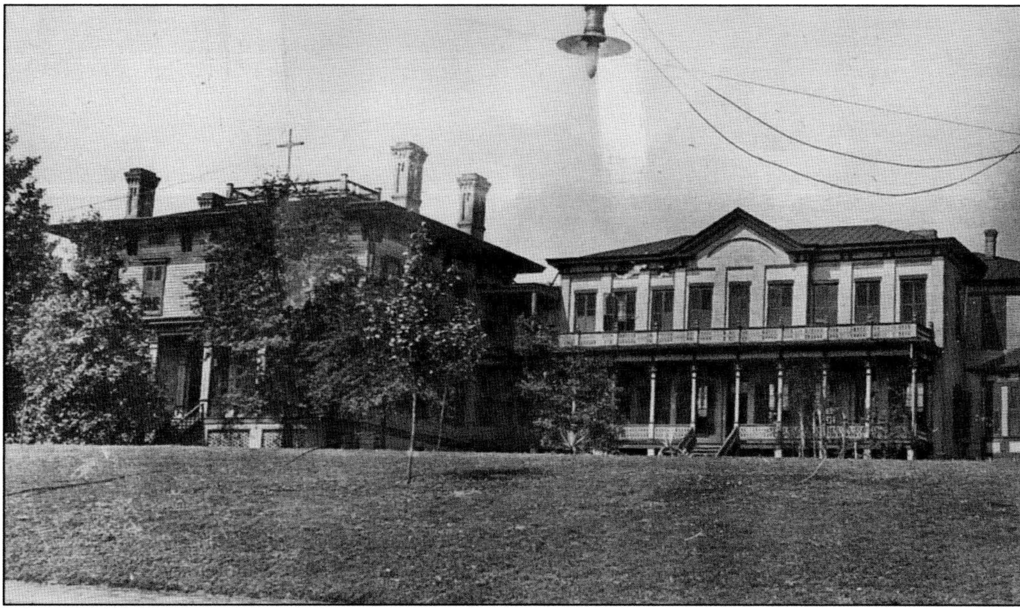

Mount de Sales Academy's, originally a small school run by five Sisters of Mercy, received its charter in 1876. A superior boarding school for young ladies, the school was located on Orange Street. (Real photograph, *c.* 1902, B/W.)

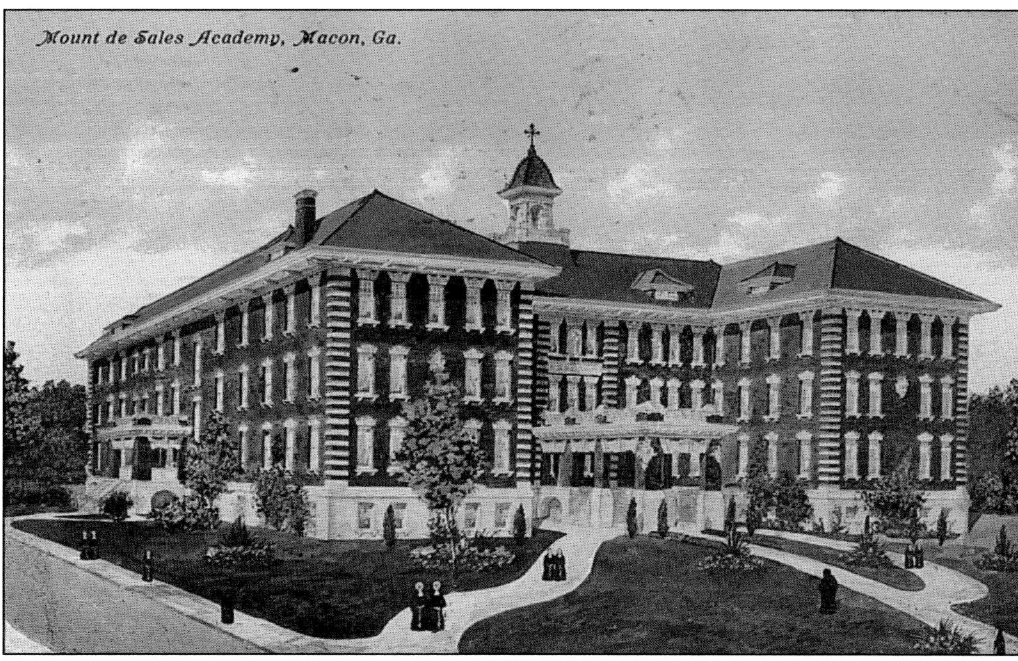

As Mount de Sales Academy's reputation and popularity attracted more pupils, increased enrollment necessitated expansion. This view, shown with a dozen nuns strolling the grounds, is of the new Mount de Sales Academy building. (S.H. Kress, Curt-Teich # A-13110, postmarked 1911, color.)

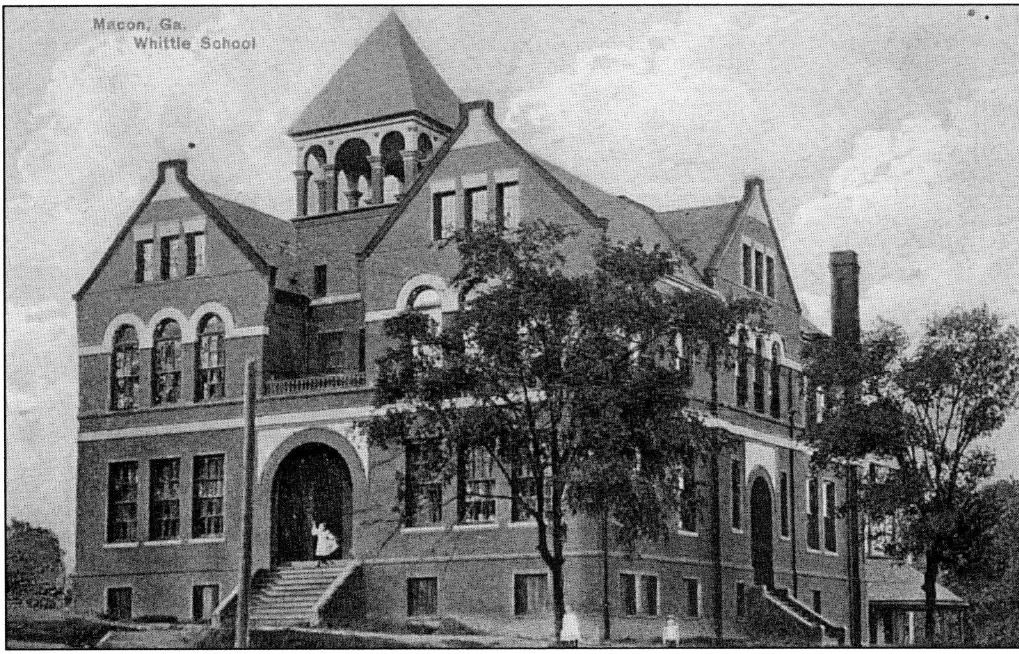

The Whittle School is shown here with several students out front. As was typical of the era, the refined girls wore dresses, while the boys wore shorts and were usually barefoot. Classrooms typically had desks that were bolted to the floor. (Peacock Series #8868, *c.* 1908, color.)

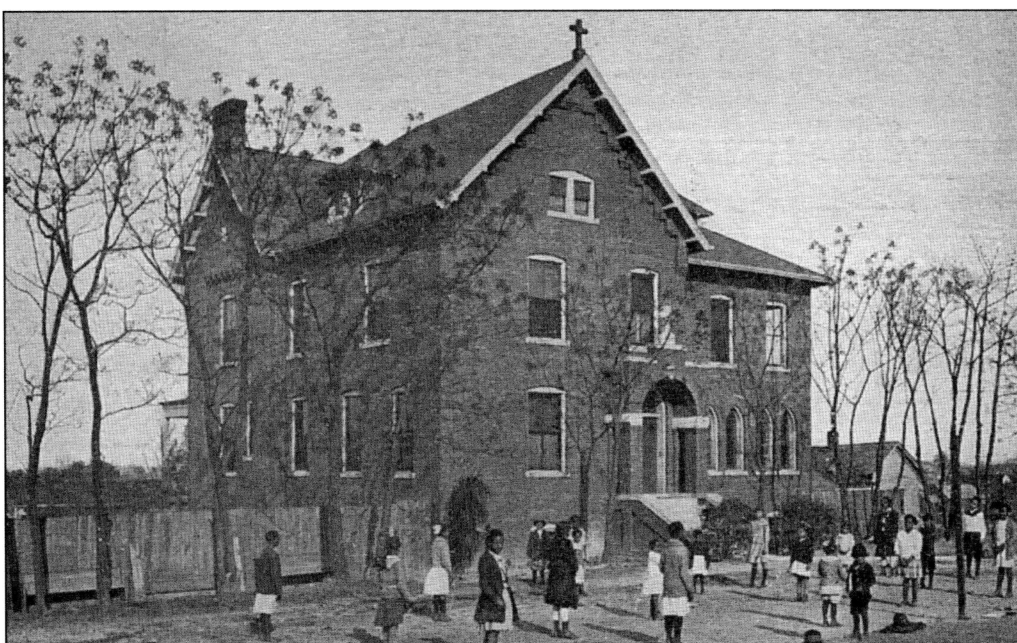

This photograph shows the house in which the sisters of the school lived and St. Peter's Claver's Rectory. A group of black students play in the yard. (Unidentified publisher, *c.* 1905, B/W.)

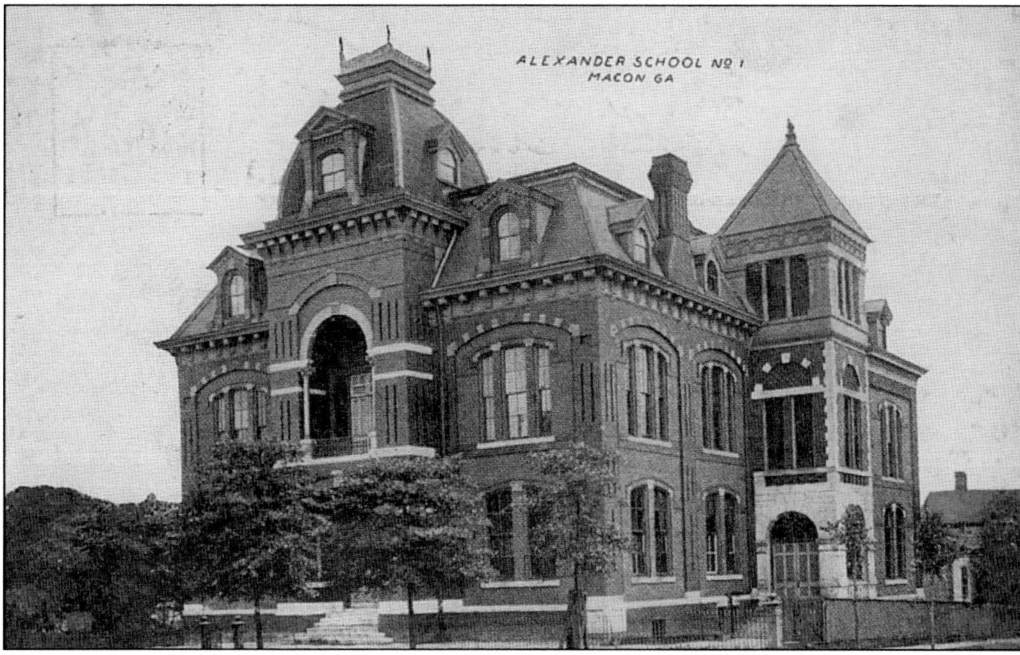

In 1892, the board of education assumed supervision over the Alexander Free School, which opened shortly after the end of the Civil War. Funding for the school was bequeathed by Elam Alexander, the architect who designed and built the original Wesleyan College building. (Unidentified publisher, postmarked 1909, B/W.)

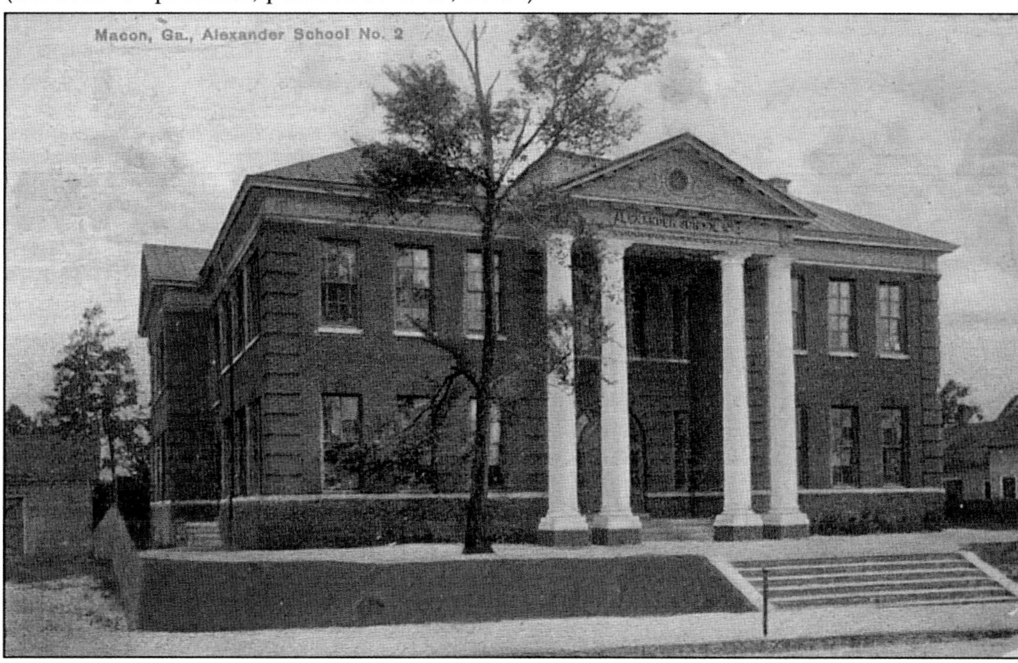

Shown here is the Alexander School No. 2; it is a beautiful school building with four large white columns. This school was constructed using more of the funds left by Elam Alexander, *c.* 1902. Other schools were built using the Alexander endowment in 1911 and 1933. (Peacock Series #8869, postmarked 1908, color.)

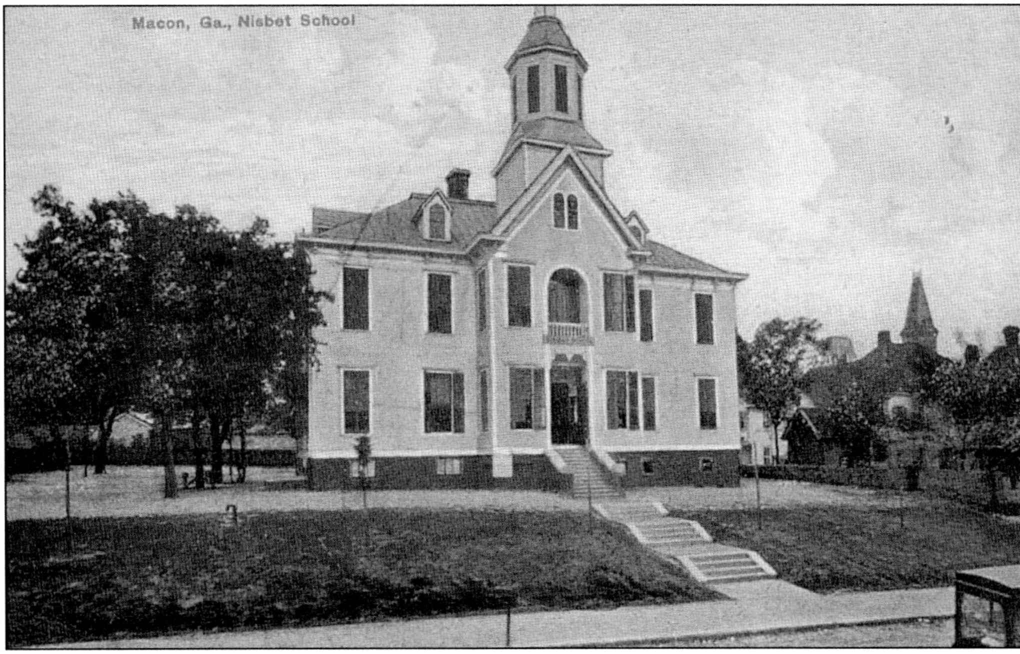

The Nisbet School was located on Orange Street. In 1893, records show that the county's total student enrollment was 2,978, which breaks down to 2,182 white and 796 black students. (Peacock Series #8866, *c.* 1908, color.)

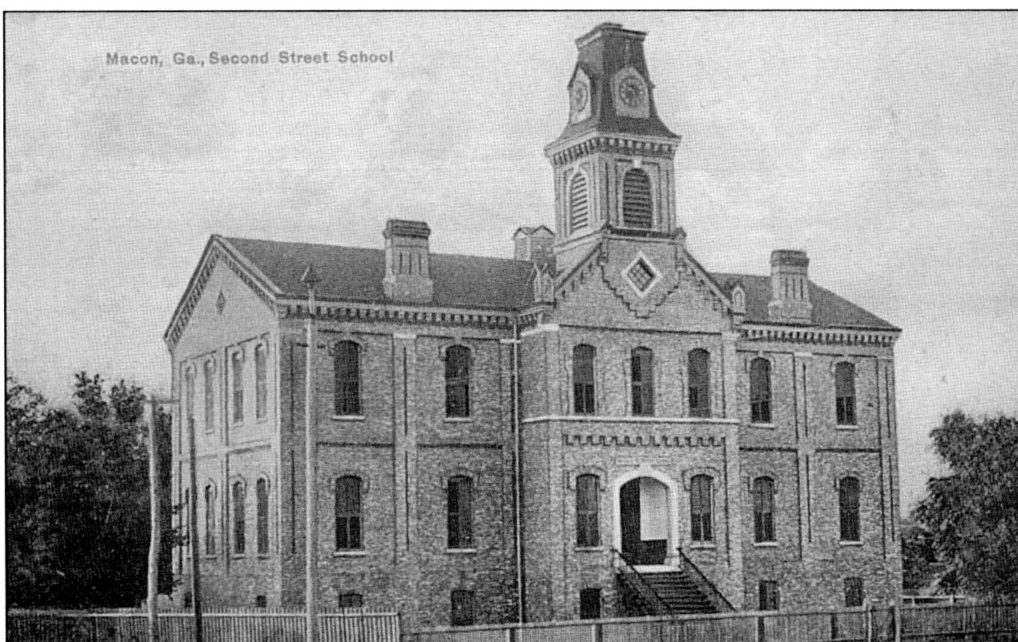

The Second Street School is a rock-faced building with a clock tower. By 1901, Macon's total student enrollment had grown to 7,310. Although the state school system only provided six months of education, Bibb County provided her children with education for nine months a year at an average cost per month per pupil of $1.36. (Peacock Series #8867, *c.* 1908, color.)

Five

Religious Diversity

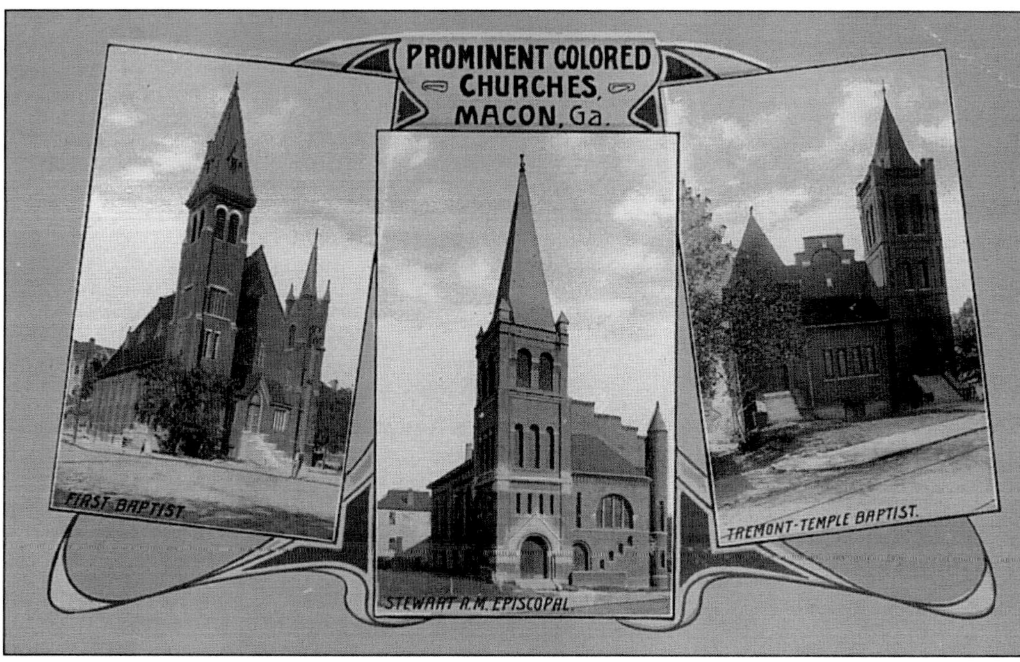

Macon's churches are said to be among the most beautiful in the state. Religious diversity is evident from the many different denominations, such as Methodist, Baptist, Presbyterian, Catholic, Hebrew, Episcopalian, Christian and others, located within Macon. Shown here are three prominent black churches, the First Baptist, the Stewart A.M. Episcopal, and the Tremont-Temple Baptist. (Power's Curiosity, Curt-Teich # A-13845, *c.* 1910, color.)

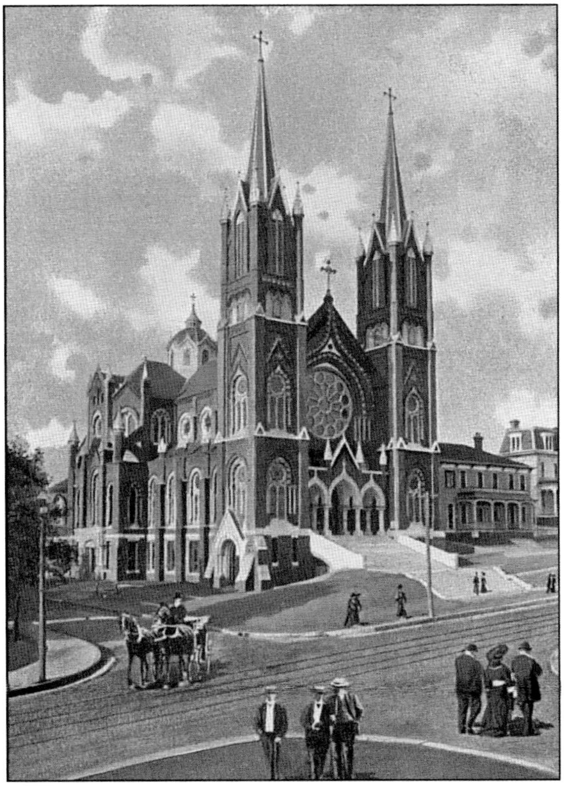

St. Joseph's Roman Catholic Church is located on the southwest corner of Poplar and New Streets. Completed in 1903, this beautiful church features two square Gothic towers supported by buttresses and topped by spires. One person writes, "This is the finest church in the south. I live about a hundred yards from it. I ought to get right don't you think?" (Raphael Tuck #2074, *c.* 1905, color.)

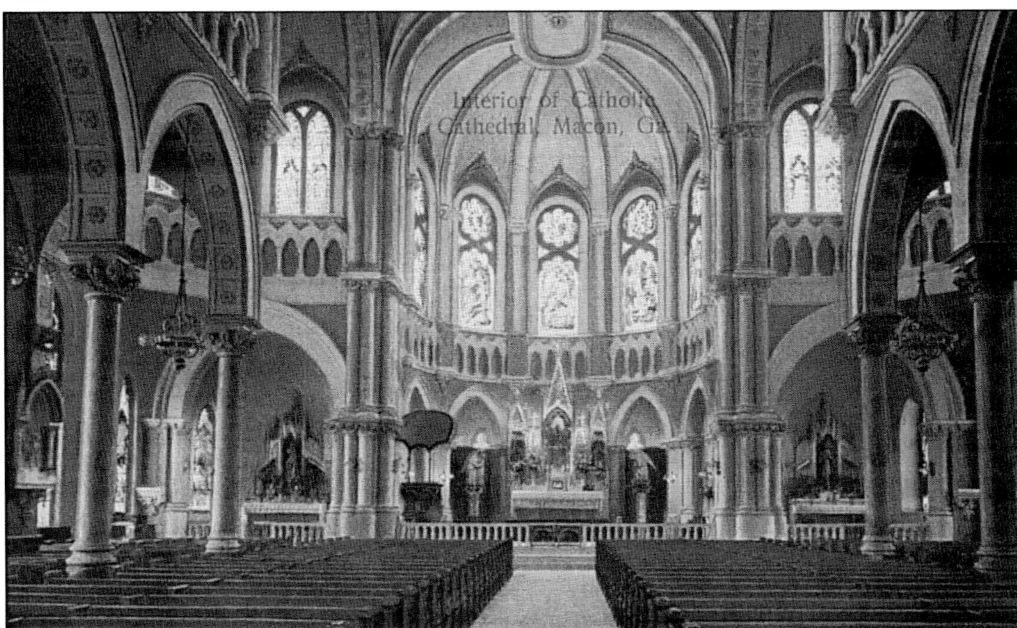

The St. Joseph Catholic Church's interior is beautiful with its graceful arches and impressive columns. In the cruciform interior, the floors and columns, as well as three alters, are all made of marble. Members of the church donated the stained glass windows and numerous statues. (International Postcard Co. #572, *c.* 1908, color.)

The Christ Church, located on Walnut Street, is a gray brick stucco structure that was built in the form of the English cross. The interior gallery, once set aside for the Negro slaves, is supported by iron pillars. Founded by Dr. Ambrose Baber, the church was established in 1825; the building was completed in 1852. (Souvenir Postcard Co. #15559, postmarked 1907, B/W.)

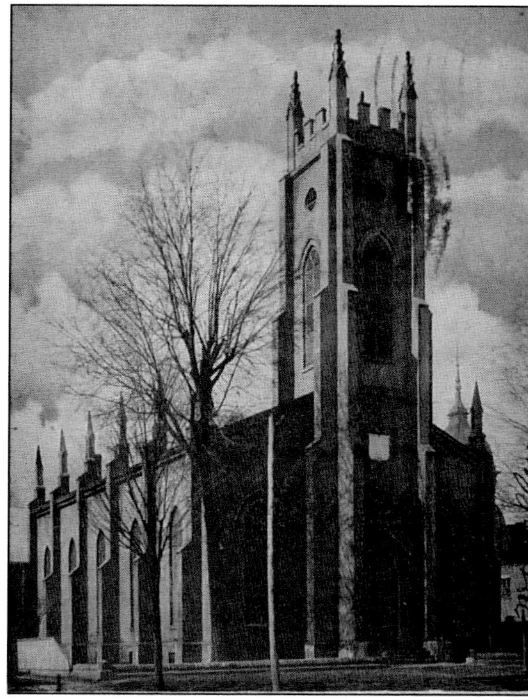

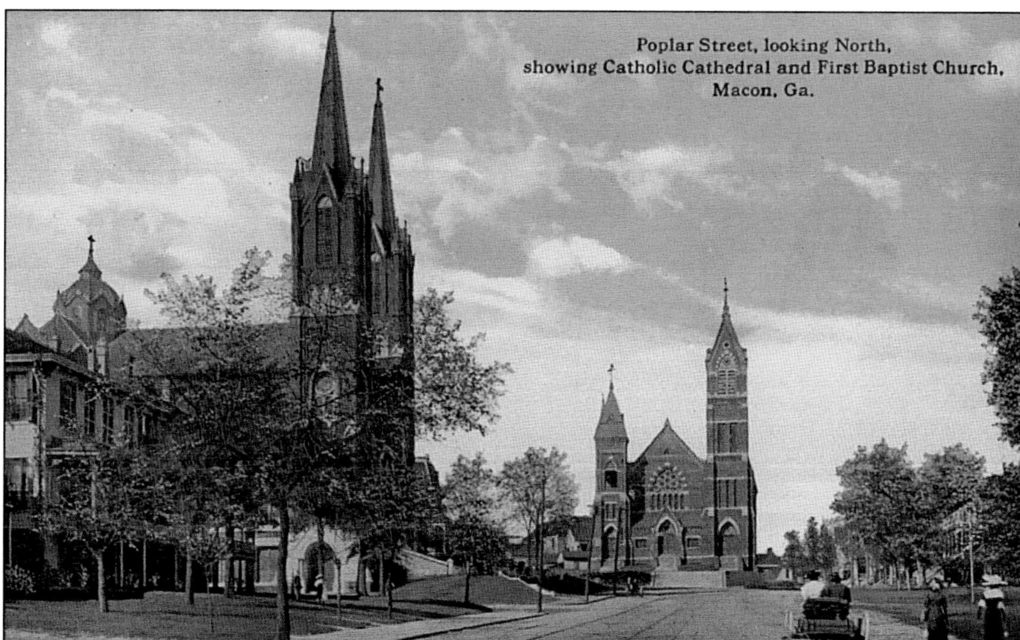

The First Baptist Church building, located at the head of Poplar Street, was built in 1887. While serving as pastor of the First Baptist Church from 1828–1830, Adiel Sherwood revised the first edition of his *Gazetteer of the State of Georgia.* This view shows both the Catholic Cathedral and the First Baptist Church. (S.H. Kress # A-27009, *c.* 1910, color.)

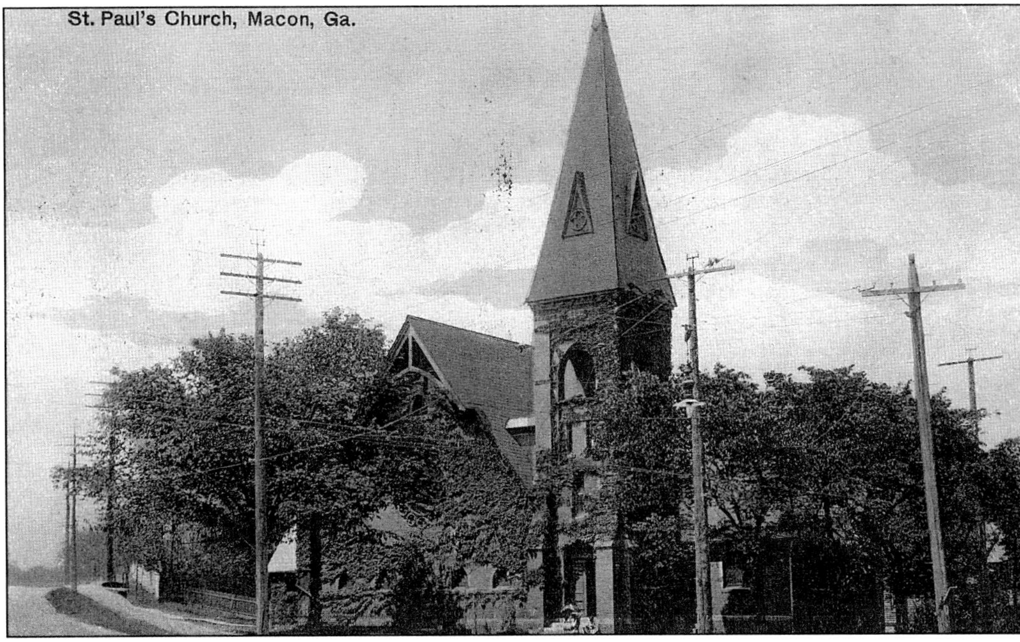

St. Paul's Episcopal Church is located on College Street. Rev. Henry Kollack Rees founded it in 1868. The Parish House is the former Appleton Orphanage, which was established by William Appleton of New York, "whose heart was full of sympathy for the destitute orphans of deceased Confederate soldiers." (S.H. Kress #74, postmarked 1908, hand colored.)

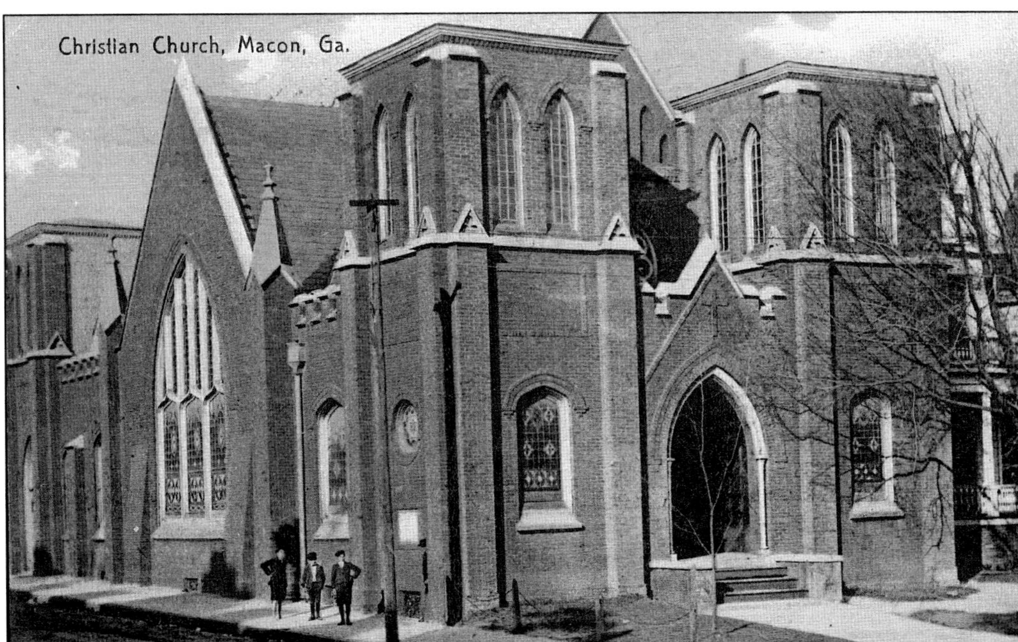

Three young men stand to the side of the Christian church on Vineville Avenue. Mildred, the sender of the card, writes of a long-standing Sunday afternoon tradition, "We have a fine day Sunday. Drove about few miles in the country and gathered a great bunch of violets." (Rotograph Co. #64293, postmarked 1909, color.)

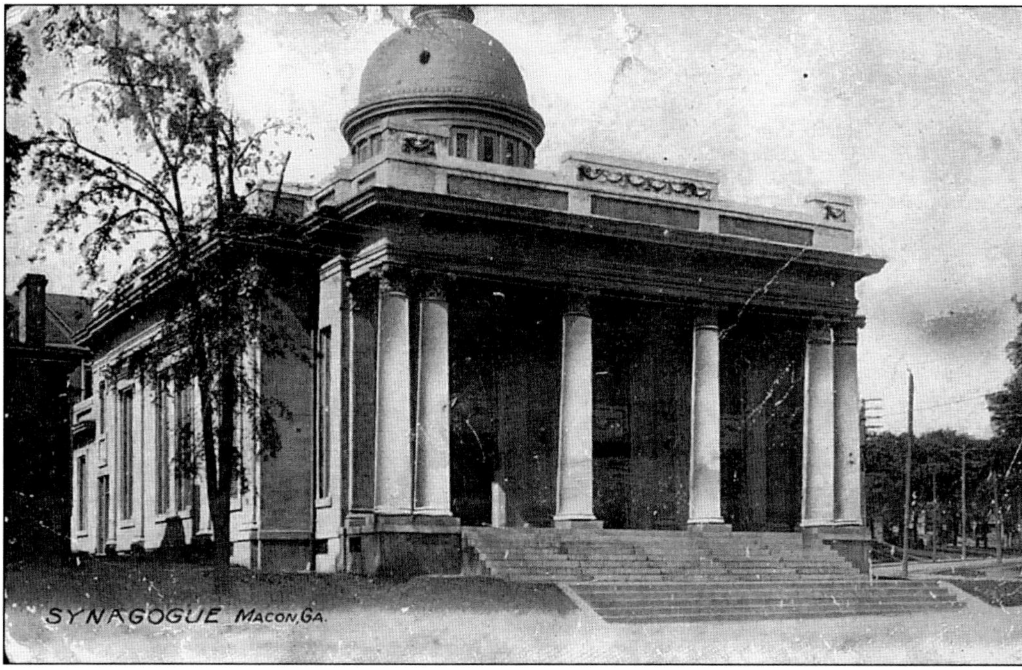

The synagogue in downtown Macon can be seen here with its six large, white columns and beautiful dome top. (J.W. Burke Co., *c.* 1910, B/W.)

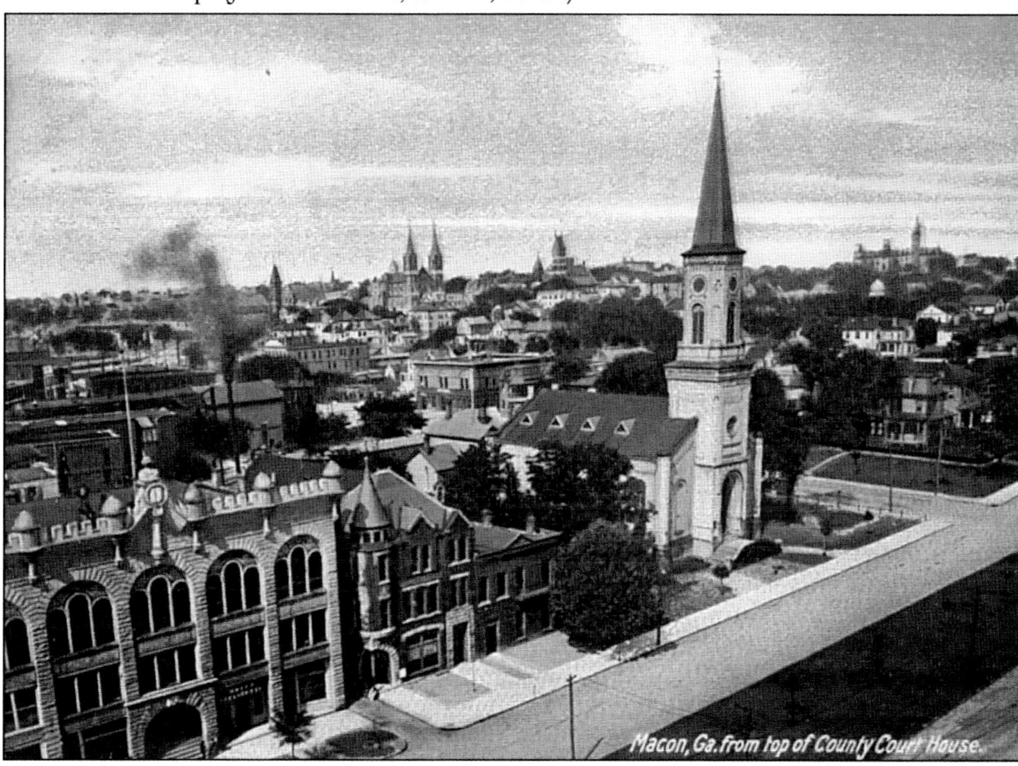

This view, from the top of the county courthouse, shows the Mulberry Presbyterian Church. (H.C. Leighton Co. # 1678, *c.* 1905, color.)

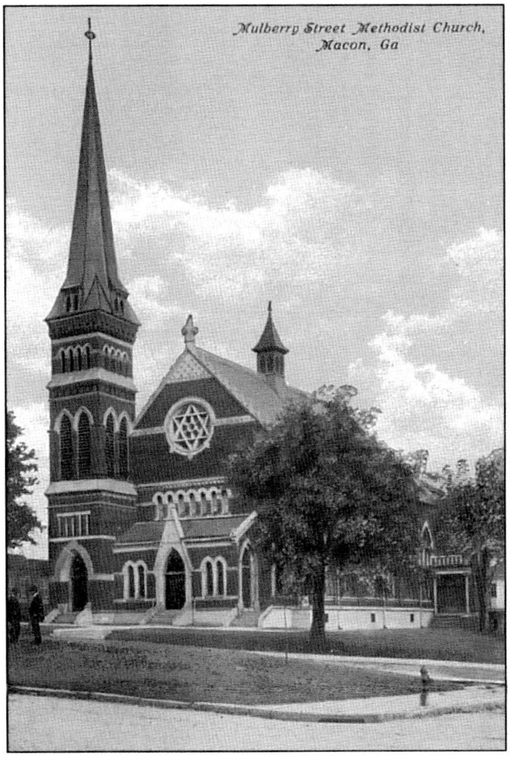

The Mulberry Street Methodist Church, located on the northwest corner of Mulberry and First Streets, is among the oldest religious institutions in Macon. Established in 1828, the congregation outgrew the original building; this building was erected in 1850. This building has since been replaced by the building shown below. (S.H. Kress #A-412, *c.* 1910, color.)

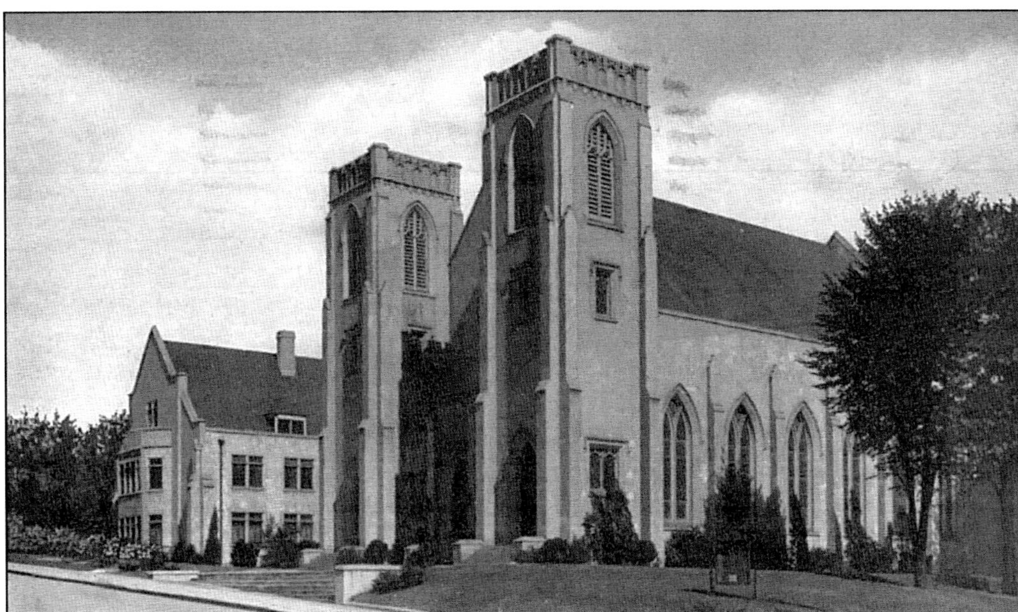

The caption on the back reads, "Mulberry Methodist Church was the first church to have a house of worship and the only church of historical interest to remain continuously on the same site." The church is built of Indiana limestone and has tall cathedral windows with pointed arches, a slate roof, and the double square towers characteristic of the Colonial-Gothic style. (Graycraft Card Co. #M-226, Free mail, postmarked 1943, B/W.)

Six

Good Times

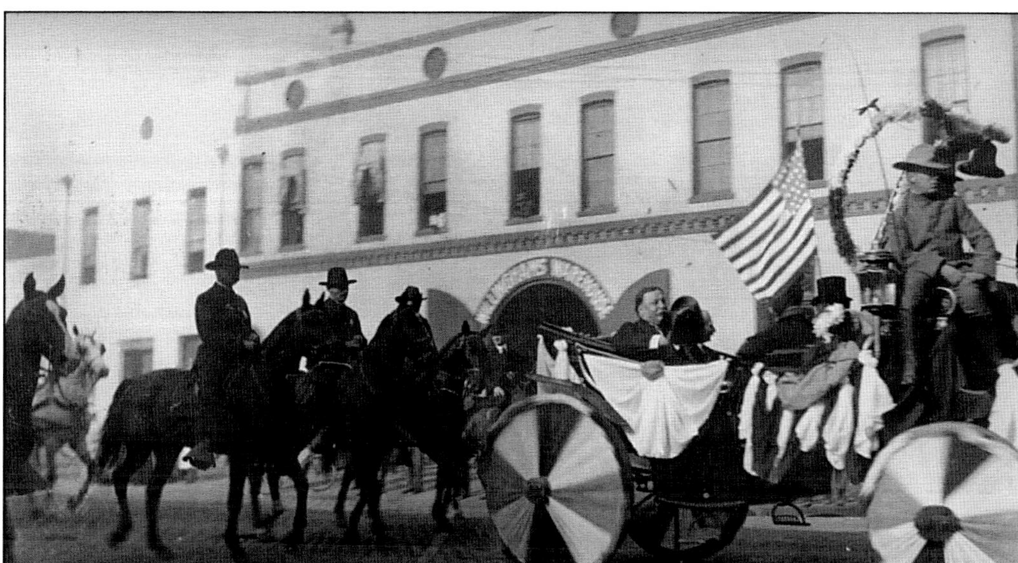

Macon has always been a lively city with a love for celebrations. From civic events, carnivals, state fairs, and Confederate Veterans Reunions to Presidential visits, Maconites have turned each occasion into grand times. The women of Macon have graced every celebration with beauty and poise as true "Southern Belles." The men have behaved as proud and honorable "Southern Gentlemen." One of Macon's fondest memories is the visit by President Taft in 1908. President Taft is shown here in a lovely decorated carriage in front of Willingham's Warehouse. (Real photograph, *c.* 1908, B/W.)

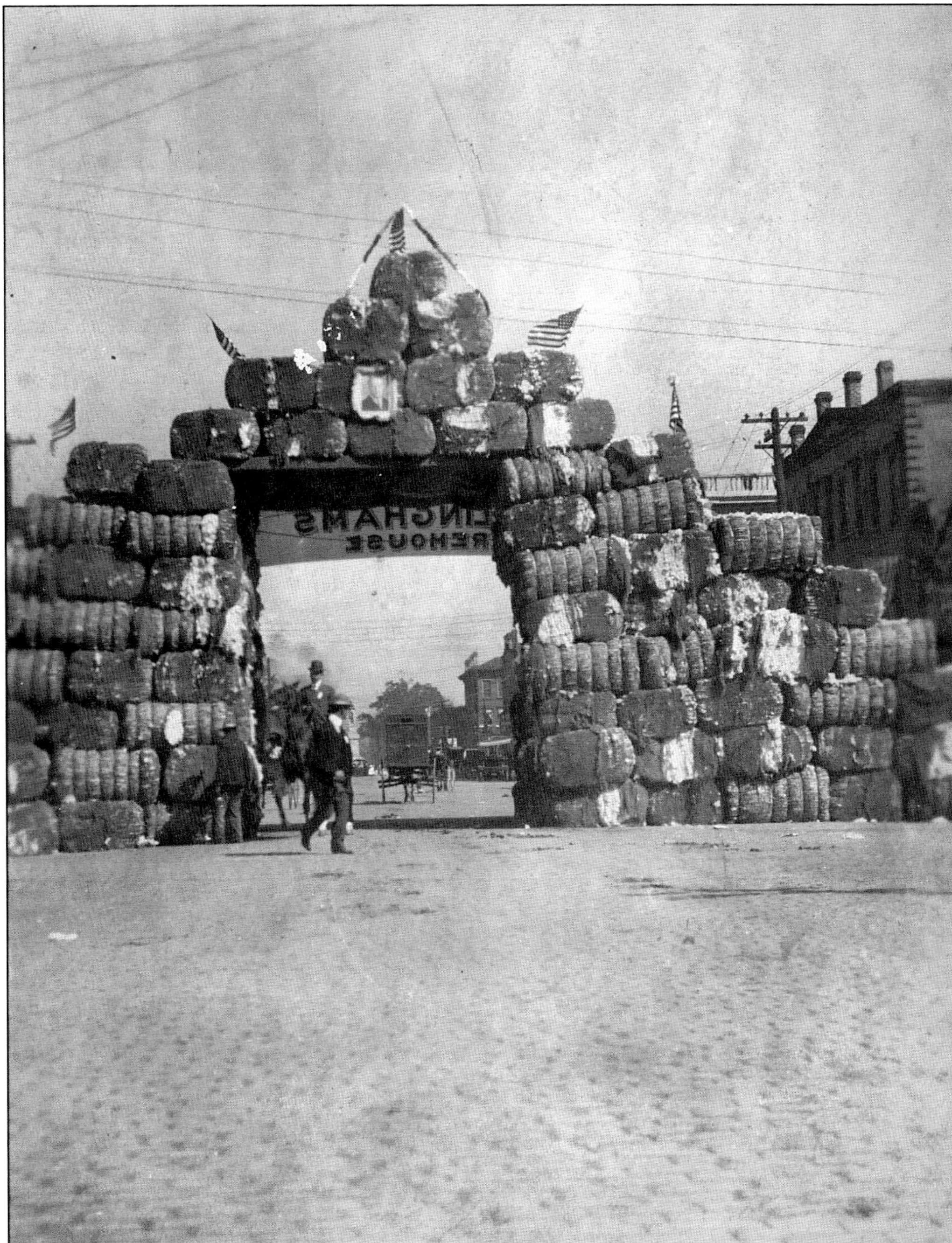

During his 5-hour visit, President William Howard Taft was driven under this cotton arch on Second Street. The arch was designed by Richard Willingham and contained 300 bales of cotton, weighting about 500 pounds each. The sign on the other side of the arch read, "Taft Prosperity-15 Cent Cotton-Willingham's Warehouse." (Real photograph, *c.* 1908, B/W.)

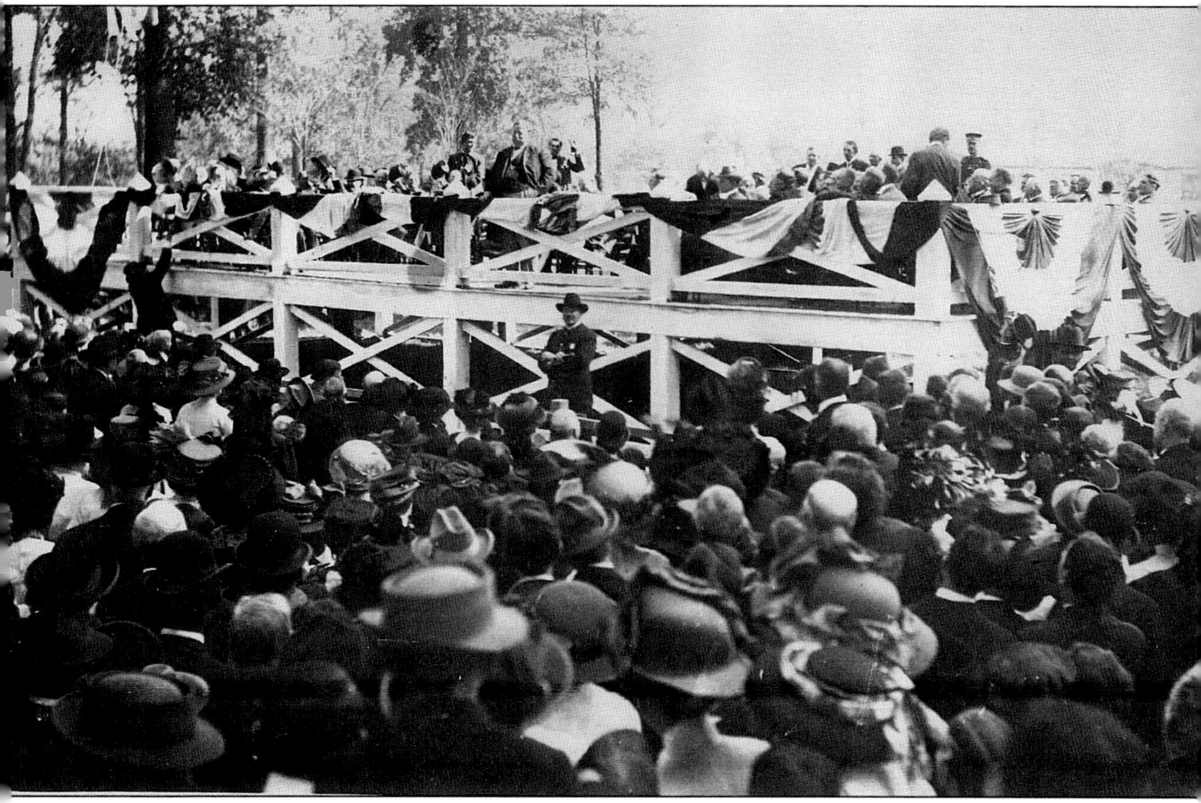

Born in 1857, the son of a distinguished judge, William H. Taft graduated from Yale and returned to Cincinnati to study and practice law. Taft rose in politics through judiciary appointments because, as he jovially wrote once, he always had his "plate the right side up when offices were falling." Taft was appointed a Federal circuit judge at age 34. Later, President Roosevelt made him secretary of war and, by 1907, had decided that Taft should be his successor. Taft disliked campaigning and complained once that it was "one of the most uncomfortable four months of my life." Taft served four years as 27th President of the United States from 1909 to 1913. Once free from the Presidency, Taft served as professor of law at Yale until just before his death in 1930. President Taft was invited to Macon by the Fair Association. Here, President Taft can be seen speaking to a crowd of citizens at Central City Park in 1908. At over 300 pounds, President Taft is easily identified on the stage. (Real photograph, *c.* 1908, B/W.)

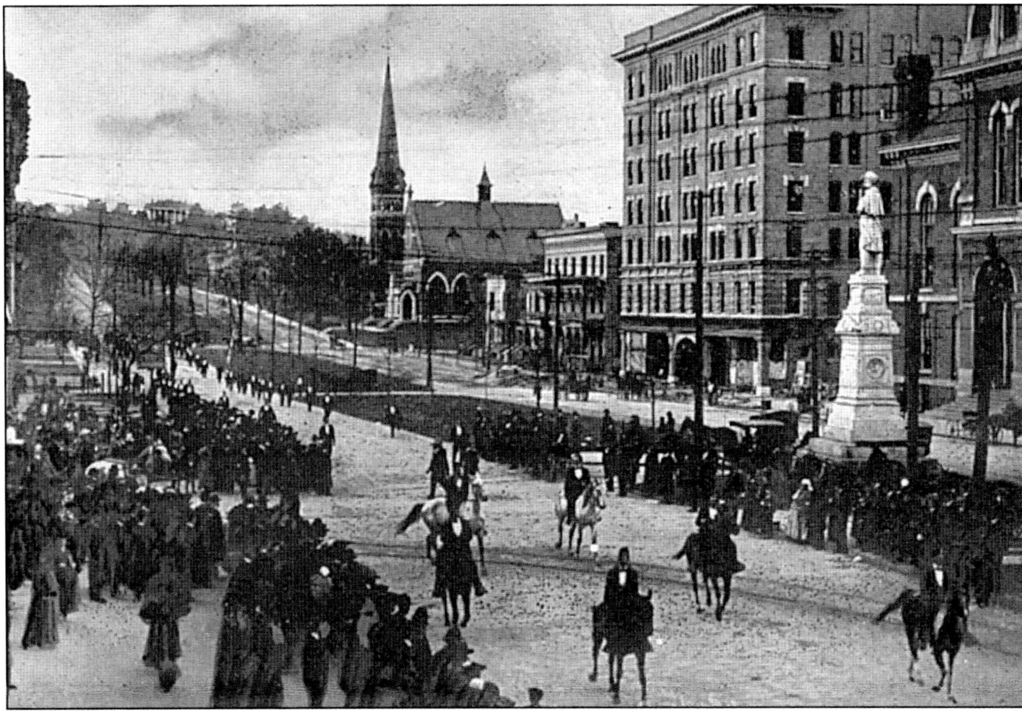

This Shriner's Parade on Mulberry Street passes in front of the Confederate Memorial and the courthouse. This parade preceded the Shriner's of Macon being granted their own temple, Al Sihah, in 1910. (Souvenir Postcard Co. #15551, *c.* 1905, B/W.)

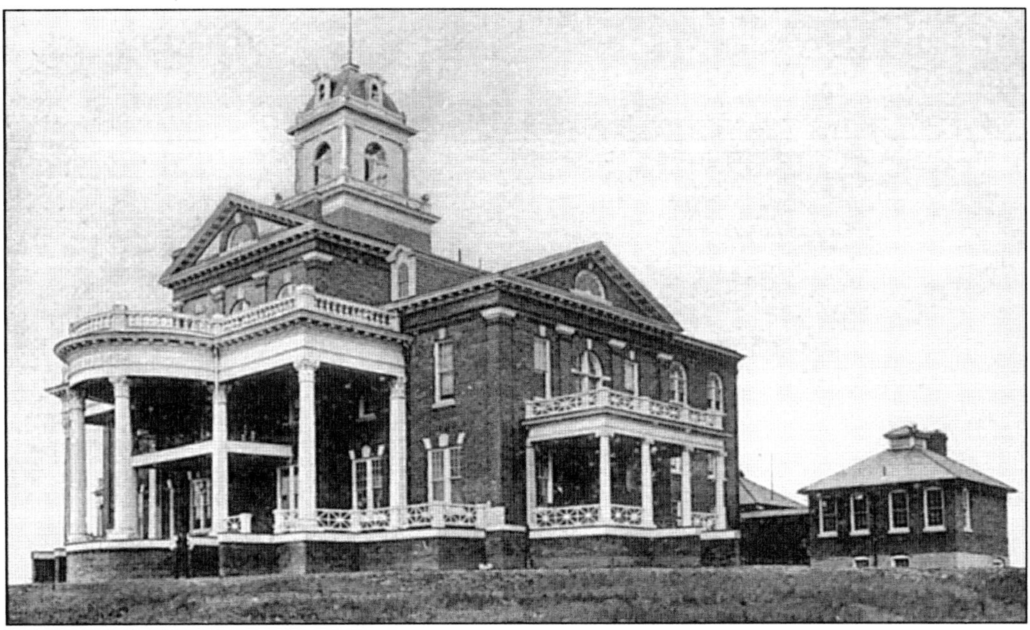

In 1825, the Free and Accepted Masons, Macon Lodge No. 5, was chartered with Ambrose Baber as worshipful master. In 1903, the Masonic Home was dedicated as a home for orphaned Masons. The land on which the house stands was donated by Senator A.O. Bacon. (McEvoy Book & Stationary, *c.* 1905, B/W.)

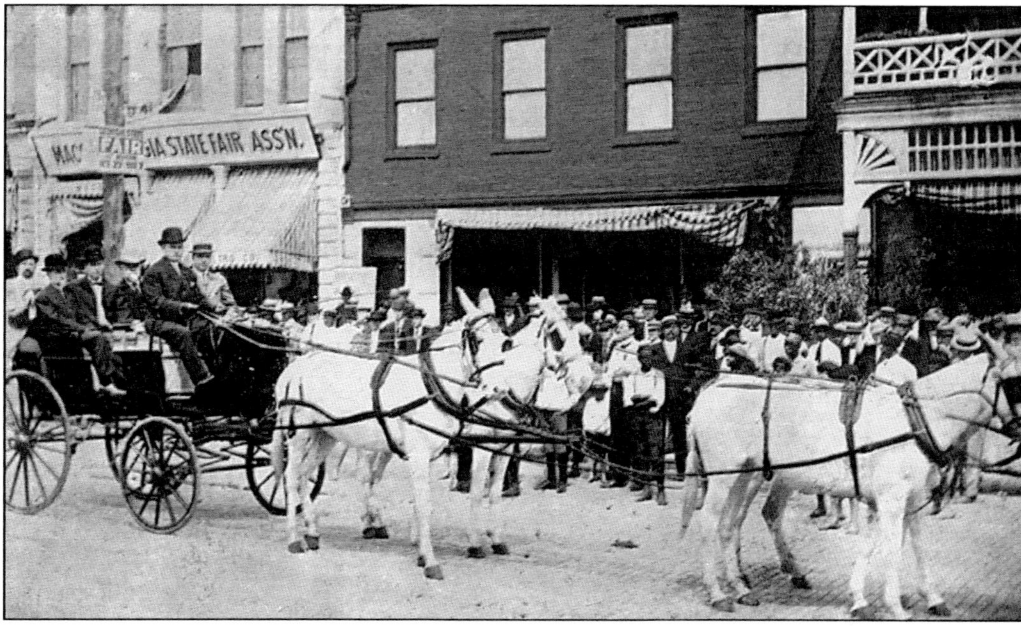

The annual Georgia State Fair, held in Macon, was a grand event. In a parade for the fair, local and state leaders rode in carriages waving at the crowds on the street. The carriage in this picture holds Georgia State Governor Joseph M. Brown. Governor Brown is driven by Ben L. Jones and accompanied by Sam Dunlap, C.R. Pendleton, Jesse B. Hart, O.C. Gibson, and John P. Ross, Macon businessmen and civic leaders. (Unidentified publisher, *c.* 1909, B/W.)

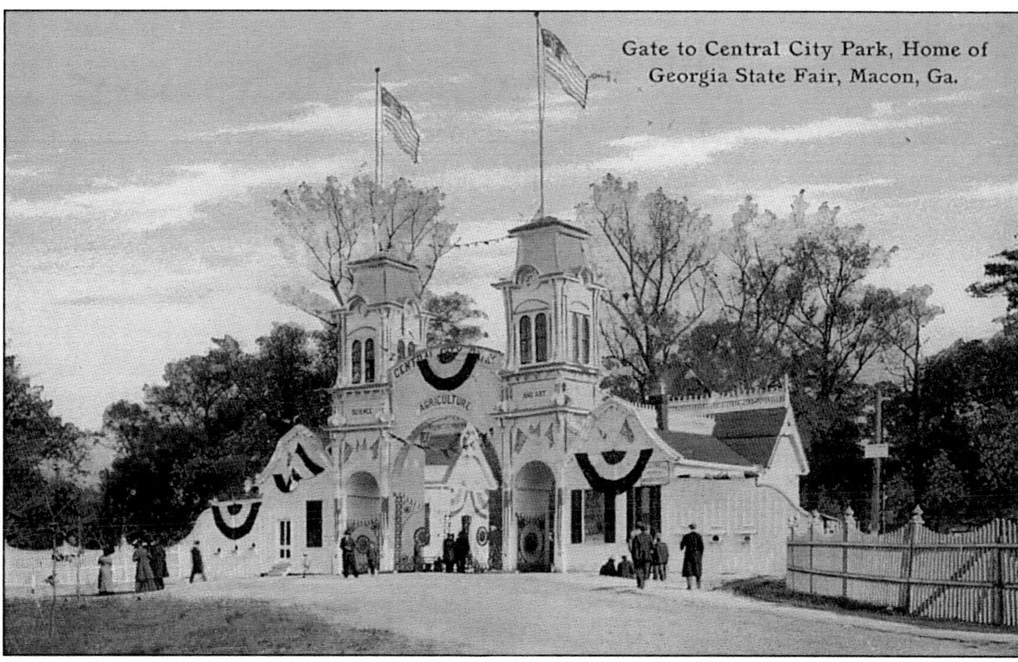

The gate to Central City Park, home of the Georgia State Fair, was designed and built to pay tribute to science, art, and agriculture, in 1871. (Power's Curiosity, Curt-Teich # A-13851, postmarked 1912, color.)

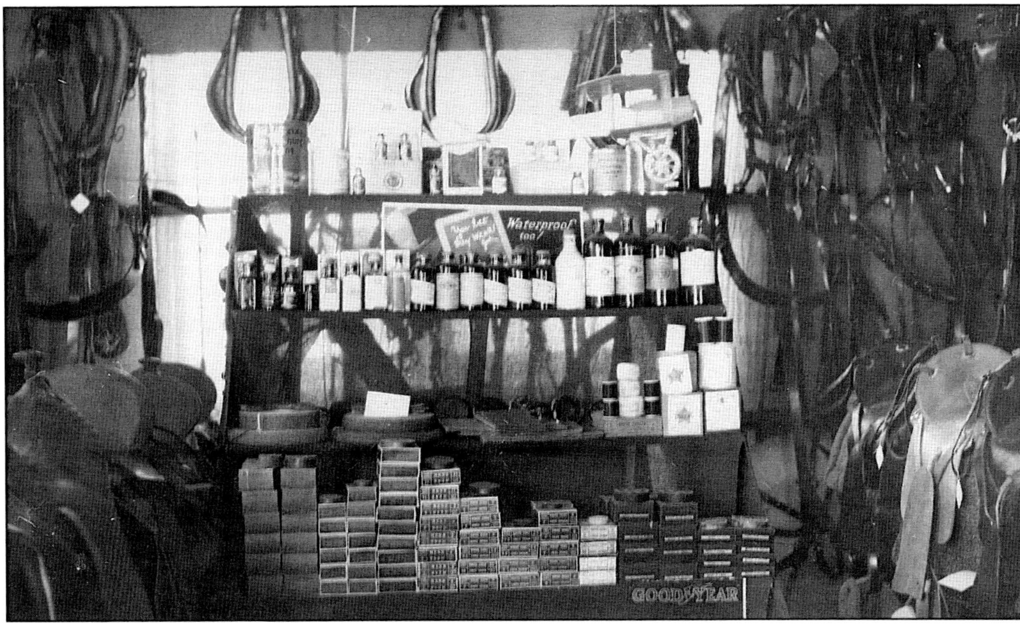

G. Bernd & Co. display their saddles, harnesses, and other horse-related products at the Georgia State Fair. The agricultural portion of the fair was always a highlight, especially the stock judging. The women of the area worked hard all year canning, pickling, perfecting recipes, sewing, and quilting for the various homemaker contests. (Real photograph, *c.* 1920, B/W.)

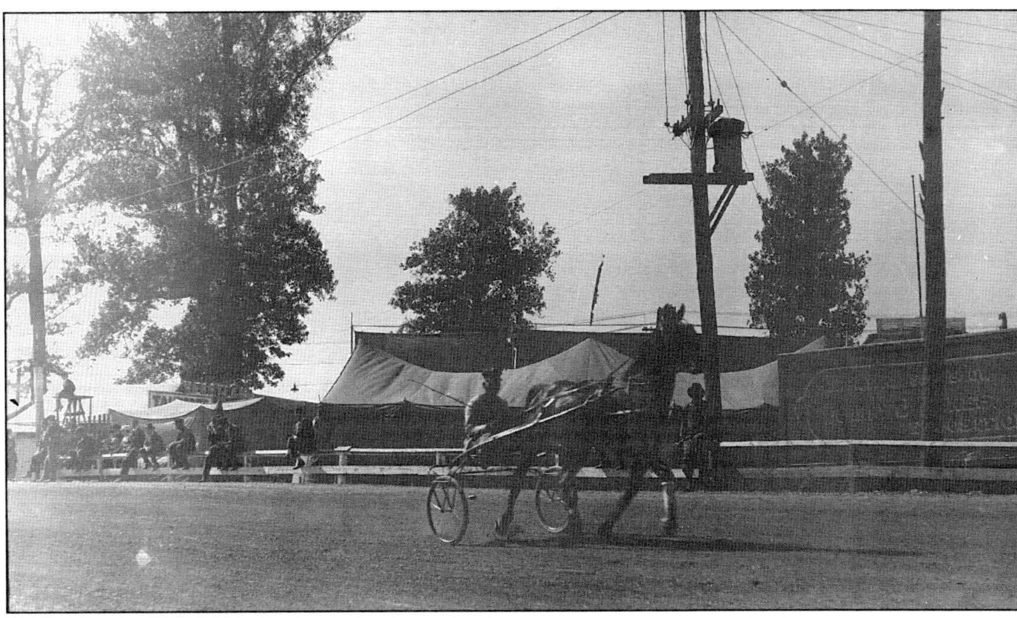

For fast paced excitement at the Georgia State Fair, crowds attended the harness races at Central City Park's racetrack. On person writes, "The Fair of the State of Georgia is on this week. It would please you, good horse races. The best was 2:15 a mile." In 1903, the celebrated harness racer, Dan Patch, established two new records here. (Real photograph, *c.* 1920, B/W.)

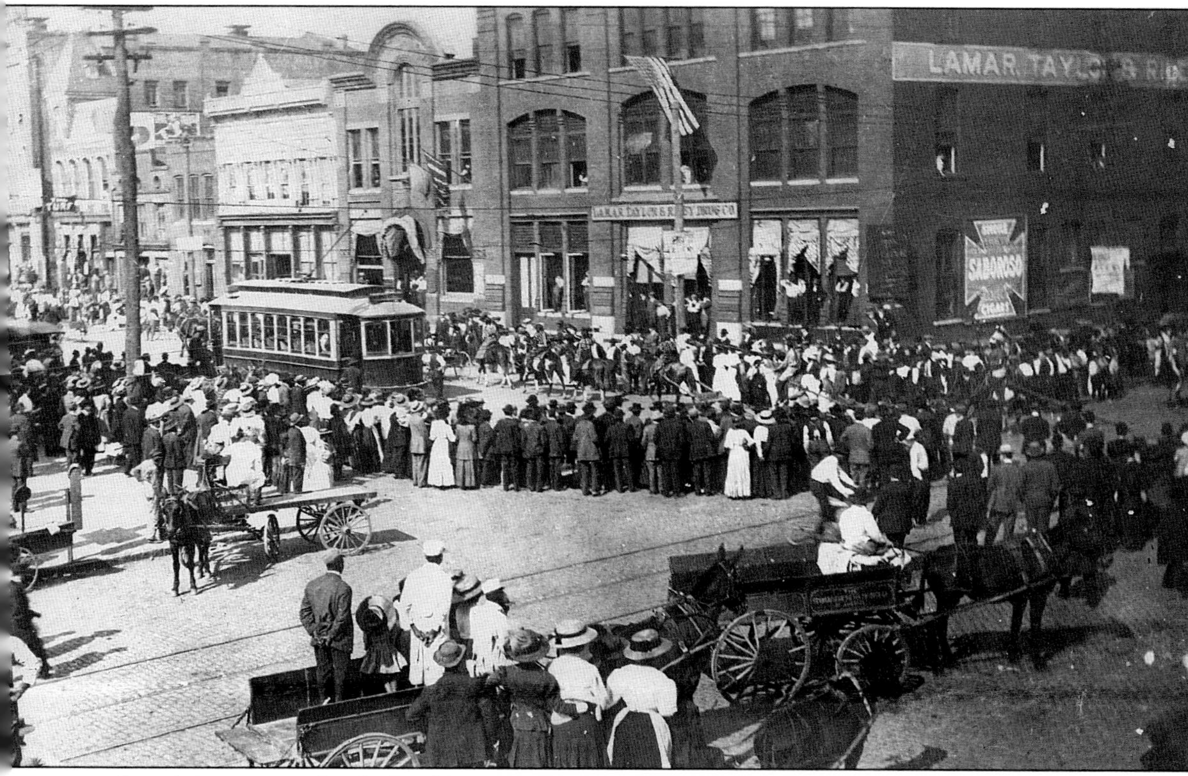

In colonial America, individual wild animals were put on display, and an admission was charged. As time went on, to beat the competition, circus owners began adding more animals to their shows. By the early 1800s, full-fledge menageries were the trend. By the 1900s, the circus was even more than just animals. Each circus promised the daring high wire acts, the strangest freaks, the best magicians, and the most beautiful assistants. The traveling circus, a sight to behold, brought excitement to every city they visited. The colorful caravans, with promises of exotic animals, magic acts, daring feats, and funny clowns, drew crowds everywhere they went. Macon was no exception. Here we see the crowds gathered in front of the Lamar, Taylor, & Riley Drug Co. to watch an approaching circus. People sought the best viewing position from the street, wagons, and even the streetcar. (Real photograph postcard, *c.* 1919, B/W.)

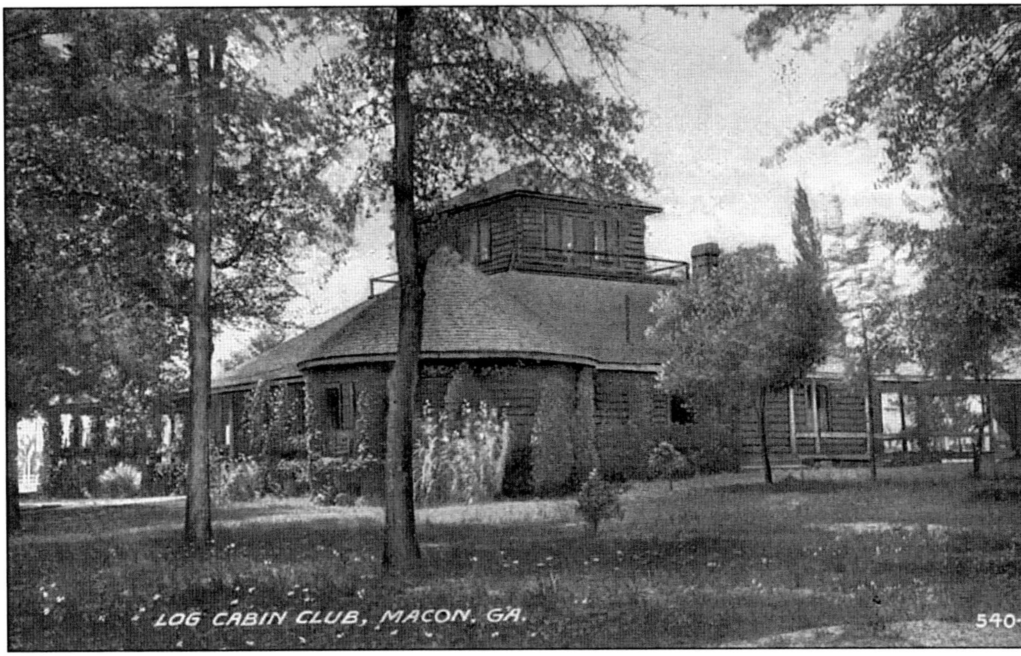

The Log Cabin Club was a men's club for informal entertaining. The building was a log structure with a spacious ballroom, big verandas, tennis courts, and a bowling alley. (Unidentified publisher, #540-12, color.)

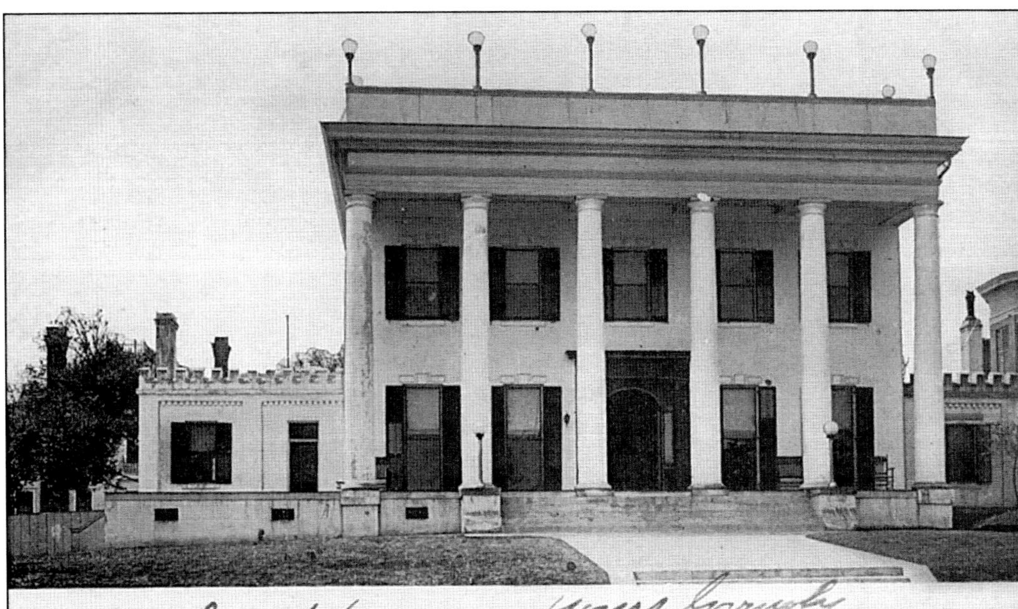

The Cherokee Club was located in the Gresham mansion on College Street. Primarily a men's club, the well-appointed drawing rooms were frequently used by the wives and sisters of its members for parties and receptions. (Curt-Teich # 2256, *c.* 1907, tinted.)

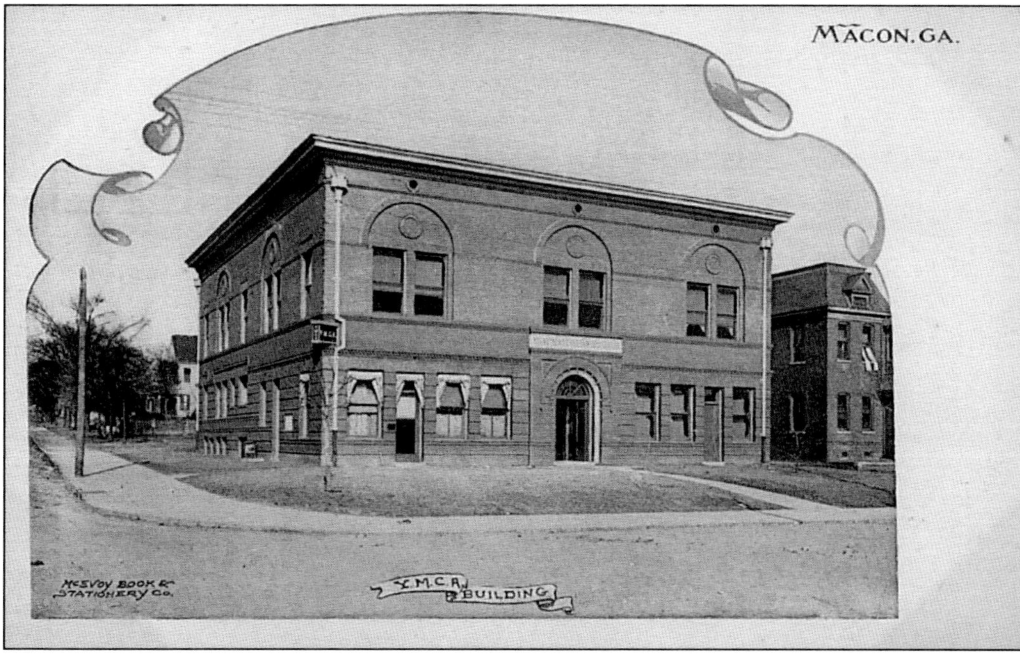

The Macon YMCA, founded in 1855, was one of the first in the country. This building was located on the corner of Cherry and First Streets. (McEvoy Book & Stationary, *c.* 1905, B/W.)

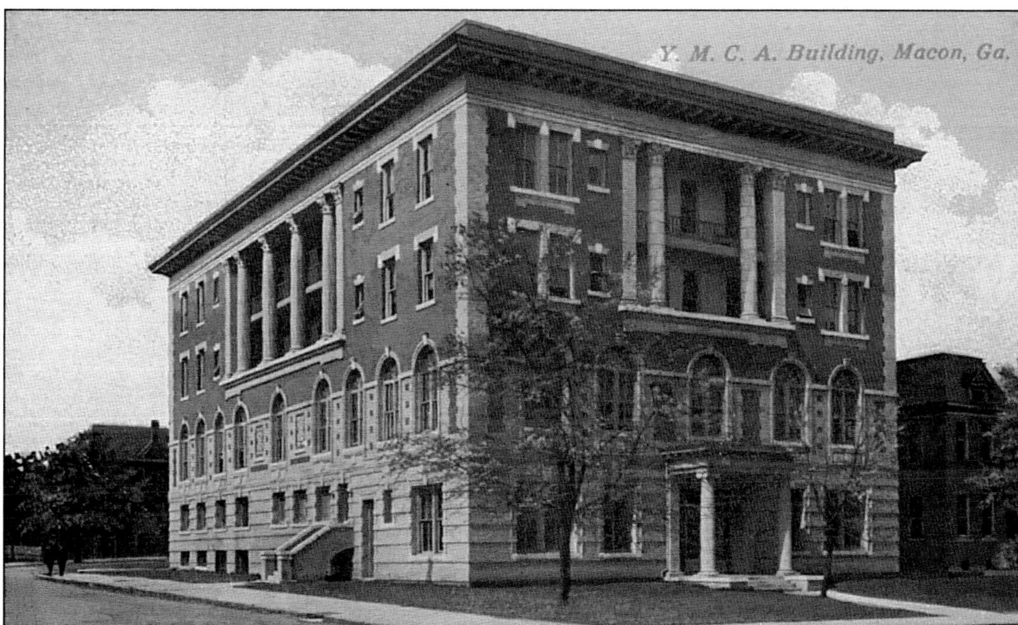

The new YMCA building was completed in 1912. It became the Macon Health Club during the 1960s, after members decided to split ties with the national organization rather than desegregate. (S.H. Kress #34262, postmarked 1914, color.)

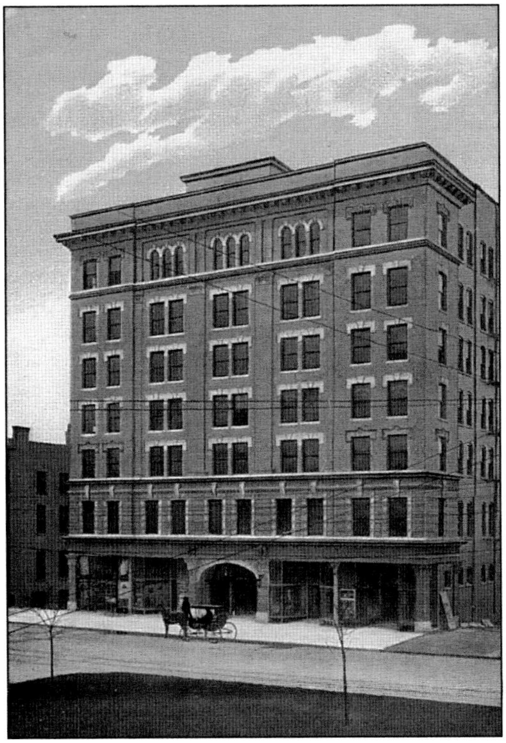

The Grand Opera House, formerly the Academy of Music, is located on Mulberry Street. Some of the world's most famous performers, such as Sarah Bernhardt and Anna Pavlova, have graced this Macon stage. (Souvenir Postcard Co. #20184, *c.* 1907, color.)

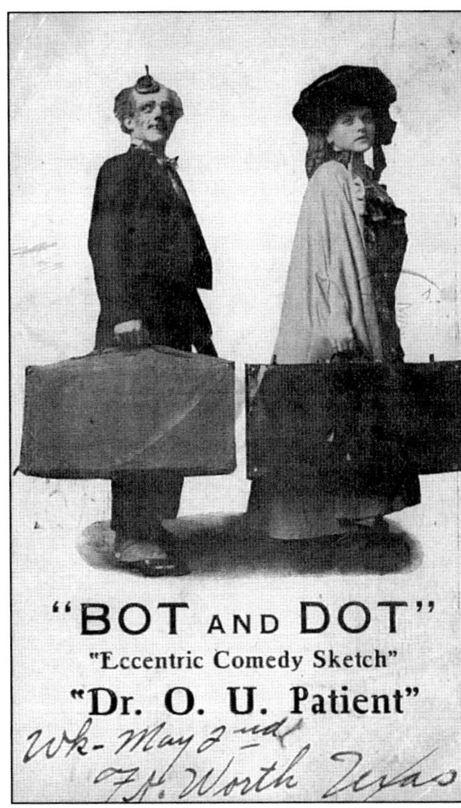

From Macon, "Bot and Dot" toured the country doing their comedy routines, while always keeping in touch with their family through postcards advertising their shows. This card is promoting their "Eccentric Comedy Sketch—Dr. O.U. Patient." On the card, they write, "wk-May 2nd, Ft. Worth Texas." (Unidentified publisher, postmarked 1910, B/W.)

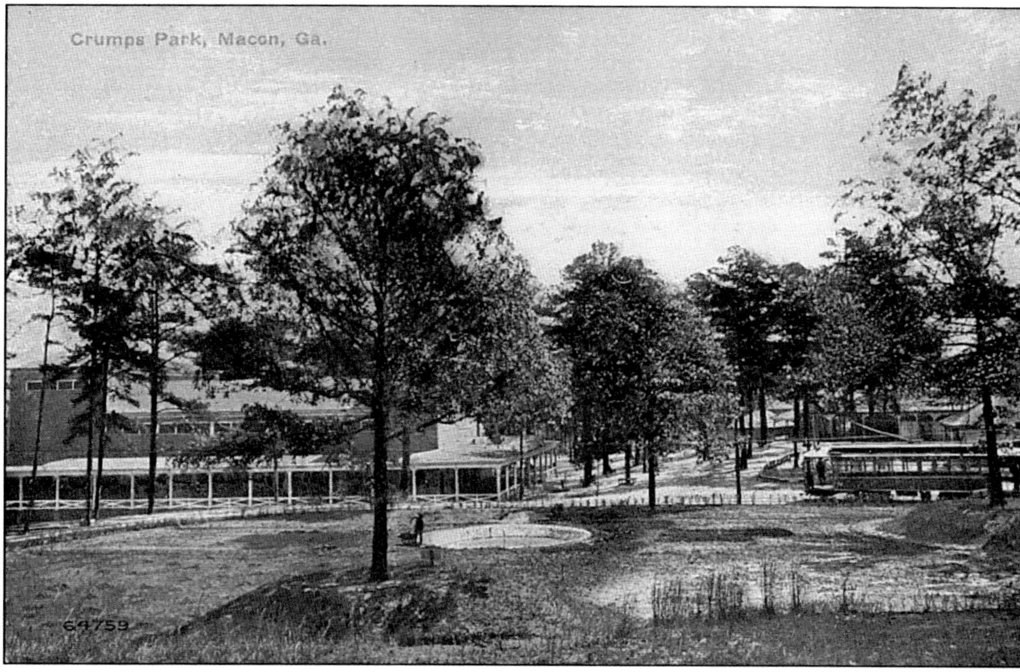

Crumps Park was a favorite summertime resort and amusement park, largely developed by the Macon Railway and Light Company. The park included a dance pavilion, a theater, a shooting gallery, and picnicking facilities. The park was located about 3 miles north of downtown, north of Vista Circle, between Vineville and Ingleside Avenues. A streetcar ran every 15 minutes during the day. The park was taken over for a National Guard mobilization camp, renamed Camp Harris, shortly before World War I. (Unidentified publisher #64759, *c.* 1910, color.)

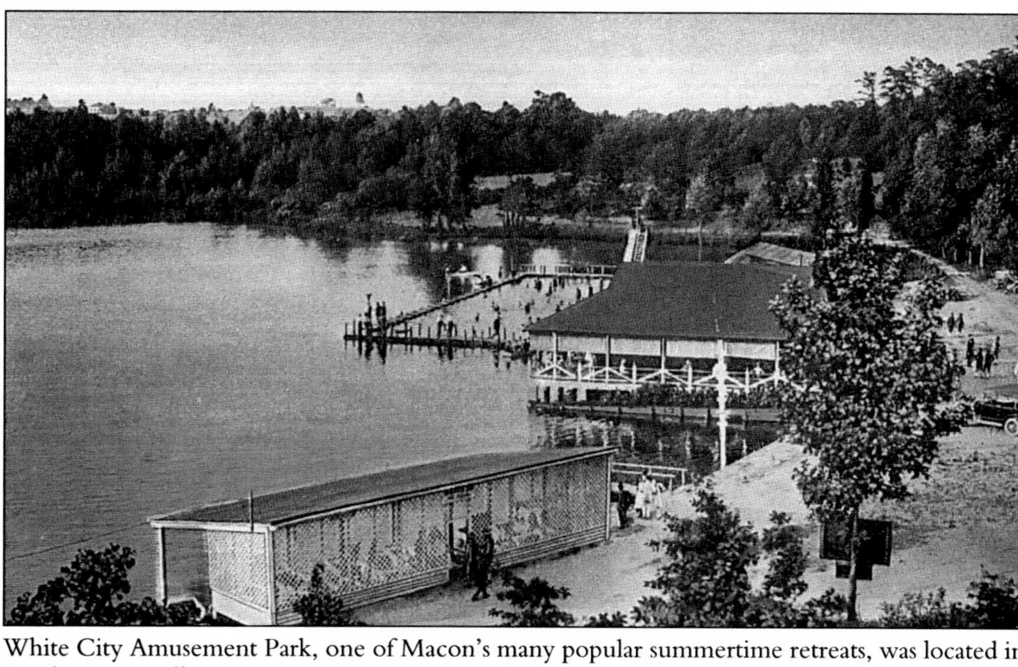

White City Amusement Park, one of Macon's many popular summertime retreats, was located in South Macon off Houston Avenue. (Curt-Teich #R-71344, *c.* 1920, color.)

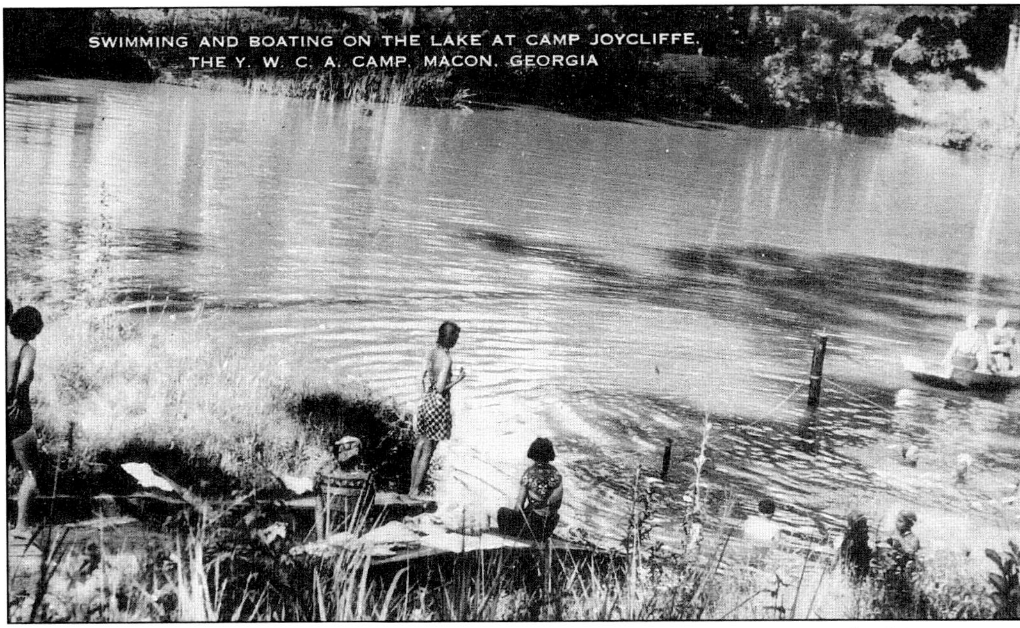

Enjoying the warm Macon weather, girls are out swimming and boating on the lake at Camp Joycliff, the YWCA Camp. (Artvue Postcard Co., *c.* 1940, B/W.)

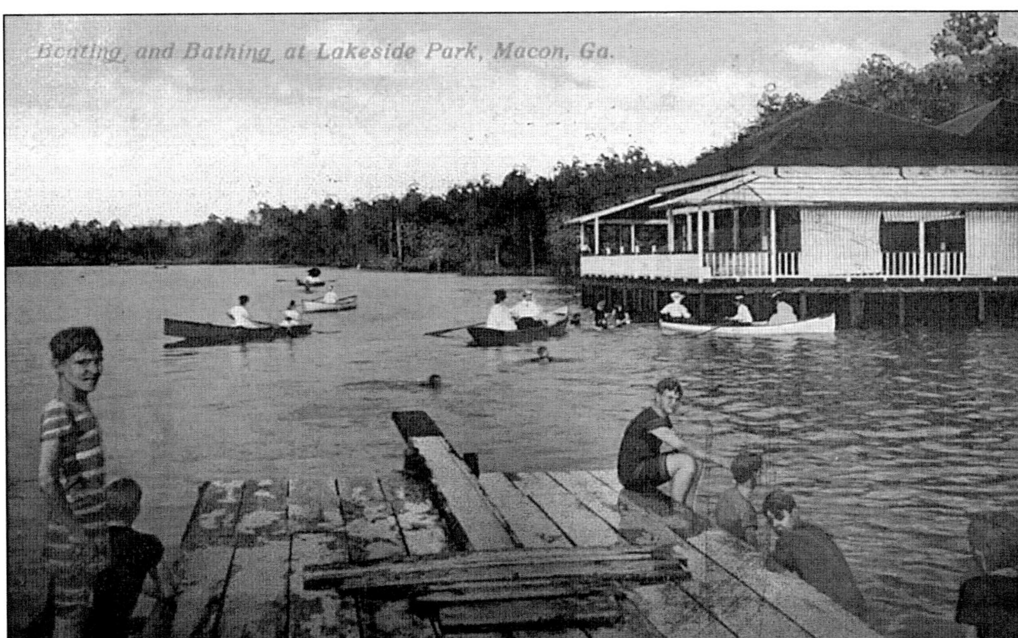

For many, favorite summertime activities included swimming at Lakeside Park. The dance pavilion, where many Macon couples courted, is shown in the background. (Octochrome #38866, postmarked 1915, color.)

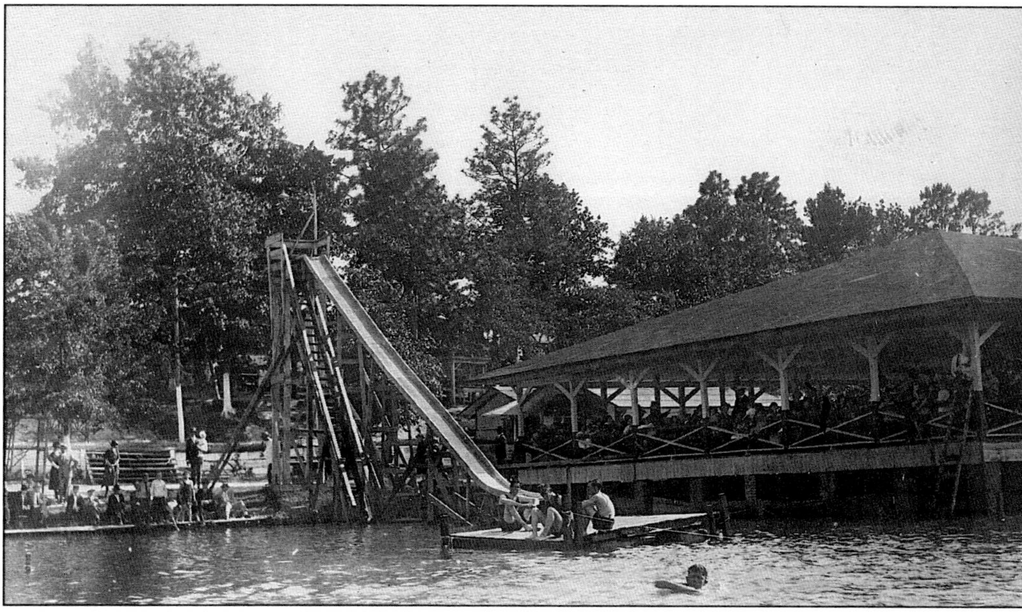

Exciting summertime fun included a thrilling slide down the giant chute at Lakeside Park. Also, another view of the dance pavilion, which was built out over the lake, can be seen in this photograph. (Real photograph postcard, *c.* 1922, B/W.)

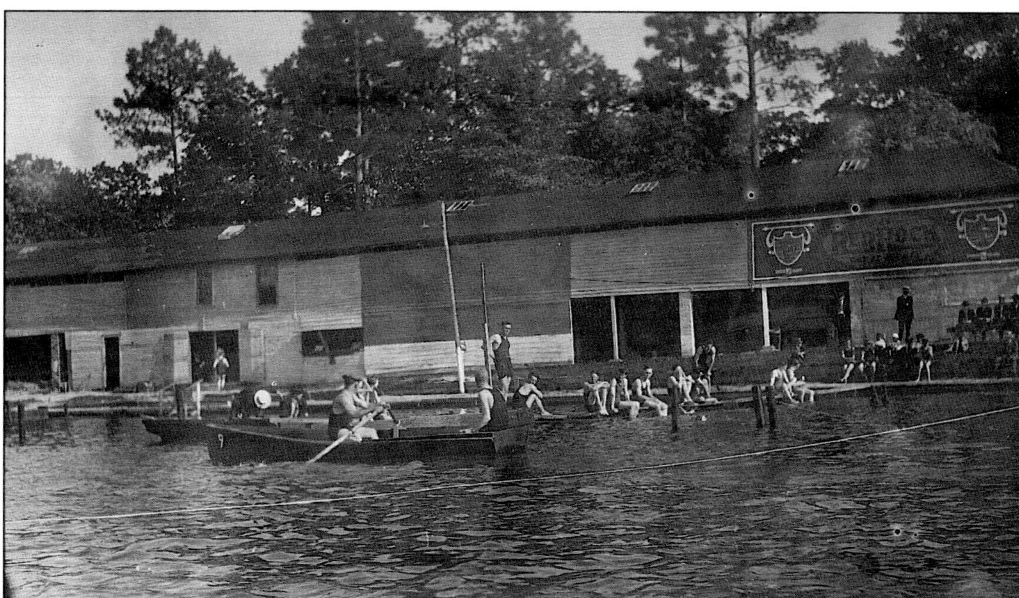

Row boating was another popular pastime at Lakeside Park. Couples would take quiet rides on the lake to talk, while the men would gather eagerly to race each other. (Real photograph , *c.* 1922, B/W.)

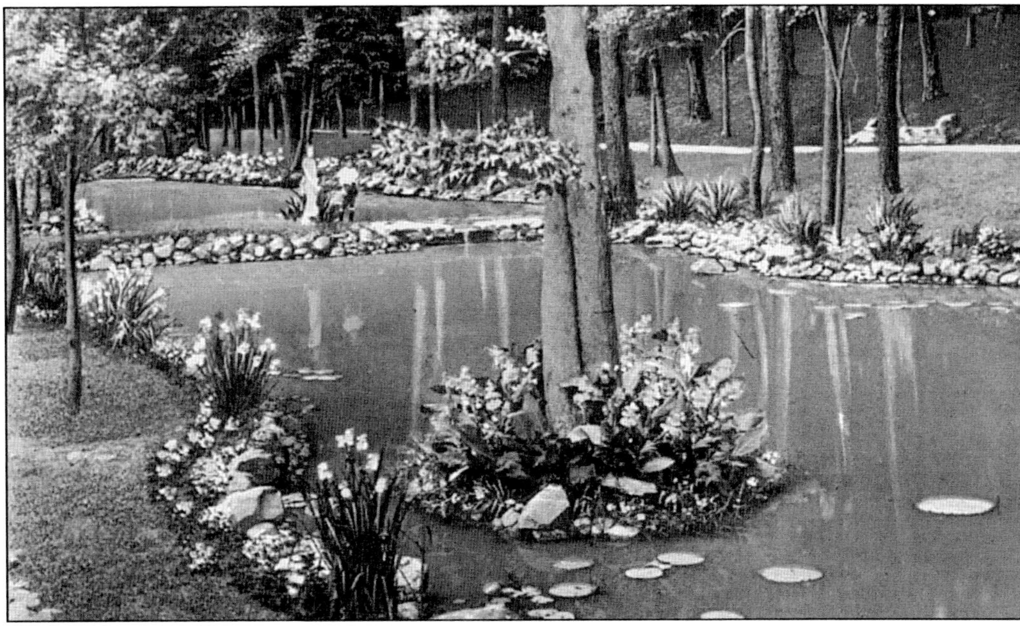

A.O. Bacon died in 1914 and left 75 acres for a park for the "white people" of Macon. This peaceful, cool scene of the ponds in Baconsfield Park is offset by the message on the back, "Hope its [*sic*] not any hotter there than it is here." (Tichnor Quality Views #64538, postmarked 1941, color.)

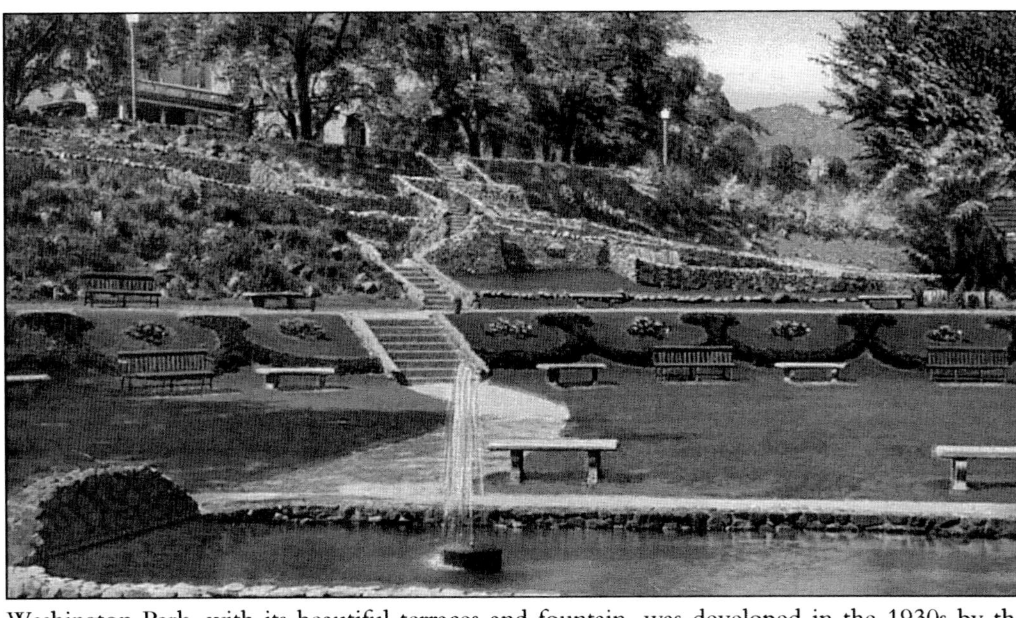

Washington Park, with its beautiful terraces and fountain, was developed in the 1930s by the Work Projects Administration (WPA) as a depression relief project. The WPA was established in 1935 by President Franklin D. Roosevelt and was the biggest economic stimulus in the history of America. (F. C. Kropp #1956N, postmarked 1934, color.)

Seven

Southern Homes

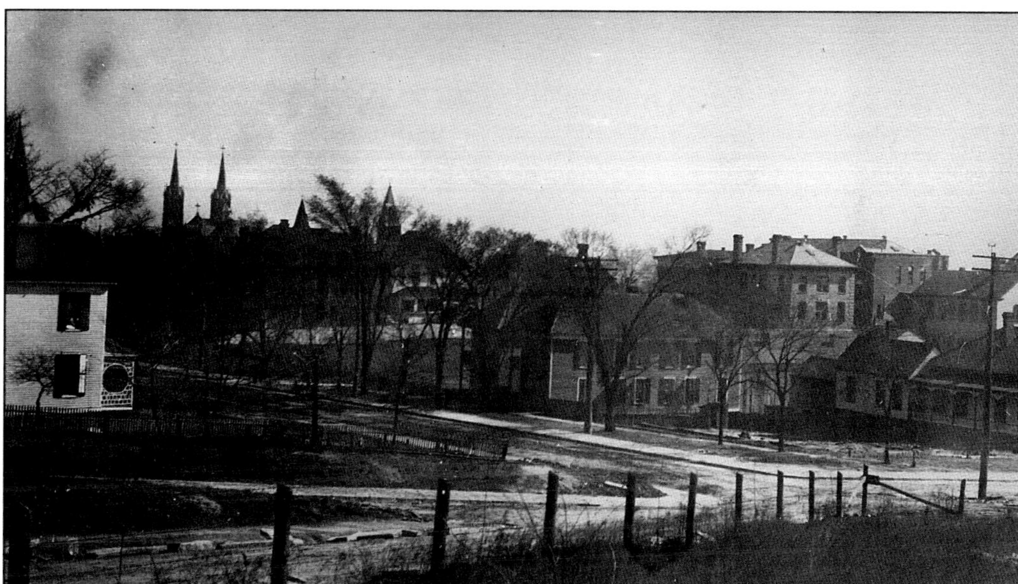

This view of Macon from Orange and Spring Streets shows a variety of residential housing. From southern Colonial and elaborate Victorian residences, from apartment complexes to rural log homes, there is definitely no such thing at monotony in Macon's residential architecture. Henry Ward Beecher once said that Macon was the prettiest city he had ever visited. Gently sloping hills and valleys combine with natural botanical beauty to accentuate the homes. (Real photograph, *c.* 1904, B/W.)

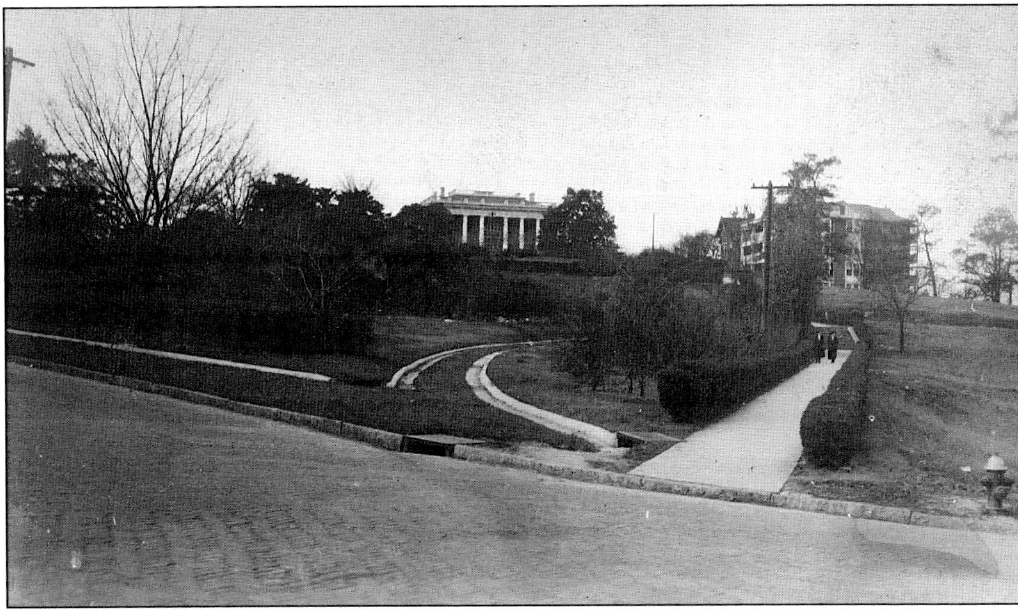

One of the most beautiful examples of a typical southern home is the residence of Mrs. S.T. Coleman. This home sits atop Coleman Hill with its broad verandas, tall white columns, and old-fashioned flower gardens. (AZO real photograph postcard, *c.* 1922, B/W.)

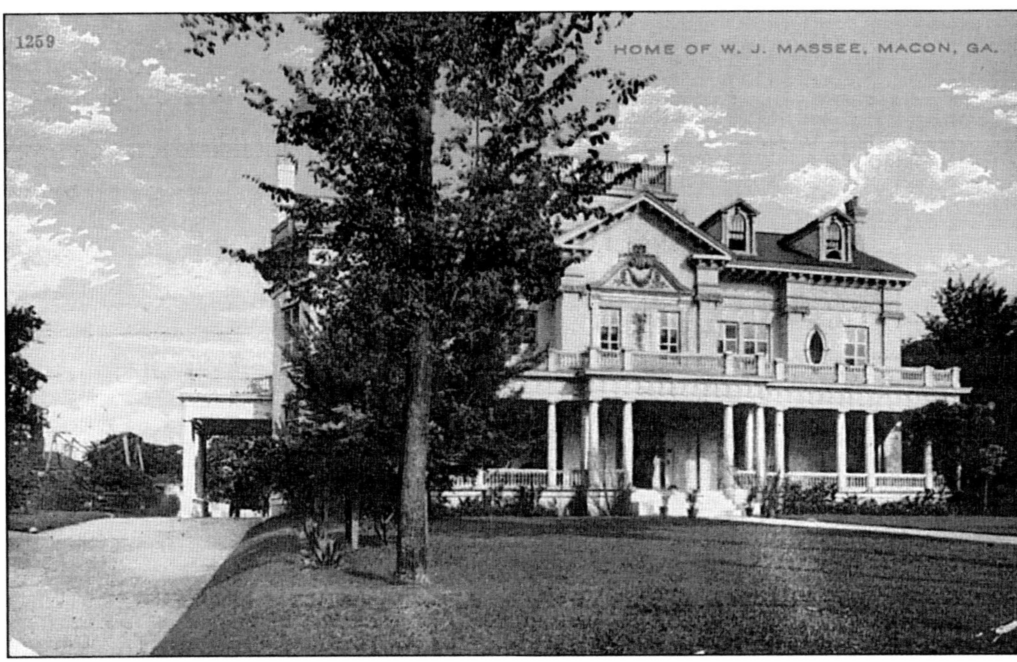

This lovely yellow house, with white columns and a widow's walk, is the home of W.J. Masse. Typical of most southern homes of the era, there was a large front porch on which to sit, capture cool breezes, and take refuge from the heat. (S.H. Kress #1259, postmarked 1912, color.)

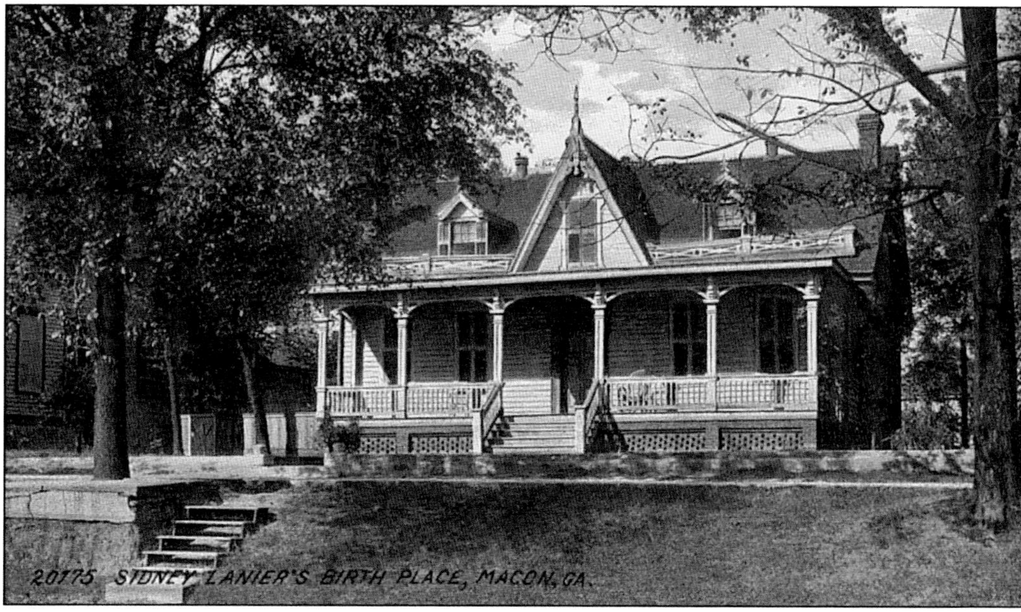

This quaint cottage is the birthplace of Sidney Lanier (1842–81), Macon's most illustrious writer. Lanier's famous series of poems on Georgia marshes begins with "The Marshes of the Glynn" and ends with "Sunrise." The cottage, located on High Street, now serves as headquarters for the Middle Georgia Historical Society and is used for a variety of social events such as wedding receptions. (Souvenir Postcard Co. # 20175, *c.* 1910, color.)

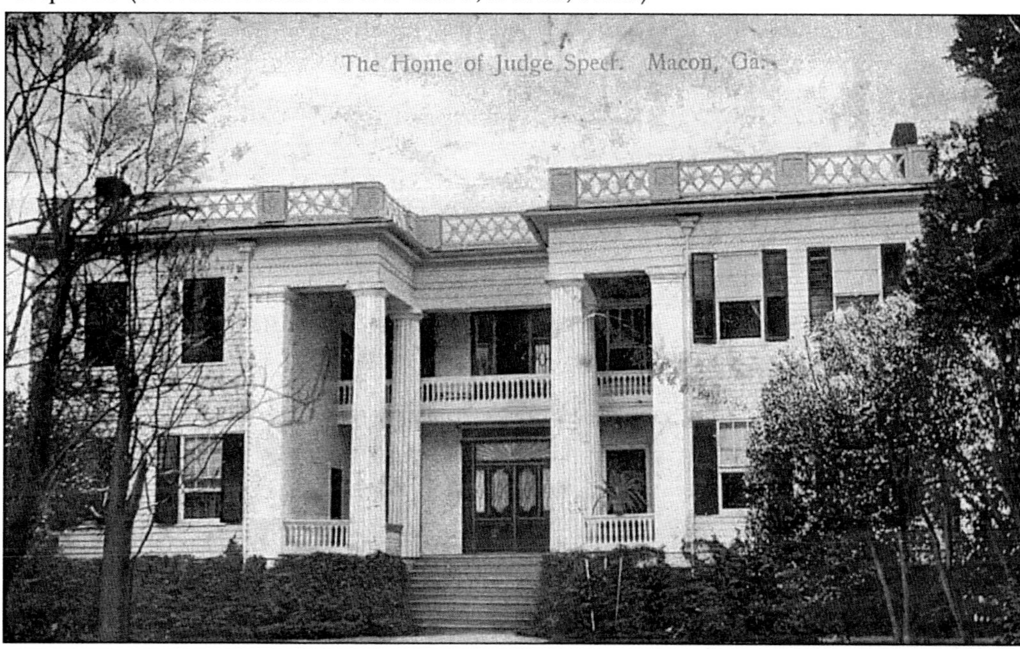

The home of prominent civic leader Judge Speer, located on Vineville Avenue, was built originally as a long frame structure by Thomas Hardeman. In 1840, it was purchased and remodeled into a Greek Revival style by Peter Solomon, and it was used by Howard Major of the American Institute of Architects to illustrate exclusively American development. (International Postcard Co. #1805, postmarked 1910, color.)

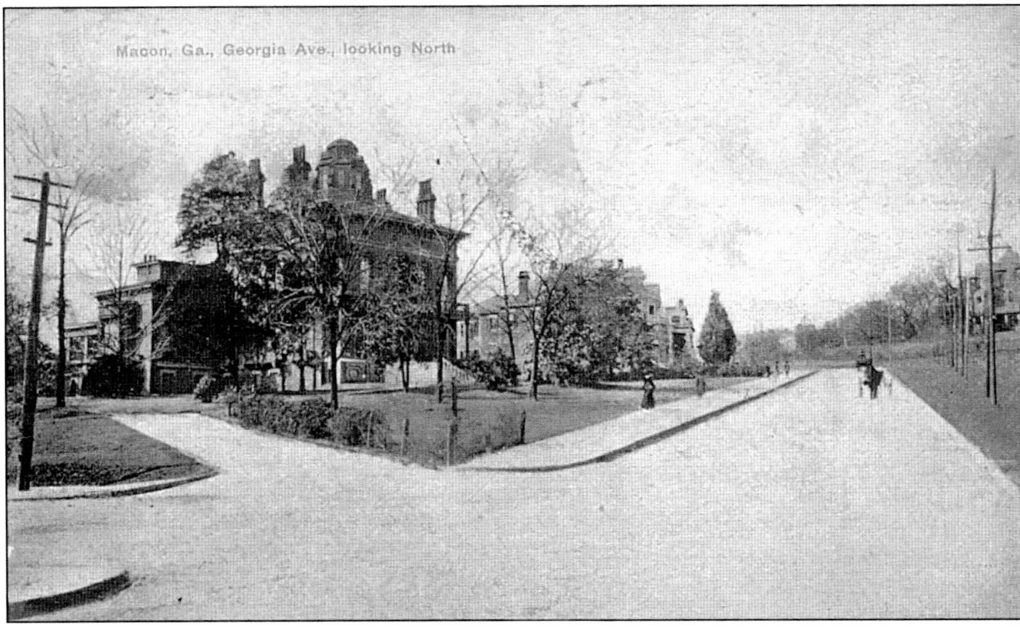

The home of Col. William B. Johnson, located on Georgia Avenue, was built in 1855 as an Italian villa; it was designed by J. Thomas & Son of New York. This home had central heat and air, indoor plumbing, an intercom system, marble steps at the entrance designed after those at the Capitol in Washington, marble floors, frescoed walls, a banquet hall, and a picture gallery. Legend has it that it was a depository during the Civil War, where Confederate gold was hidden from the invading Union soldiers. Renamed the "Hay House," it is now owned by the Georgia Trust for Historic Preservation. (Peacock Series #129317, postmarked 1908, color.)

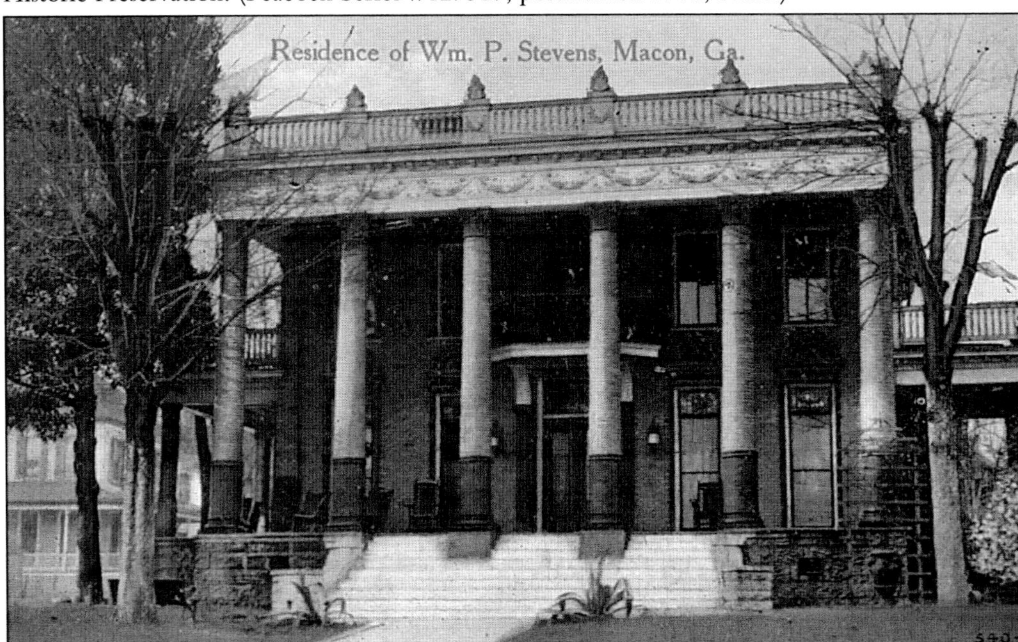

This beautiful home was the residence of William P. Stevens. (Unidentified publisher, #540-4, *c.* 1910, color.)

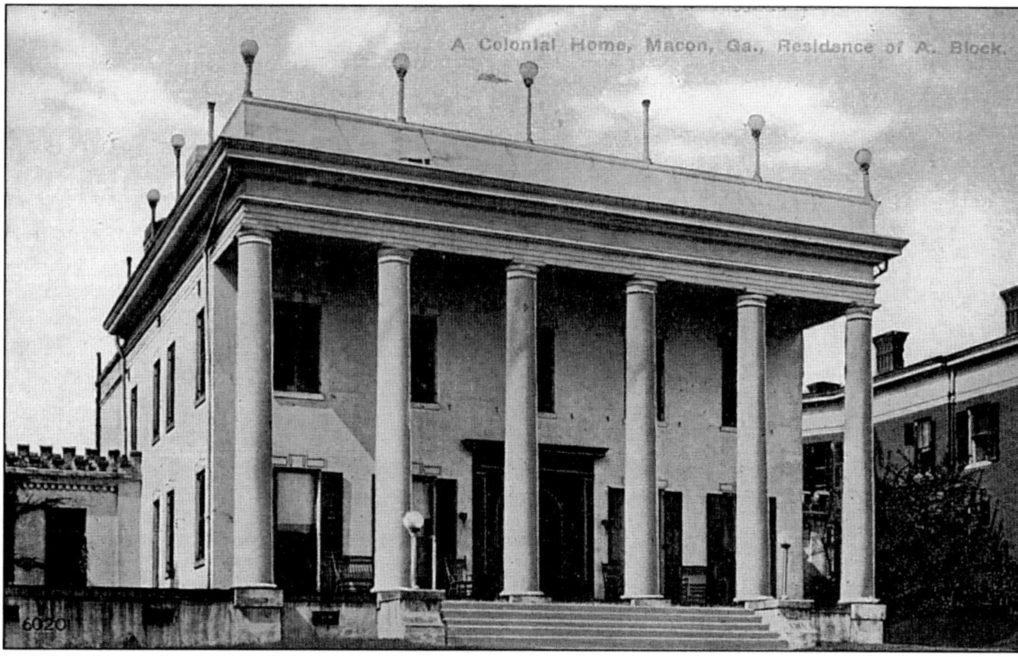

This impressive Colonial home is the residence of A. Block. Rocking chairs and benches invite visitors to sit and visit on the porch. There, they could watch and wave as people passed on the street in front.(Unidentified publisher #6020, *c.* 1910, color.)

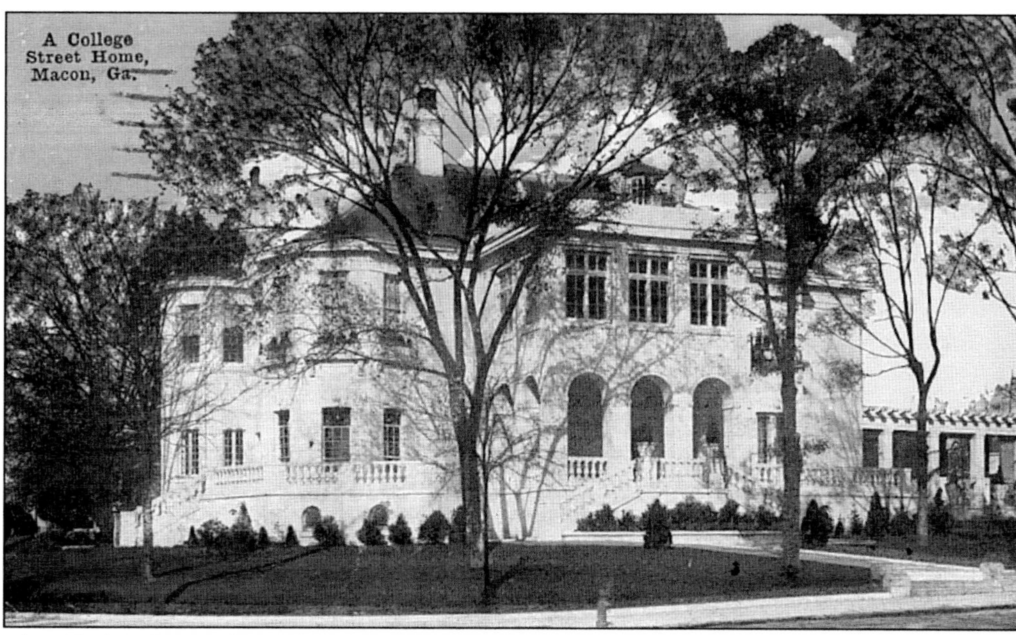

This fabulous house, located on College Street, features a double staircase leading to an entrance porch with arched columns. Above the porch is a sunroom with seven large windows on three sides. (E.C. Kropp & Co. #2422, postmarked 1919, color.)

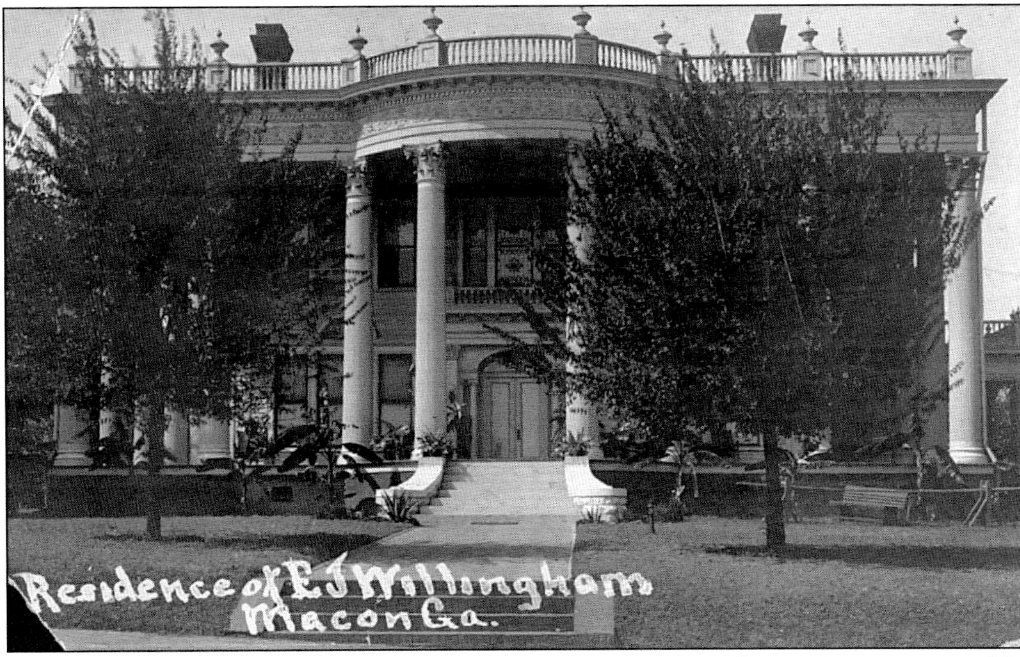

The residence of E.J. Willingham displays Southern elegance at its finest. The curvature of the entrance steps and entablature softens the facade and visually beckons one to visit. Potted plants on the porch as well as the bench in the yard differ from the formal plantings of typical grand houses of the era. (Real photograph postcard, postmarked 1908, B/W.)

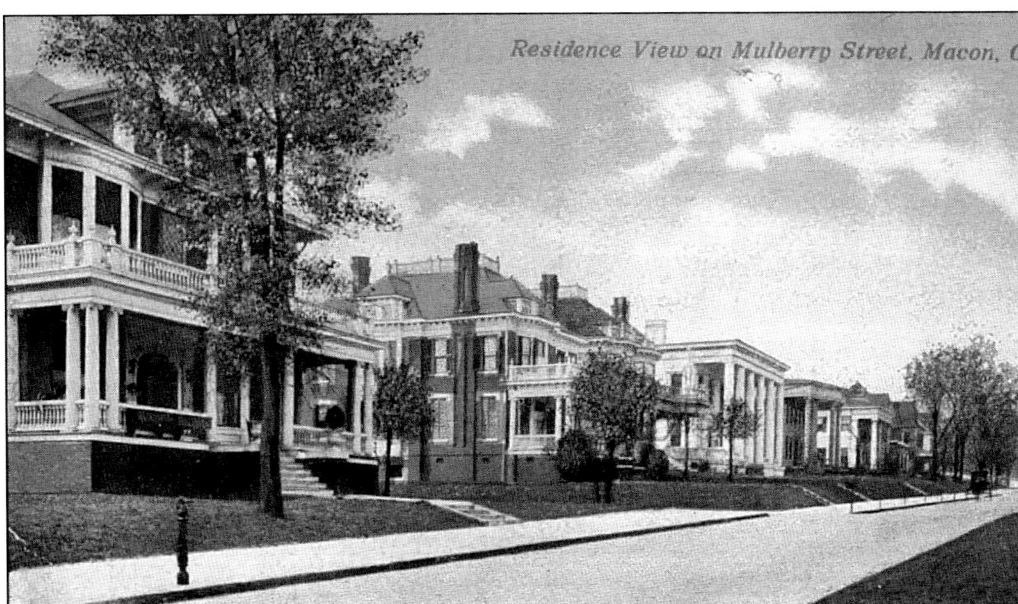

Shown here is a residential view on Mulberry Street. The card's sender writes in December, "We arrived here last evening. This is a pretty place, weather just like June. Flowers in bloom and kids barefoot everywhere." (Power's Curiosity, Octochrome #38659, postmarked 1920, color.)

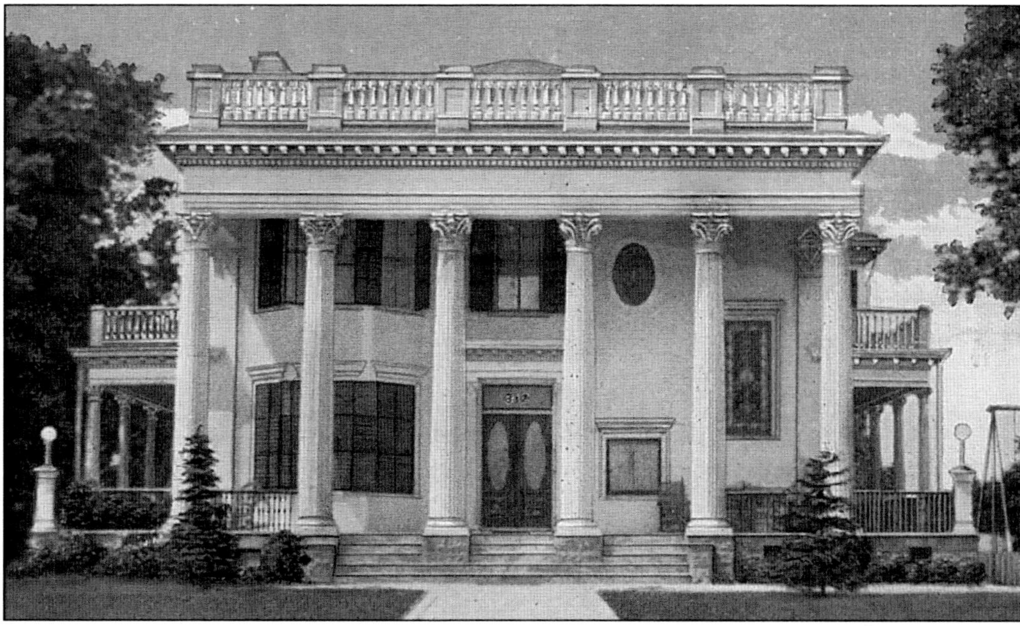

Seen here is the home of R.G. Jordan on Vineville Avenue. This beautiful Georgian-style residence has six huge columns across the front porch, balconies, and bay windows. (Curt-Teich #R-79428, *c.* 1920, color.)

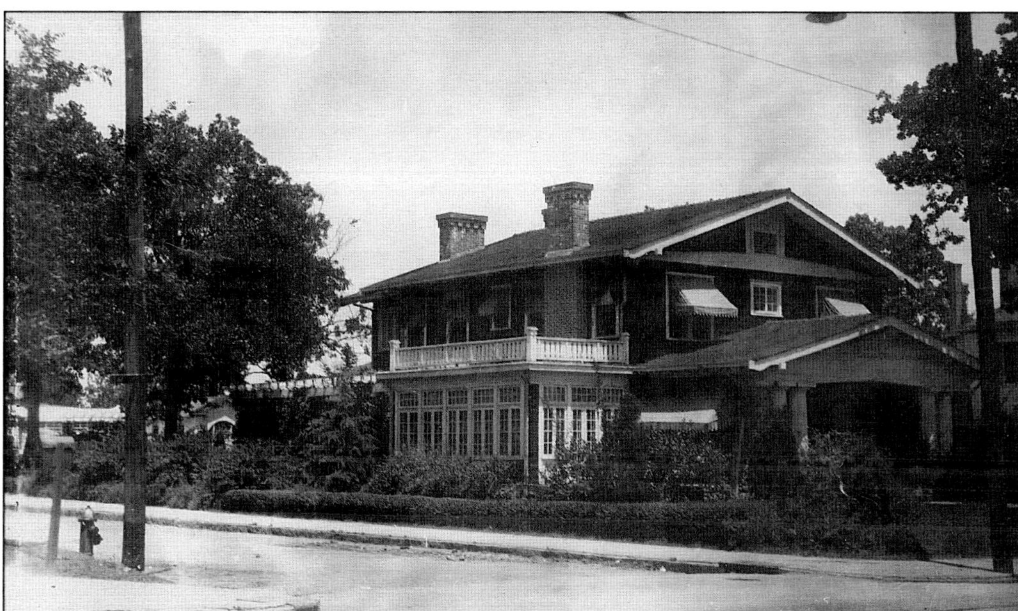

The Perry residence on Vineville Avenue was described as palatial by the photographer. The house features a small front porch with four white columns as well as a sunroom with 12 tall windows. Note that over the windows in the rest of the house are awnings. Awnings became very popular in the 1920s as a means of controlling the heat of the summer sun. (Real photograph, *c.* 1922, B/W.)

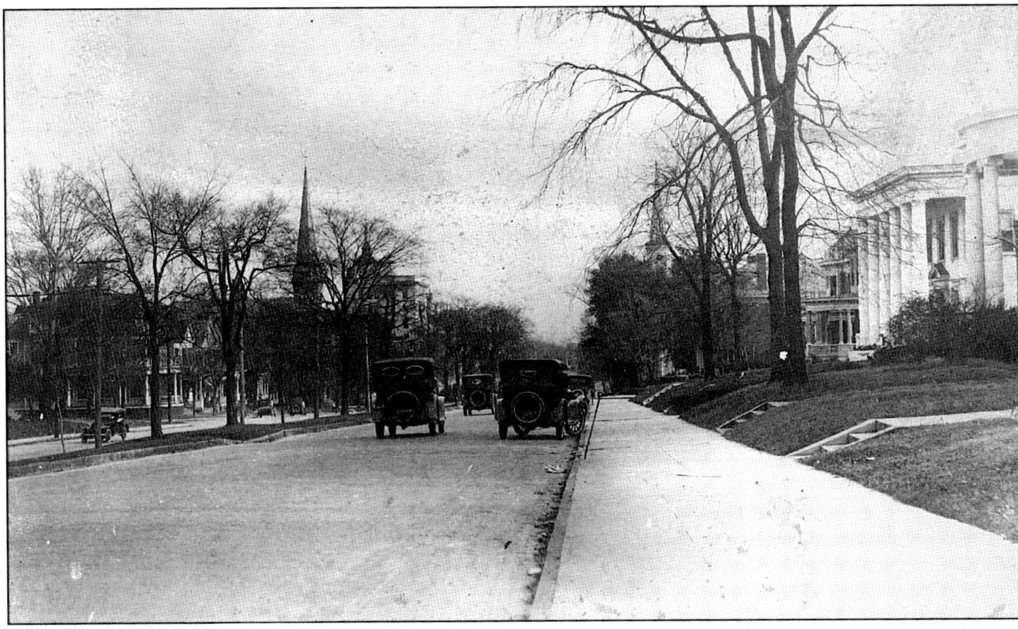

This picture shows several automobiles in the residential section of Mulberry Street. On the right side of the street, white columns of several houses are visible. Residents enjoyed the wide sidewalks bordering the street and the tree-lined median separating the center of the street. (AZO real photograph postcard, *c.* 1922, B/W.)

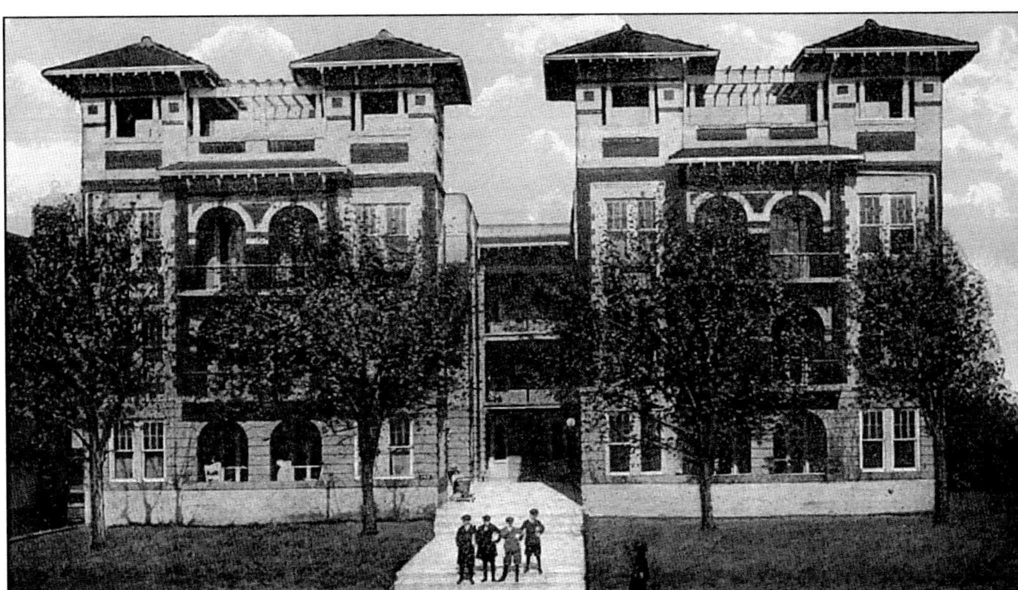

A group of residents pose in front of Katherine Court, one of Macon's many nice apartment buildings. Each apartment had its own small private balcony area on the street side of the building. (E.C. Kropp #10191, *c.* 1910, color.)

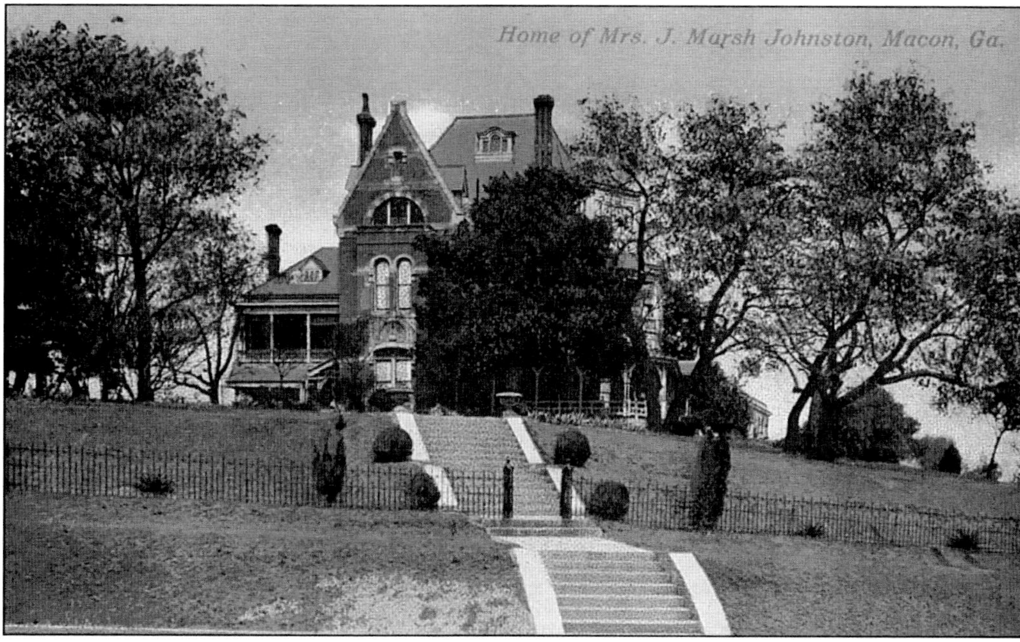

"Hill Crest," the home of Mrs. J. Marsh Johnson, is located on the northwest corner of Georgia Avenue and Bond Street, on a high hill overlooking Macon. An old iron fence surrounds the wide lawn setting for the red brick house with gray trim. The elaborate house is in Victorian Gothic style with gables, turrets, balconies, and bay windows. The house was built in 1883. (Octochrome #38875, *c.* 1910, color.)

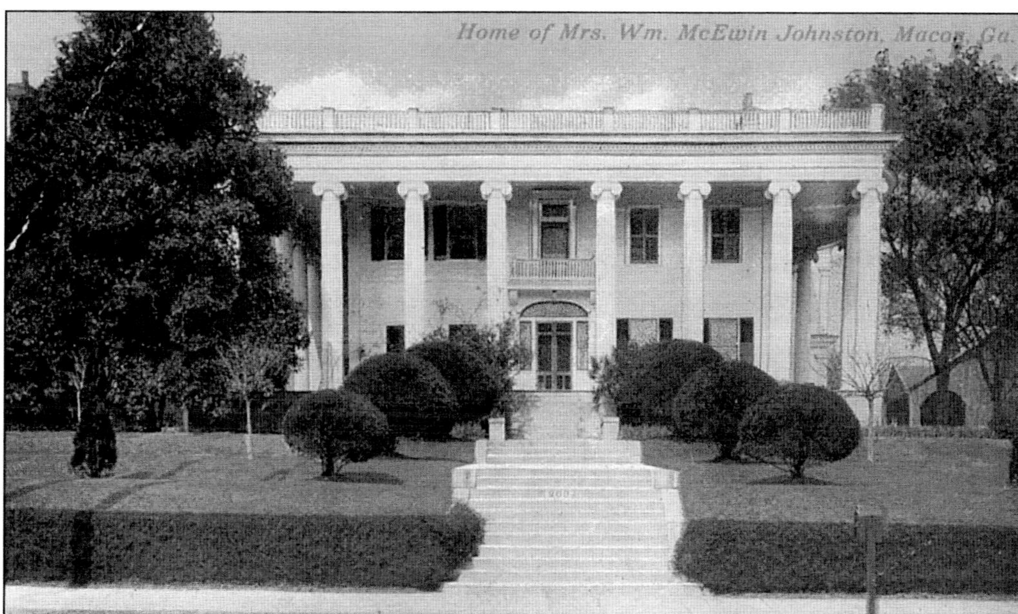

"Bonnybrae," home of Mrs. William McEwin Johnson, is located next door to "Hill Crest." This house is most noted for its Egyptian-style library with pictures and draperies bought by Mrs. Johnson during an extended Eastern tour. (Octochrome #38872, *c.* 1920, color.)

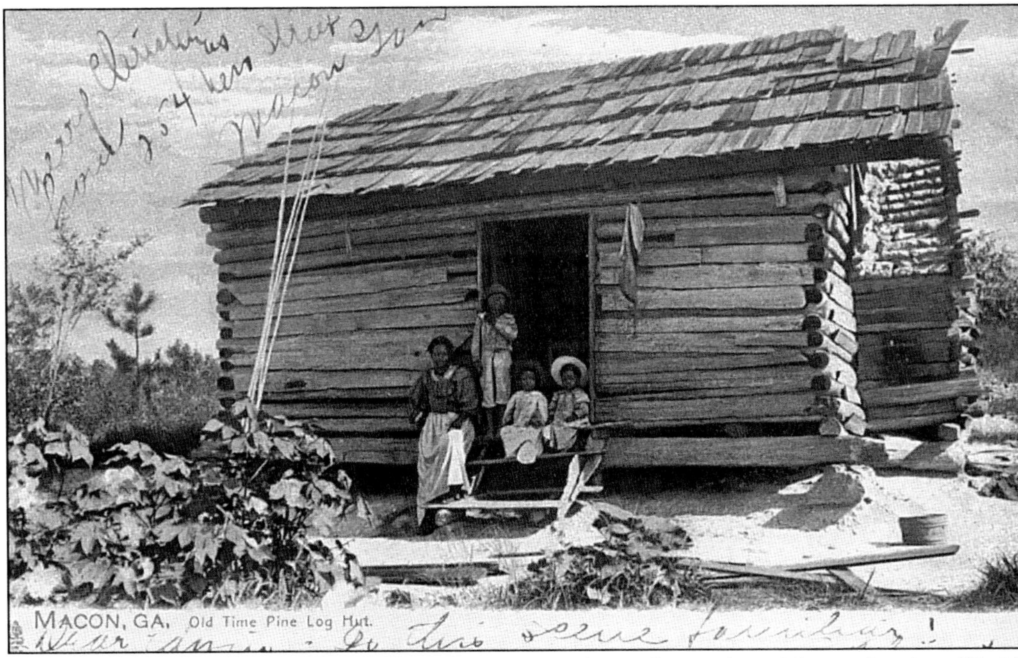

A black family sits on the steps of an old-time pine log hut. The sender of the card writes, "Is this scene familiar?" (Raphael Tuck #2074, postmarked 1905, color.)

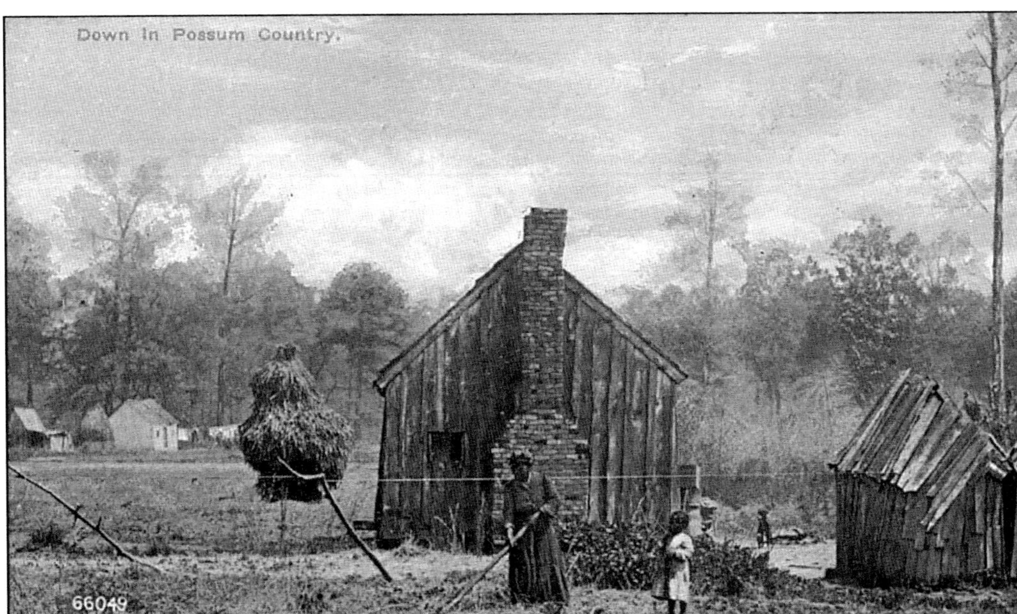

This rural scene in middle Georgia was typical. Popular postcards of the era tended to show black people in small frame houses or pine log huts. While such housing was typical for poor southern families, such housing was not limited to only black people, but white people as well. Yet, you will find few, if any, commercially printed cards showing poor white living conditions. (Unidentified publisher #66049, postmarked 1908, color.)

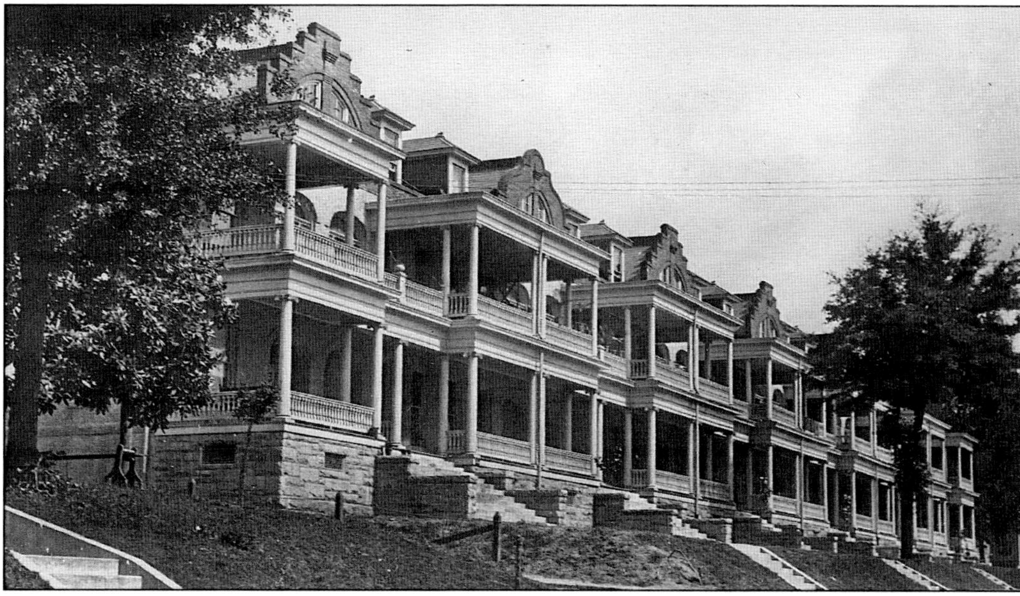

Macon's housing needs included multi-family complexes. The Navarro Apartments provided living space in lovely buildings with nice white column porches and verandas. (Real photograph, *c.* 1920, B/W.)

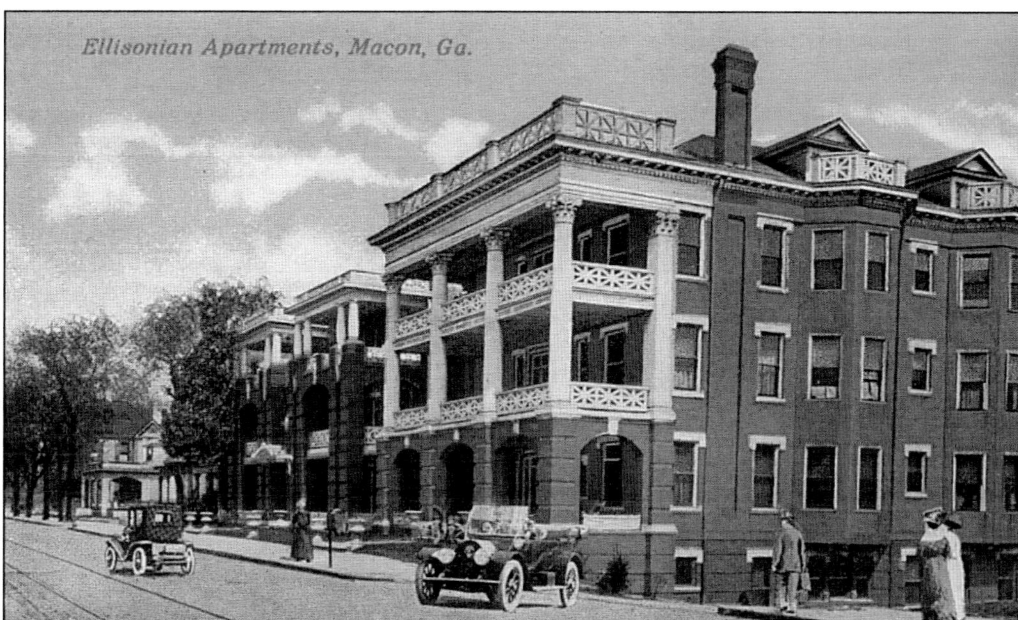

The lovely apartment complex shown here was the three-storied Ellisonian Apartments. Conveniently located near downtown businesses, the complex was a popular multi-family residence. The man in the picture is carrying a satchel and is most likely returning from a day of work. (Powers Curiosity, Octochrome #38652, *c.* 1920, color.)

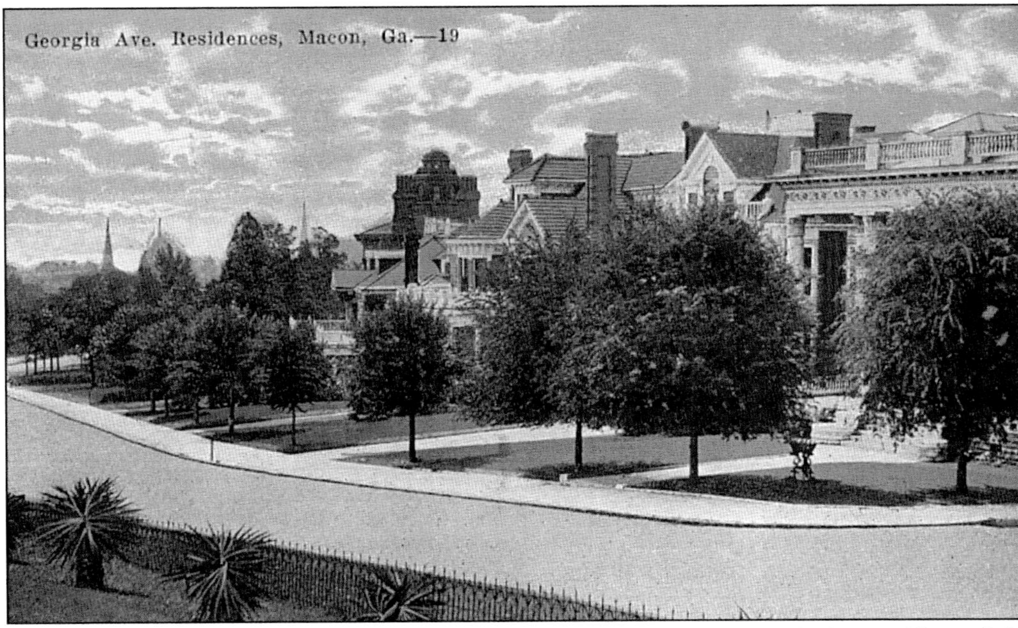

This card shows the lovely homes along tree-lined Georgia Avenue, with the roof line of the "Hay House" clearly visible. The sender of this card writes, "Georgia seems to be made up of cotton fields, pickaninnies, and peach orchards and today we have run into the turpentine belt... Macon is a beautiful place and hustling." (E.C. Kropp # 26389N, postmarked 1923, color.)

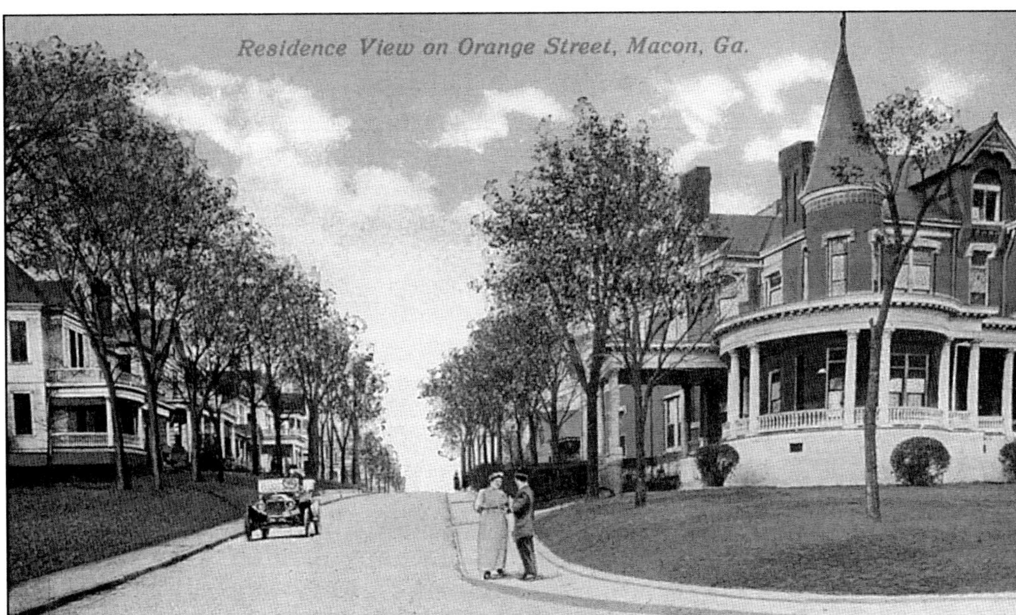

Always ready to socialize, neighbors stop to chat on the sidewalk in front of residences on Orange Street. The house shown to the right features a lovely round porch with columns. (Octochrome #38658, *c.* 1920, color.)

Eight

Wish You Were Here

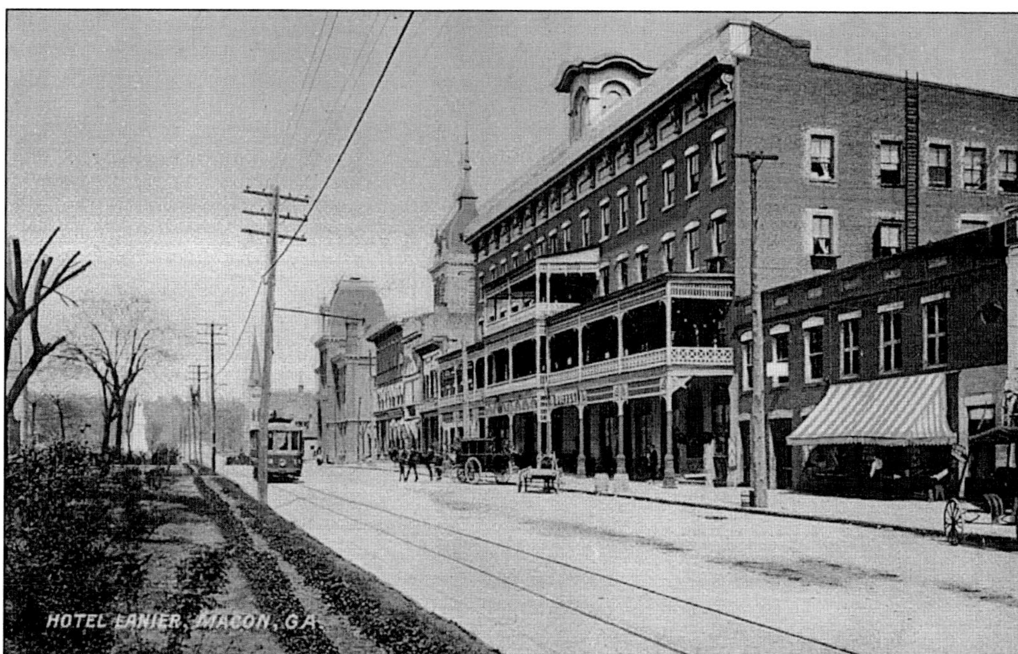

Macon has long been a popular place for visitors to come and enjoy. Postcard messages echo the words, "Wish you were here." Thus, it is of no surprise that Macon should have many fine modern hotels in which to stay. The Hotel Lanier was a grand structure, located on Mulberry Street between Second and Third Streets, just down the street from the county courthouse. This view of the hotel shows the streetcar line and the courthouse in the background. (Rotograph #E-13573, *c.* 1905, color.)

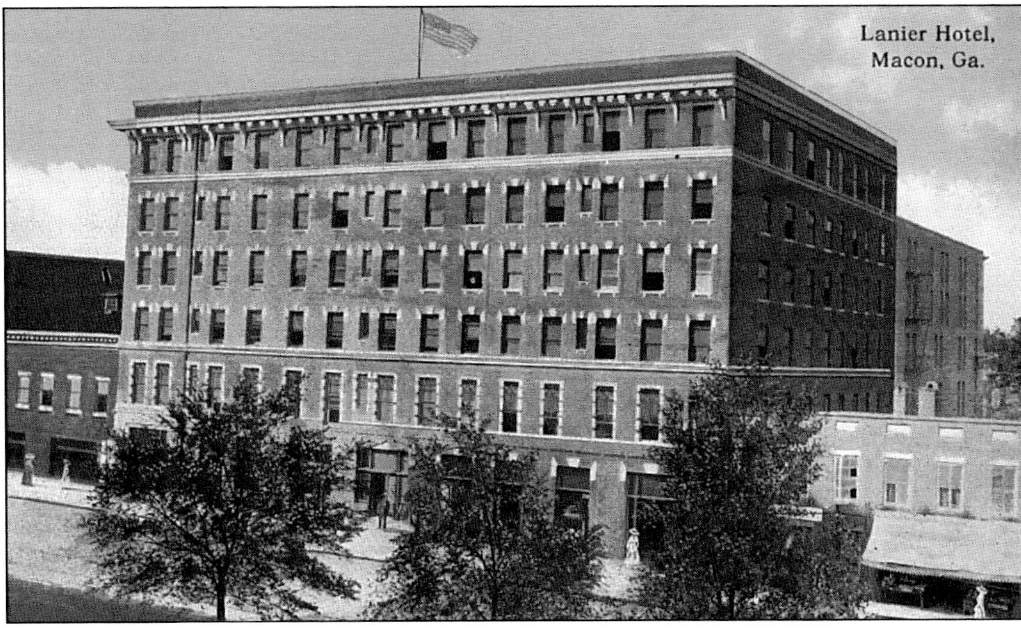

Gov. Joseph E. Brown made his home at the Hotel Lanier from 1864–1865, when the Macon City Hall was used as the Georgia State Capitol. Then on May 13, 1865, Jefferson Davis stayed there after his capture at Irwinville. This picture shows the Hotel Lanier after the verandah was removed from the front of the building. (Power's Curiosity, Curt-Teich # A-26987, *c.* 1915, color.)

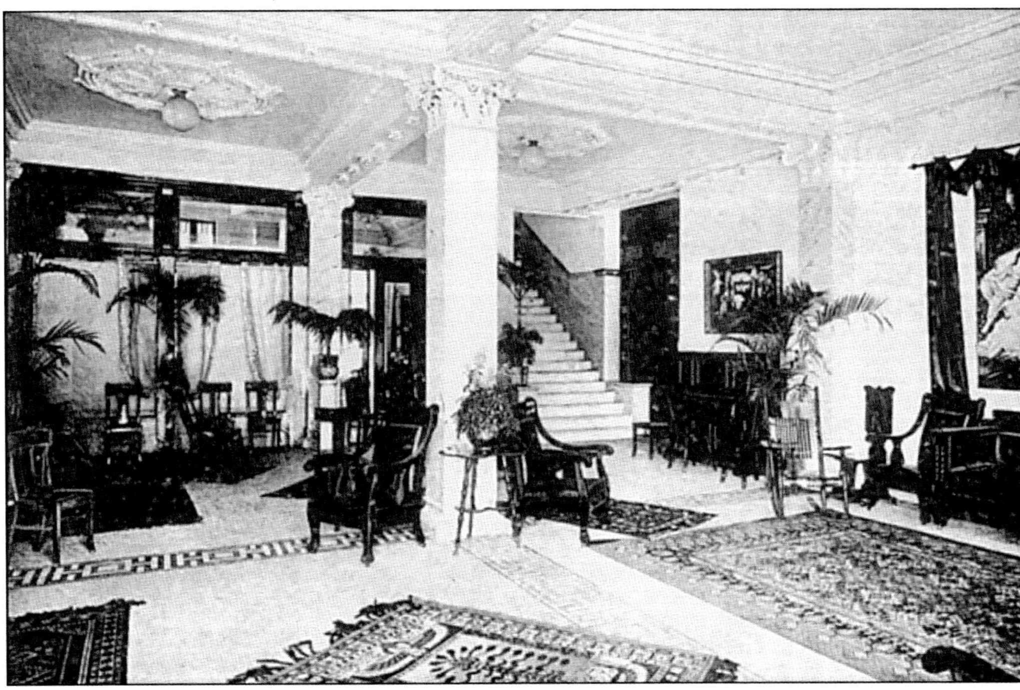

C.C. Clay, charged with conspiracy in the Lincoln assassination, learned he was wanted by Federal authorities and came to the Hotel Lanier to surrender. Shown here is the elegantly appointed lobby of the Hotel Lanier Cafe. (McEvoy Book & Stationary, *c.* 1905, B/W.)

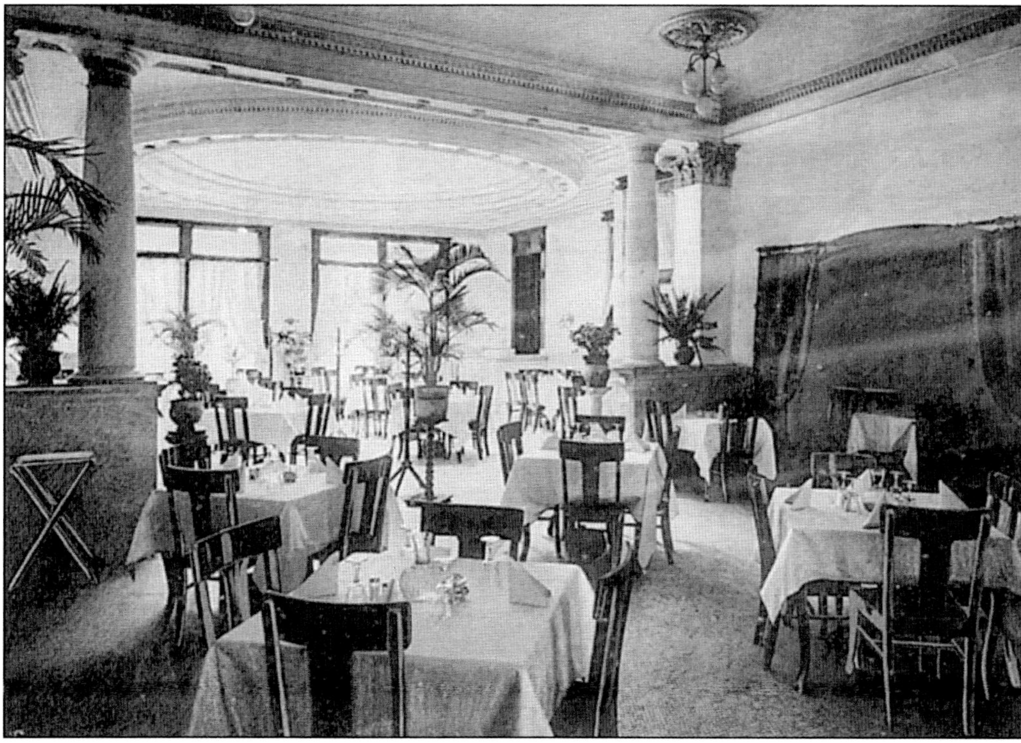

The Hotel Lanier Cafe provided a lovely spot to dine for guests and visitors. In 1907, one visitor wrote, "I am enjoying myself. You ought to see me eat! I like Macon very much." (McEvoy Book & Stationary, *c.* 1905, B/W.)

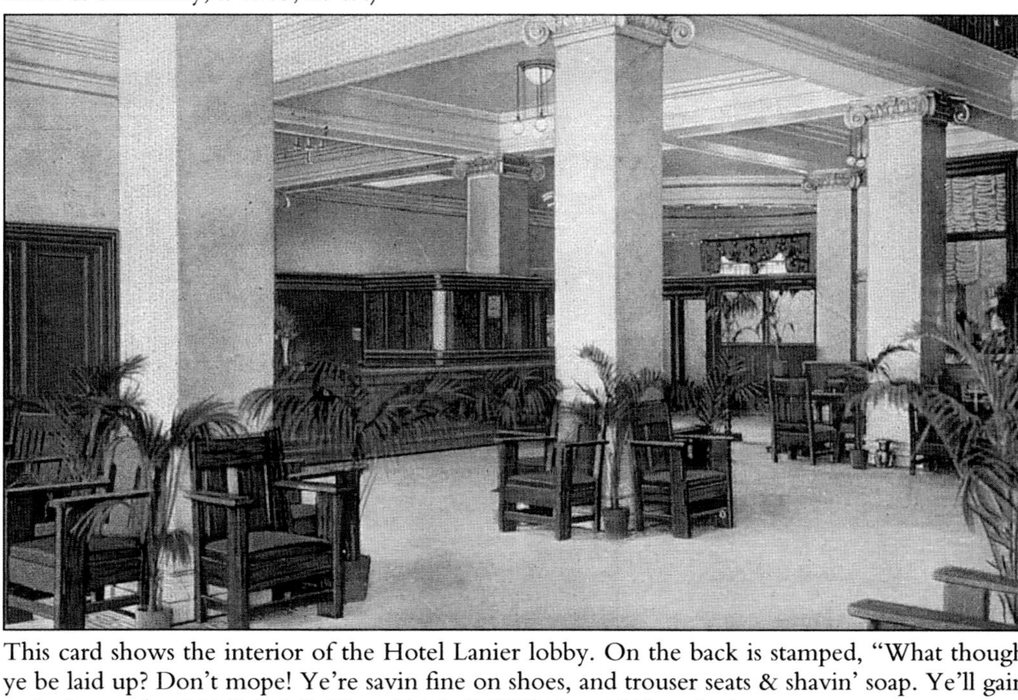

This card shows the interior of the Hotel Lanier lobby. On the back is stamped, "What though ye be laid up? Don't mope! Ye're savin fine on shoes, and trouser seats & shavin' soap. Ye'll gain mair than ye lose! M.E.R.L." (Curt-Teich # 107946, *c.* 1915, color.)

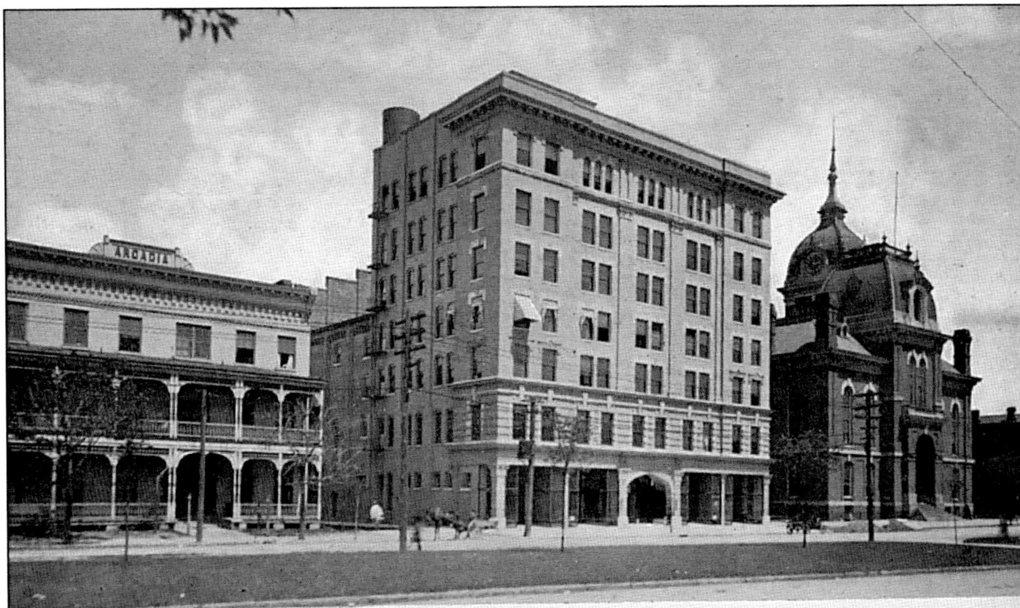

Grand Building and Court House, Macon, Ga.

The Hotel Arcadia was located on Mulberry Street next to the Grand Building and the county courthouse. Under the proprietorship of A.J. Sparks, the hotel was popular with many visitors to Macon. (Unidentified publisher, *c.* 1905, B/W.)

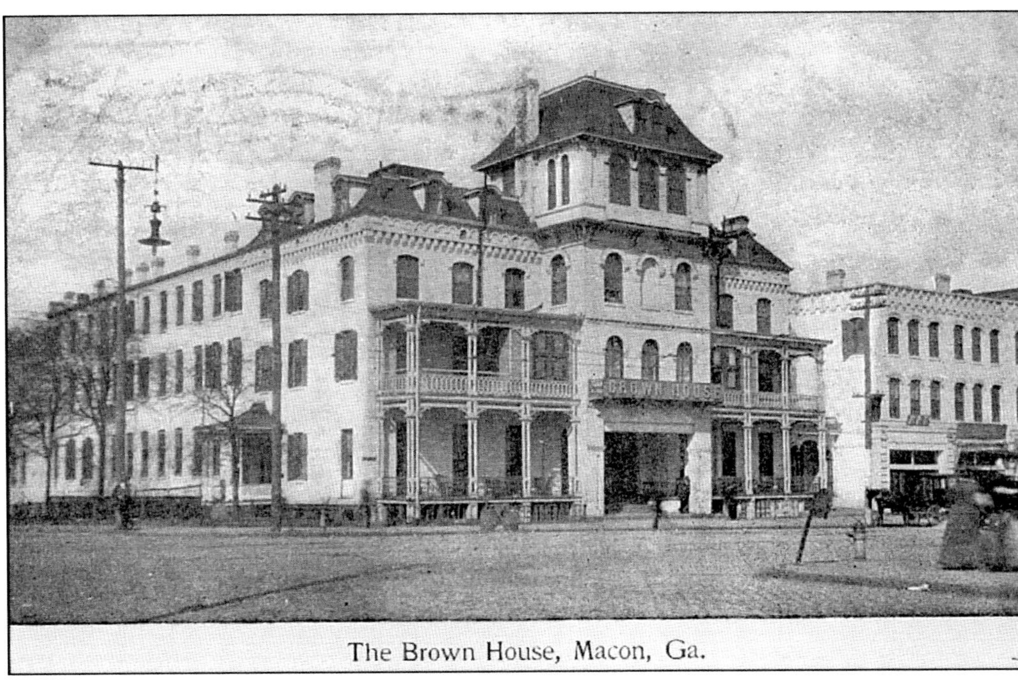

The Brown House, Macon, Ga.

The Brown House was located on Fourth Street, across from Union Depot, and was said to be a "first-class establishment." This building was erected after the original 1855 structure burned in 1878. (Unidentified publisher, *c.* 1907, B/W.)

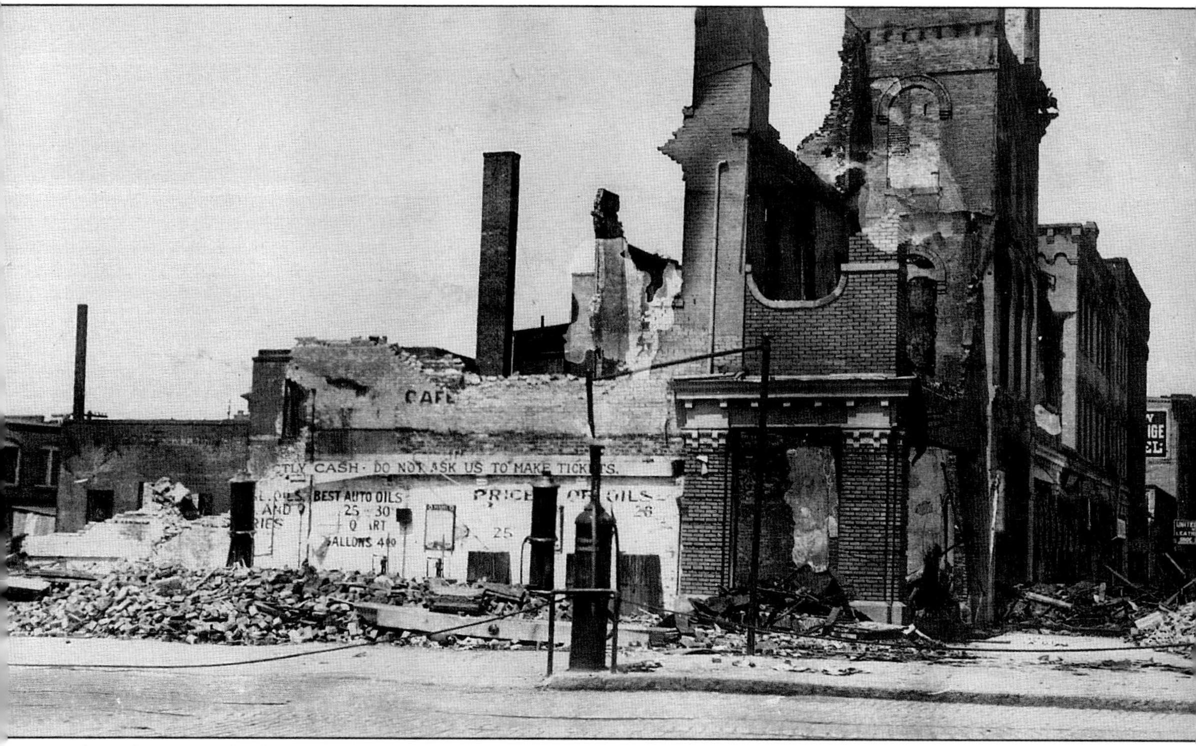

This photograph shows the shell remains of the Brown House after it was destroyed by fire in 1921. Ironically, the same hotel had burned on the same date, July 22, 43 years before in 1878. There were six deaths in the 1921 fire. Macon suffered other losses from fire in 1921 including the loss of most of the physical plant of Central City College, an institution for African-American youth, and the total destruction of Saint Stanislaus College, the Jesuit school. The Brown House and Central City College were both rebuilt; however, Saint Stanislaus was abandoned, and the land was sold. (Real photograph, *c.* 1921, B/W.)

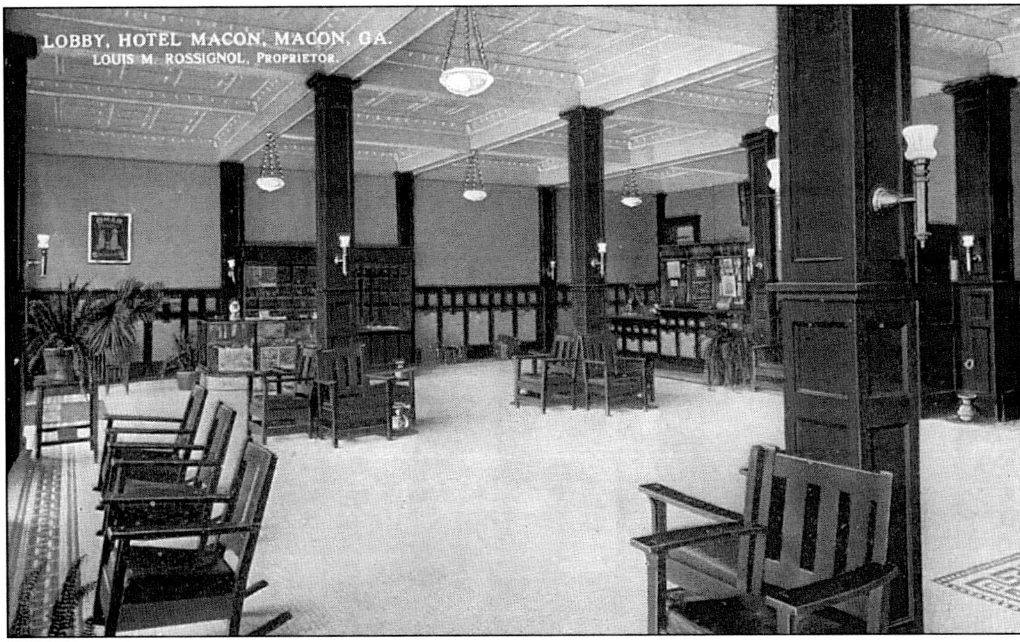

Rocking chairs and brass spittoons await guests in the beautiful lobby of the Hotel Macon. Under the proprietorship of Louis M. Rossingnol, the hotel offered many modern conveniences. (Curt-Teich #R-64490, *c.* 1910, color.)

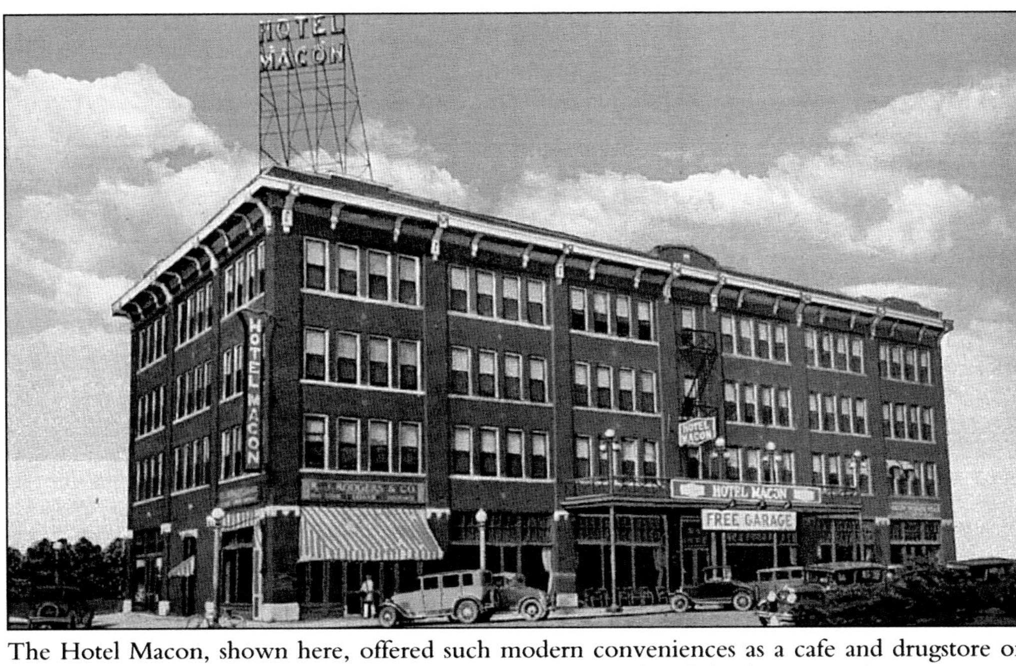

The Hotel Macon, shown here, offered such modern conveniences as a cafe and drugstore on site as well as a free parking garage. As the automobile replaced the horse as primary means of transportation, businesses quickly learned to cater to the new needs. (Tichnor Quality Views # 130944, *c.* 1920, color.)

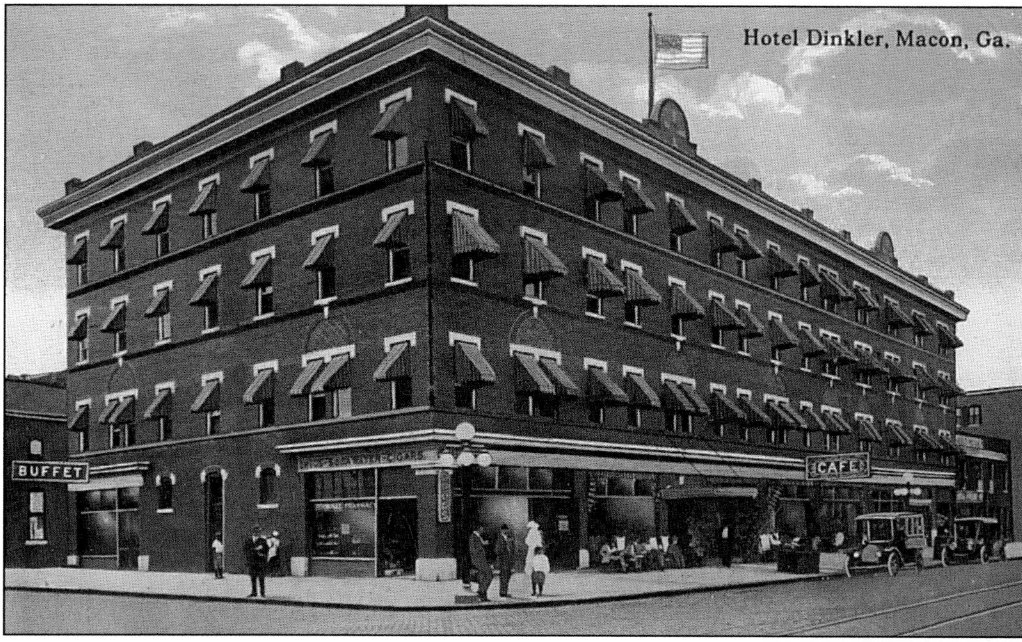

The Hotel Dinkler, an European-style hotel complete with cafe and drugstore, was located on the corner of Fourth and Mulberry Streets. (Powers Curiosity, Curt-Teich #R-36712, *c.* 1910, color.)

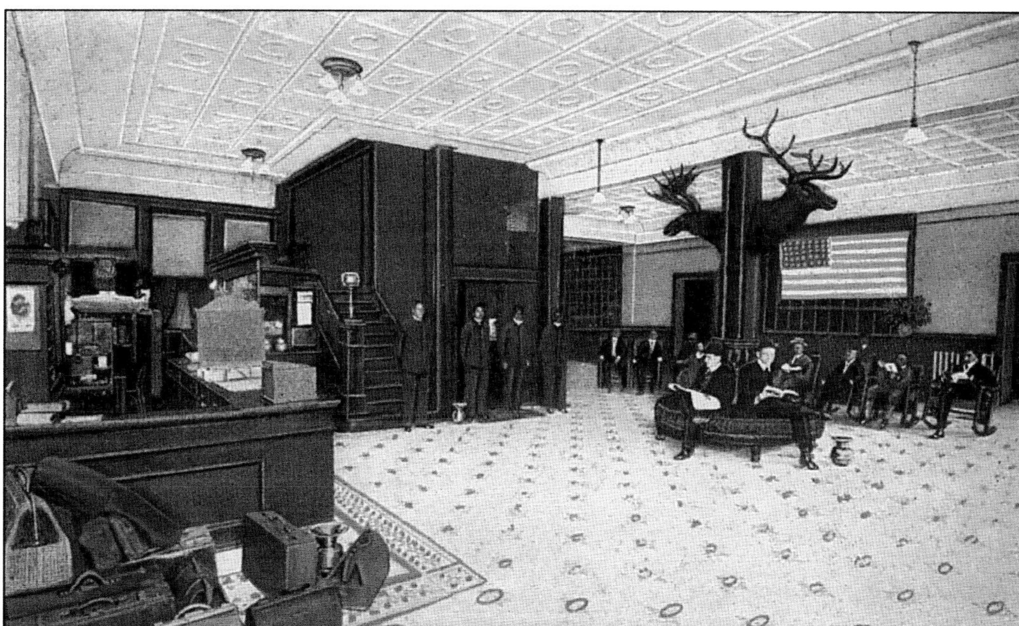

It was in the lobby of the Hotel Dinkler "where special attention [was] given to visitors of soldiers." Suitcases piled up and brass spittoons, deer heads, bellhops, and visitors resting in the lobby are all typical of any day at the Dinkler. (Curt-Teich #R-71408, *c.* 1910, color.)

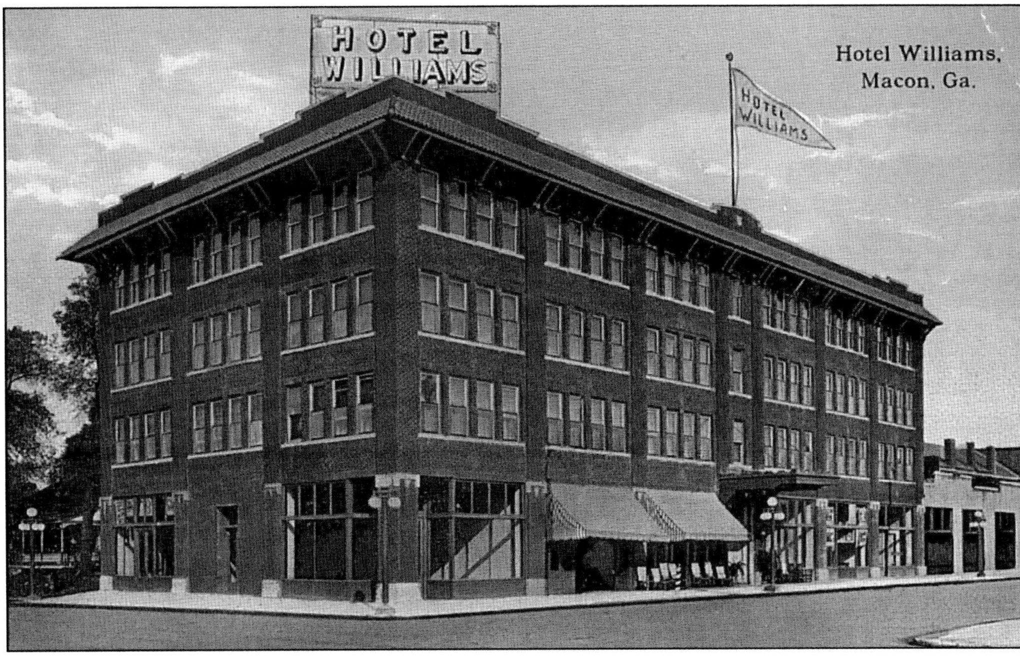

Shown here is the Hotel Williams. The sender of this card writes, "Good Hotel, up to date in every respect." (Powers Curiosity, Curt-Teich #R33733, postmarked 1913, color.)

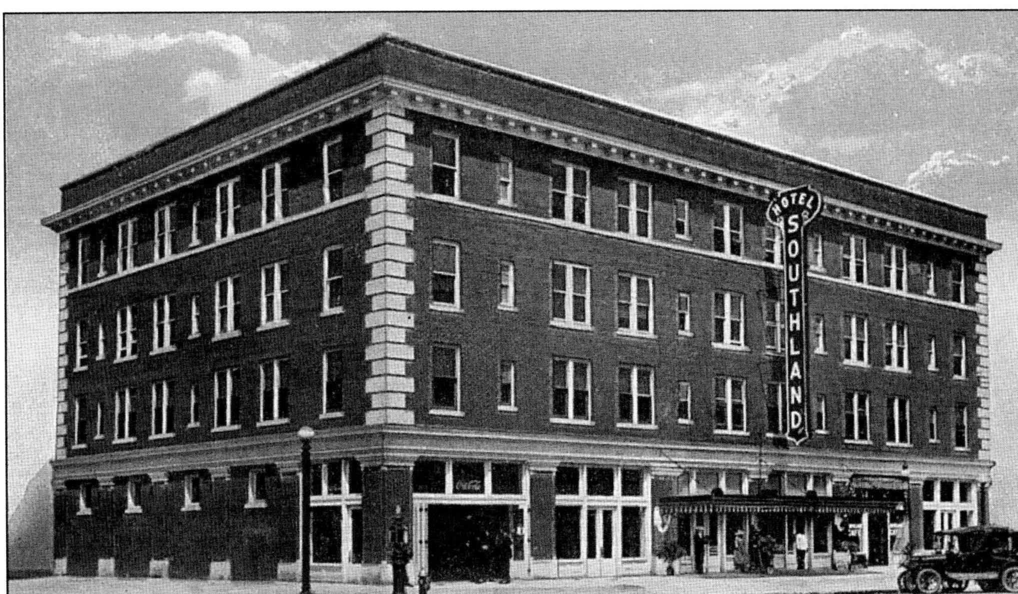

Hotel Southland billed itself as "Macon's only new hotel." It is interesting to notice the similarities in the building styles of most all the new modern hotels of the *c.* 1910–1925 period. They tend to all look alike, and all usually had a cafe in the bottom floor. These cafes catered not only to guests of the hotel, but also to the nearby business employees. (E.W. Freene #R-93322, *c.* 1910, color.)

Excavation for the Hotel Dempsey started in 1912. The hotel was to be Macon's finest facility for tourists, conventions, and social gatherings. For decades, the Dempsey was the premier place to stay in Macon. (Powers Curiosity #R-36371, postmarked 1913, color.)

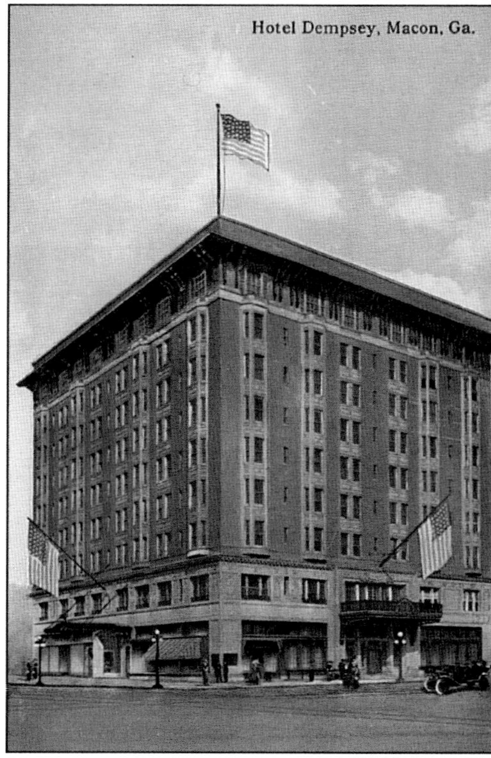

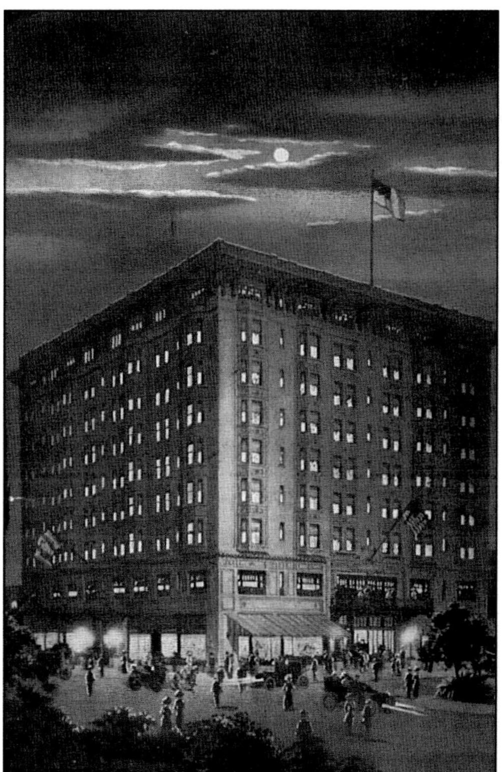

This night view of the Dempsey Hotel shows the streets active with people and motorists. Beautiful moonlight night strolls along the streets, window shopping, was a popular pastime in a age before television. People often stopped into the hotel cafe for refreshments. (Power's Curiosity Store, Curt-Teich # A 26995, postmarked 1913, color.)

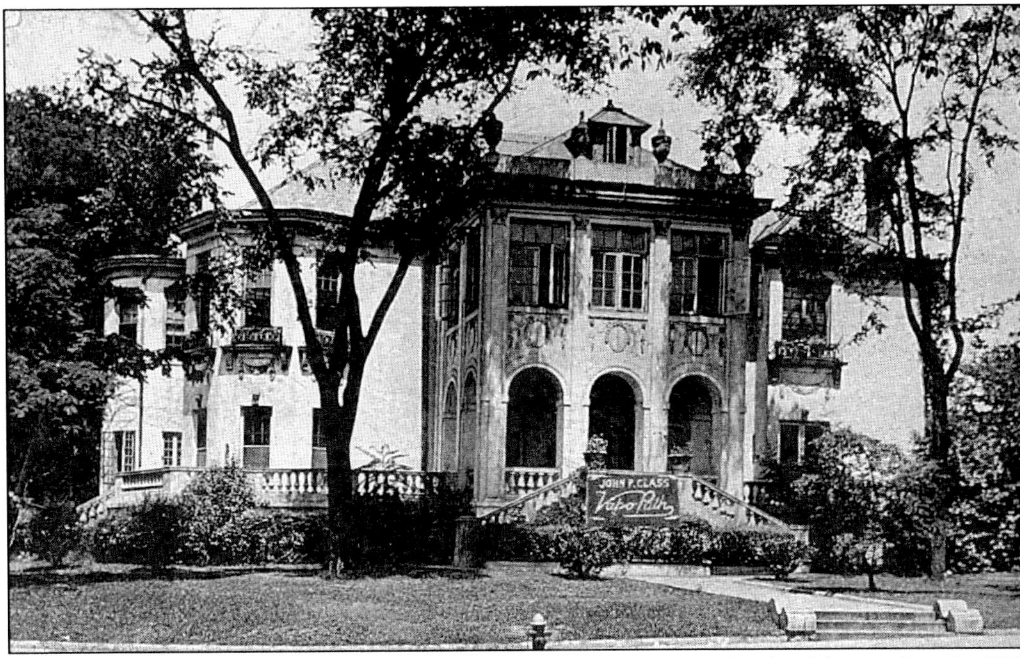

The College Inn is a grand Italian-style house. The message on the back of this card reads, "We are staying here for 2 days at this beautiful place, which was formerly the mansion of a great 'Peach King.' It is now a popular price tourist house." (Unidentified publisher, postmarked 1931, B/W.)

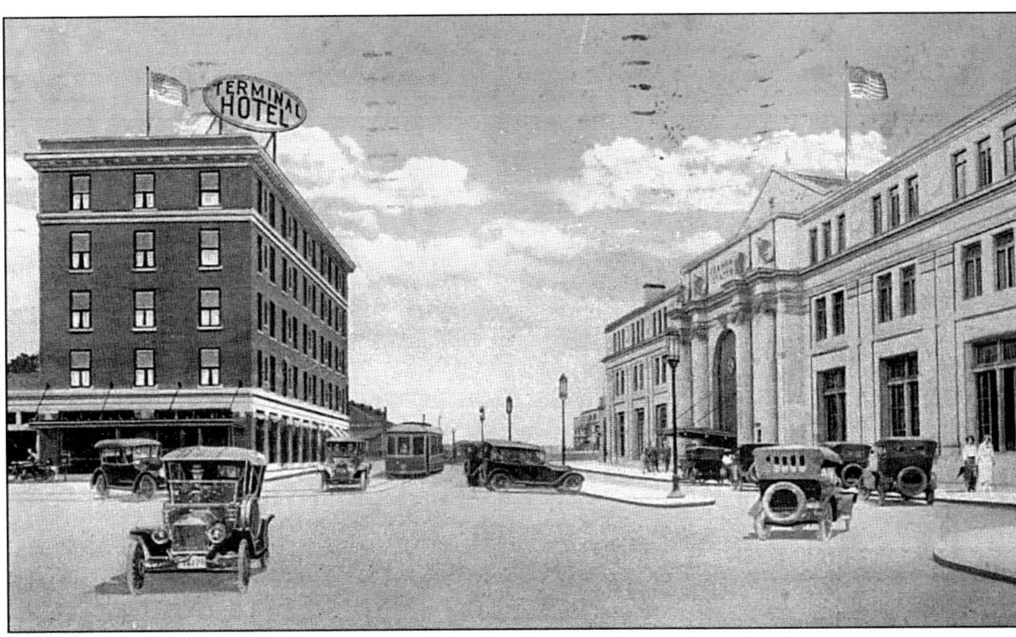

This card reads, "The Terminal Hotel, opposite the Terminal Station on the main business thoroughfare and within two blocks of the center of the city. Every room with a private bath and one price only, $2.00." (Curt-Teich #R-71343, postmarked 1921, color.)

Nine

A Thriving Business Center

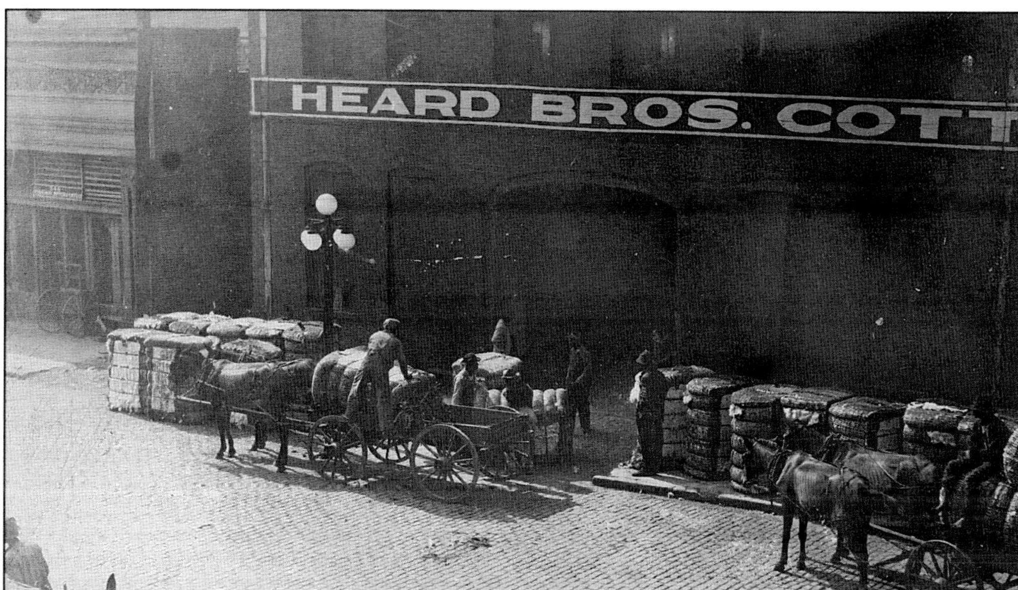

While Macon continued to grow and prosper as a bustling city with modern conveniences, it remained an agricultural center for regional farming in the early part of the century. This is evidenced by the continued presence of horse-drawn wagons, which brought cotton into the massive downtown warehouses to unload. Such action is depicted in this typical Macon Street scene. During cotton time in Georgia, wagons lined up, waiting to unload bales at the Heards Warehouse. (Real photograph postcard, *c.* 1919, B/W.)

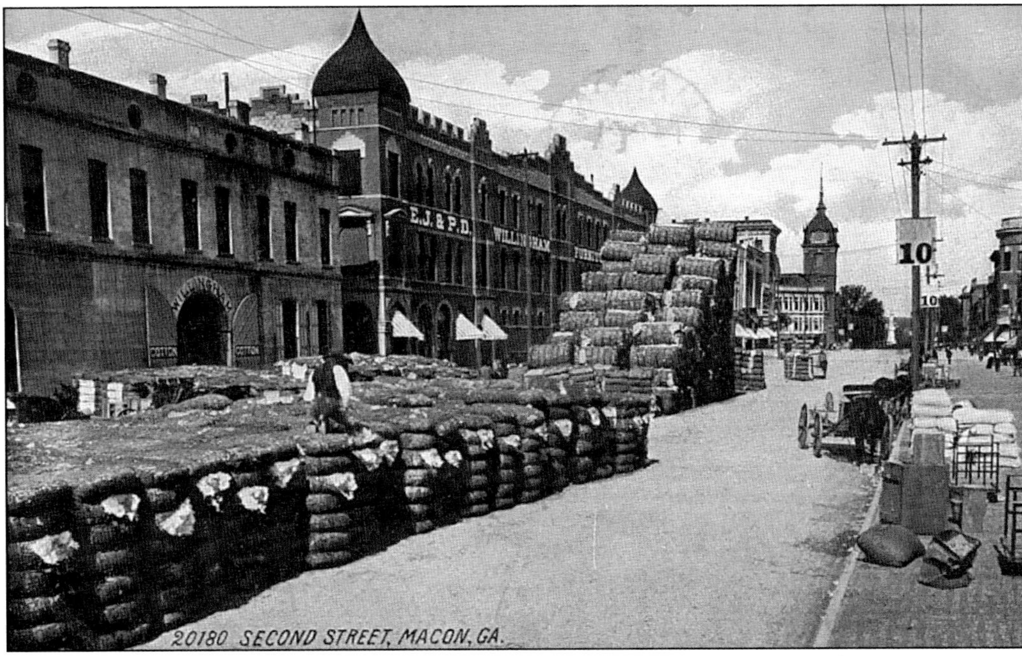

Here, bales of cotton are piled high in front of the Willingham cotton warehouses on Second Street. The message on the back of the card reads, "This is great cotton country. In fact the natives think it's the garden spot of the world." (Souvenir Postcard Co. #20180, postmarked 1910, color.)

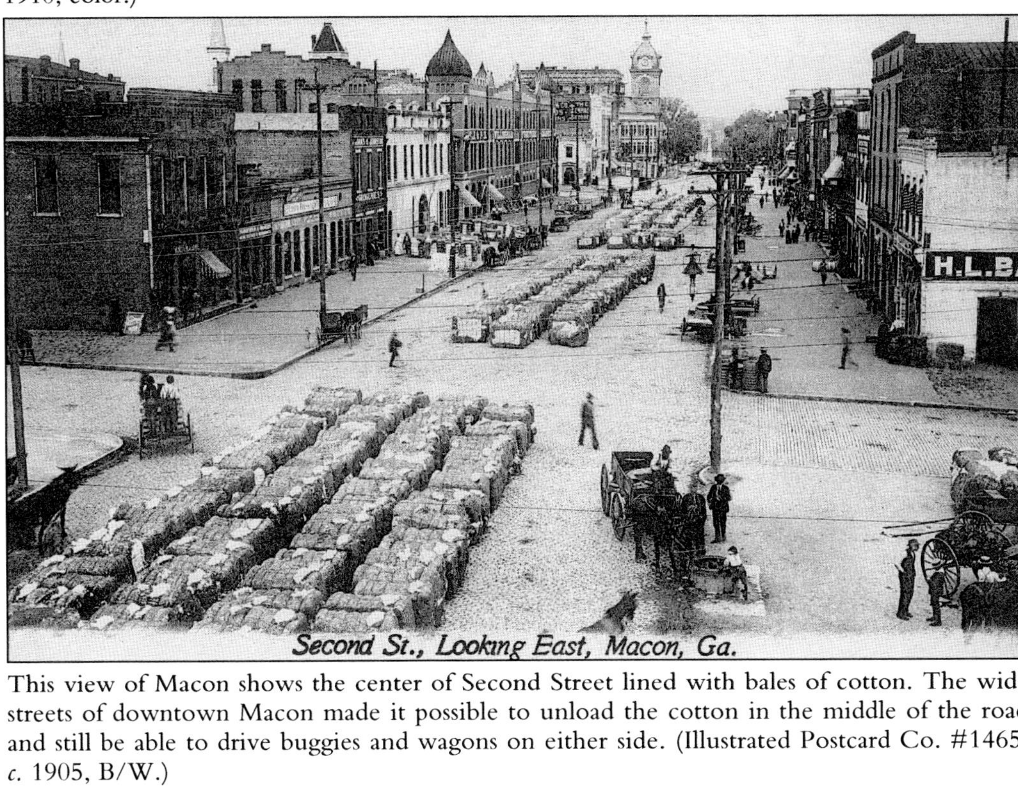

This view of Macon shows the center of Second Street lined with bales of cotton. The wide streets of downtown Macon made it possible to unload the cotton in the middle of the road and still be able to drive buggies and wagons on either side. (Illustrated Postcard Co. #1465, *c.* 1905, B/W.)

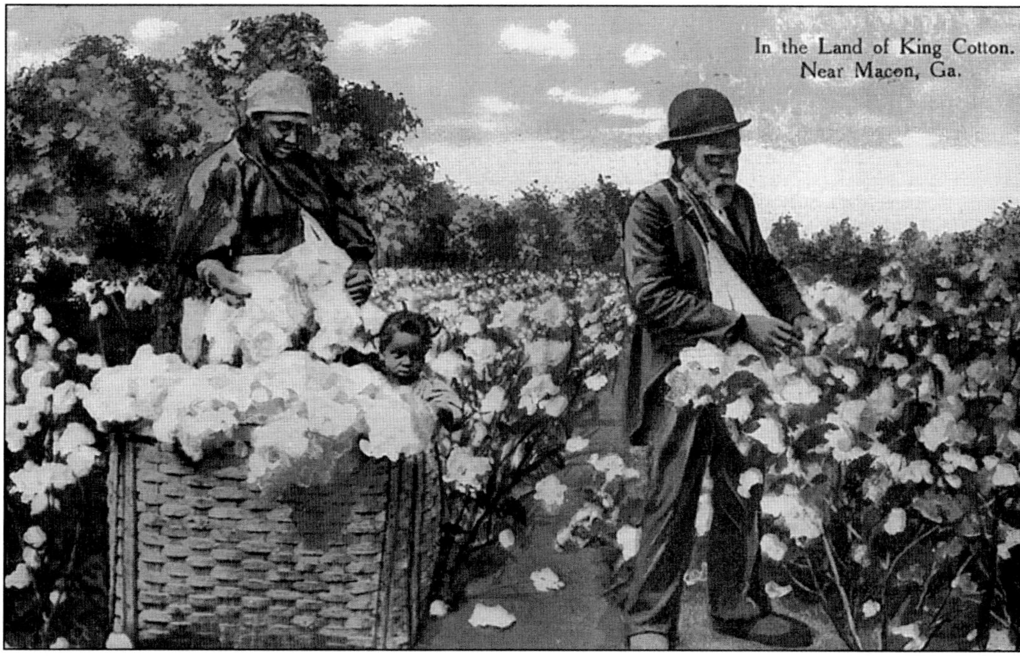

This family is picking cotton near Macon. The sender of the card writes, "You ought to be in the South and see all of the colored people and how they halft to work." (Curt-Teich #A1922, postmarked 1911, color.)

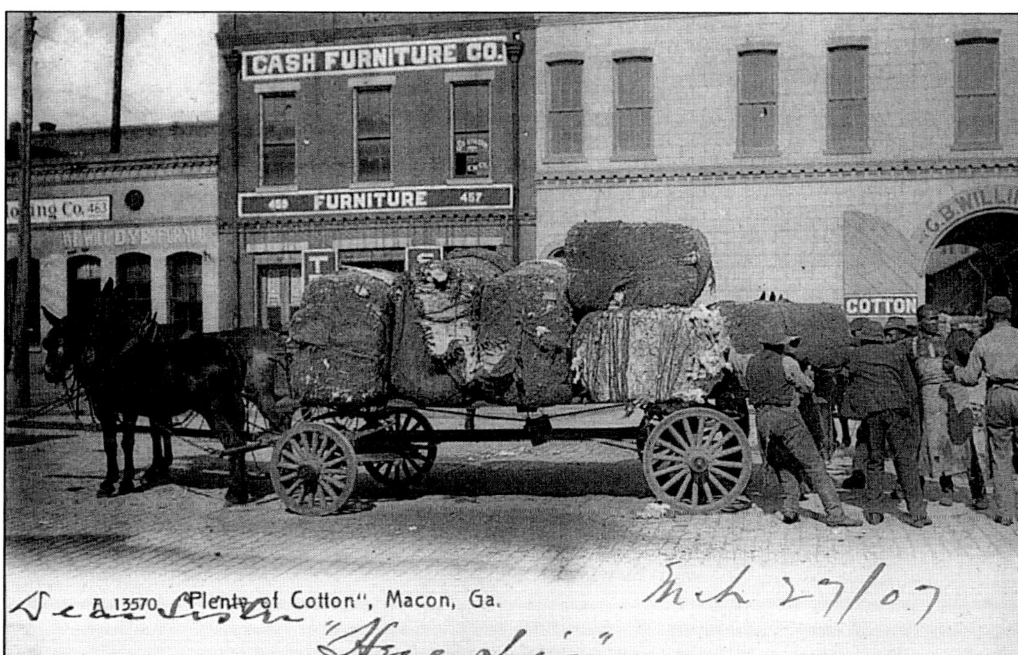

Willingham's Warehouse was one of the largest and busiest cotton warehouses in the city. Shown here is a group of black men unloading cotton bales from a horse-drawn wagon. (Rotograph Co. #A-13570, postmarked 1907, B/W.)

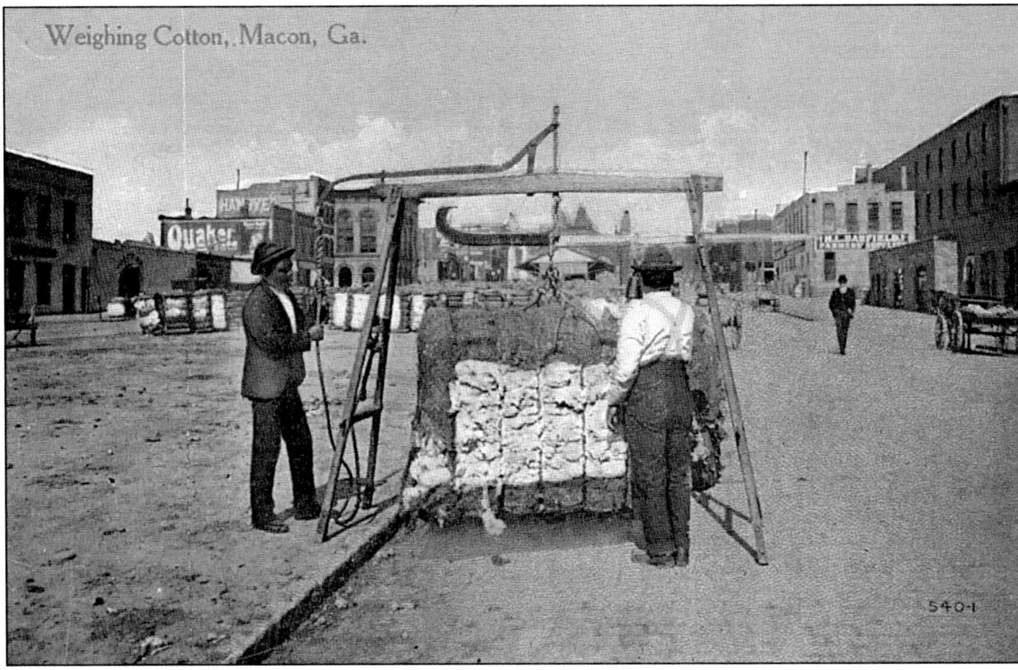

These two men are weighing cotton on Poplar Street. An average bale of cotton weighed about 500 pounds. It took approximately one acre of cotton plants to produce one bale. (Unidentified publisher #540-1, *c.* 1910, color.)

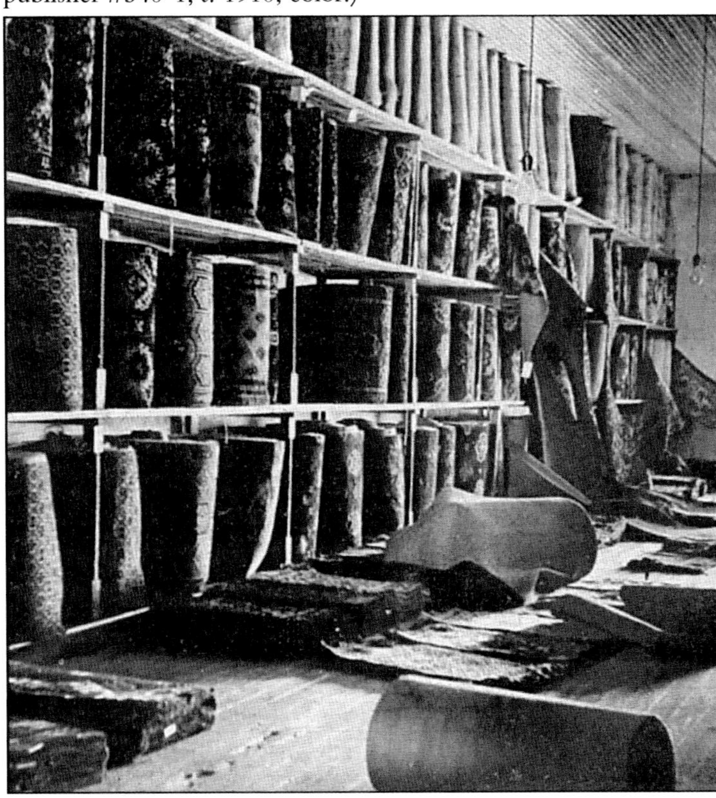

Most of Macon's cotton was shipped off to be made into consumer products; later, those finished products were shipped back to Macon for sale. Here, we see the carpet room of the L. McManus Company, located on Cherry Street. (E.C. Kropp, *c.* 1910, B/W.)

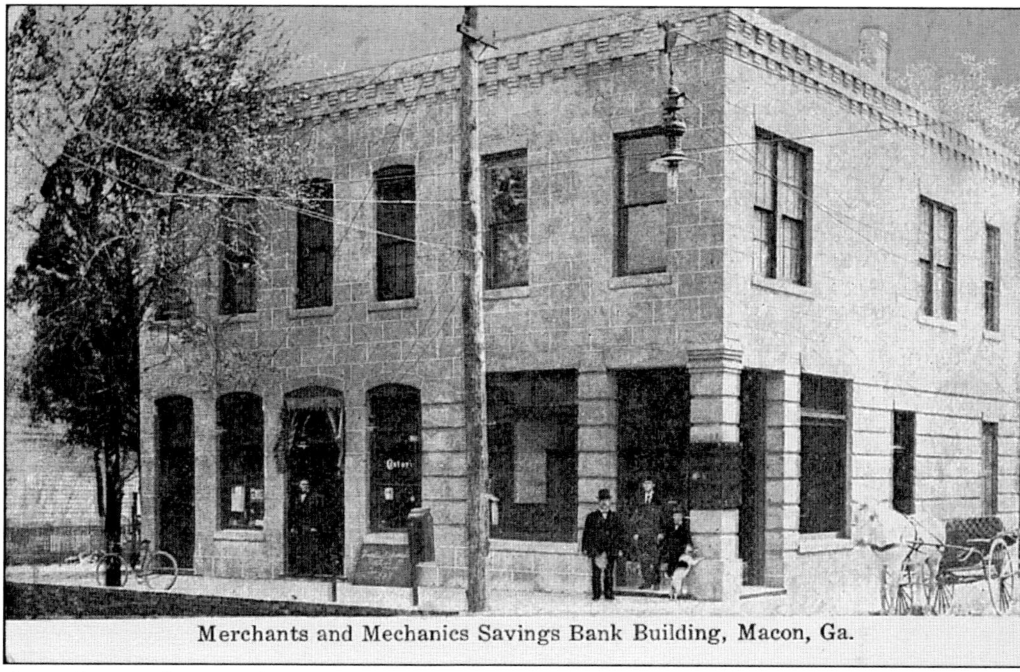

One of Macon's many financial facilities, the Merchants and Mechanics Savings Bank, is shown here. (Unidentified publisher, *c.* 1907, color.)

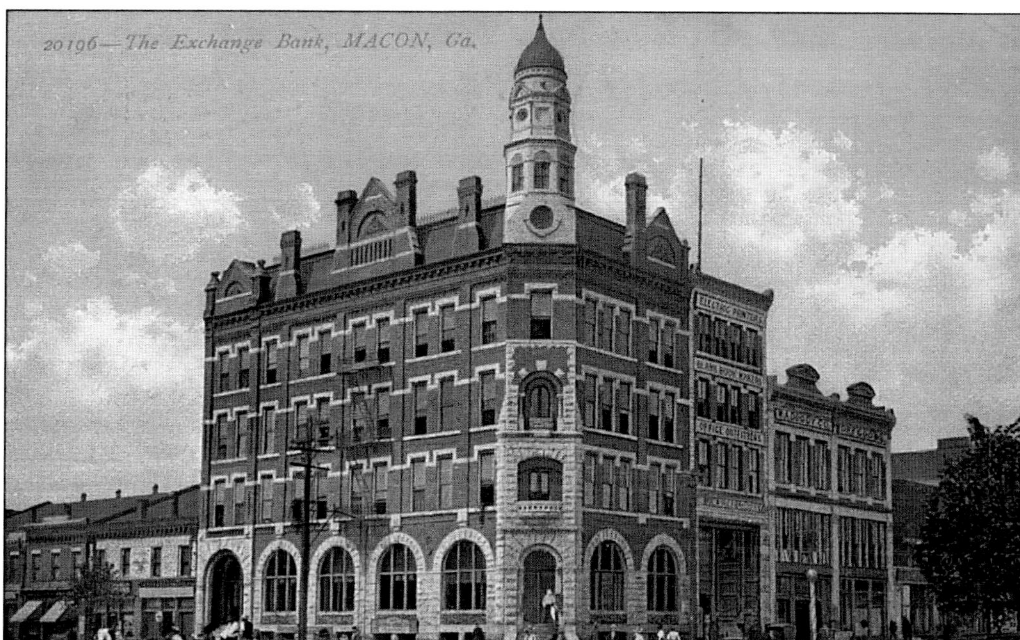

This large, impressive building on Cherry Street is the Exchange Bank, chartered in 1871. In an early advertisement, the Exchange Bank states it, "Throughout the long financial depression has adhered to its policy of assisting and sustaining the commercial interests of the city and section, as far as consistent with sound banking principles." (Souvenir Postcard Co. #20196, postmarked 1908, color.)

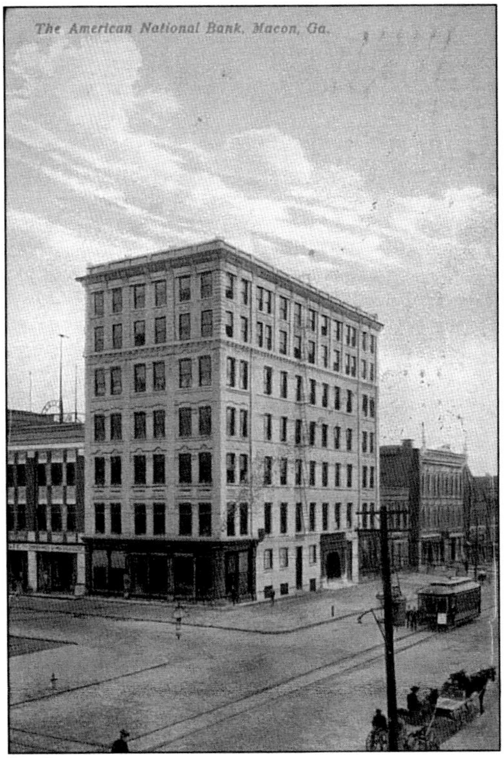

This seven-story building on the corner of Third and Cherry Streets is the American National Bank, which opened its doors for business on April 23, 1891. Note the streetcar boarding passengers as well as the horse-drawn wagon in the lower right corner. Irvine's Music House, which incidentally published and sold many postcards of Macon, is located next door to the bank. (Souvenir Postcard Co. #20191, postmarked 1912, color.)

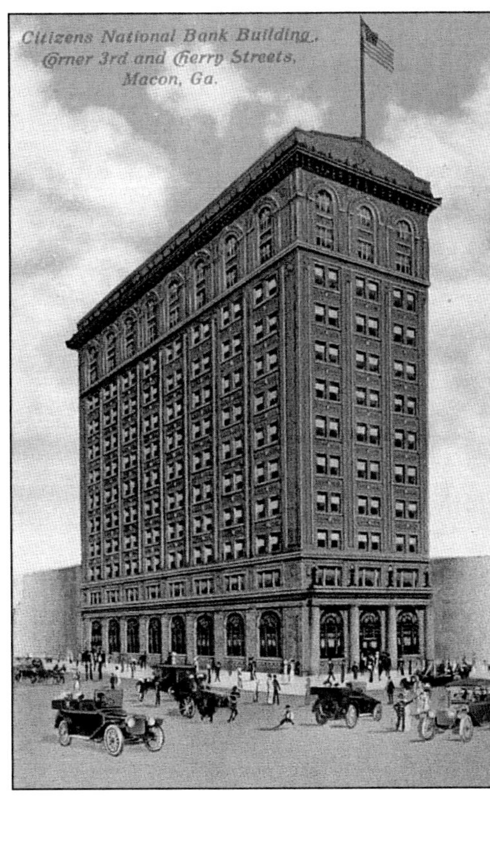

The Citizens National Bank Building, located on Cherry Street was built in the 1890s. At the turn of the century, Macon had eight banks and four security and loan associations. In 1897, total bank clearing in Macon amounted to $32, 147, 000, and only 56 cities in the U.S. made a better showing. (Powers Curiosity, Octochrome #33973, *c.* 1910, color.)

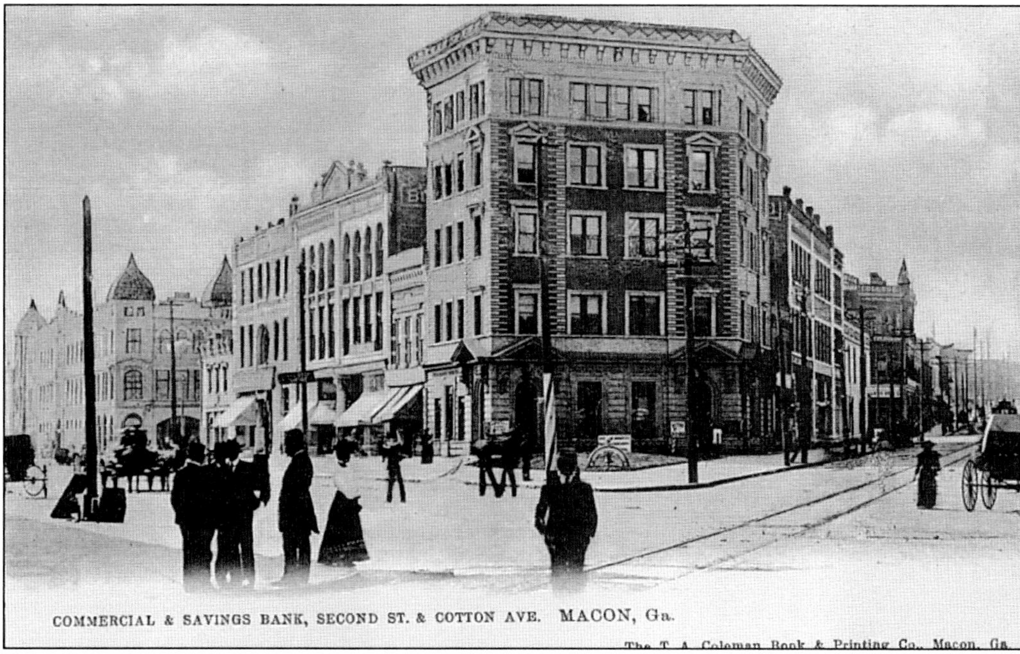

The streets are busy in front of the Commercial Bank Building at Second Street and Cotton Avenue. On the lawn in front of the bank, you can see the riverboat bell before it was moved to Central City Park. (Raphael Tuck #1022, *c.* 1905, B/W.)

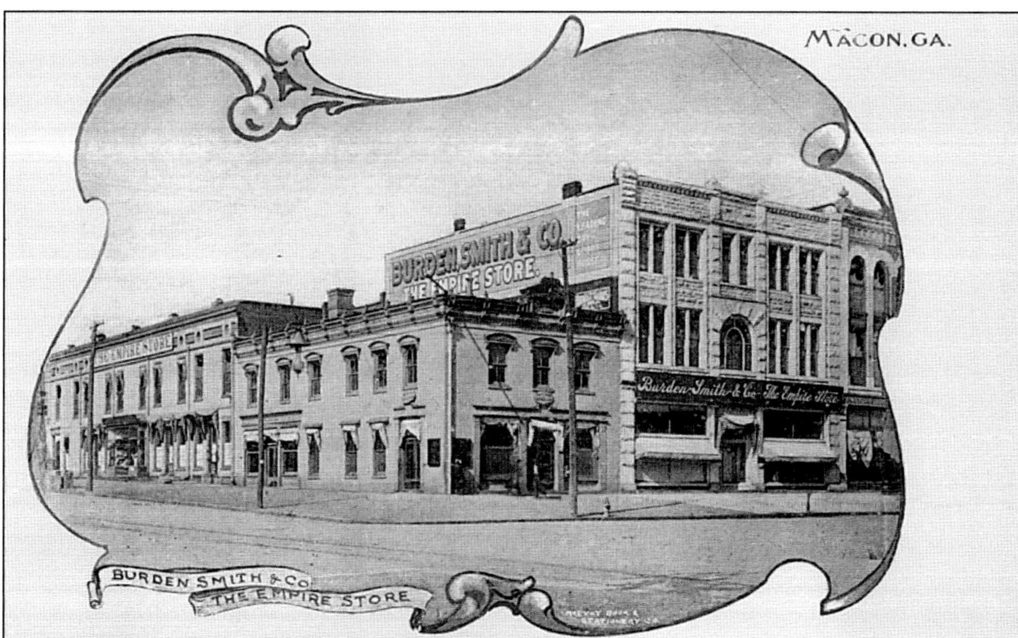

Burden Smith & Co., known as the Empire Store, was located on Second Street. It advertised the following: "Artistic dress making a specialty. Staple and fancy dry goods sold." (McEvoy Book & Stationary, *c.* 1905, B/W.)

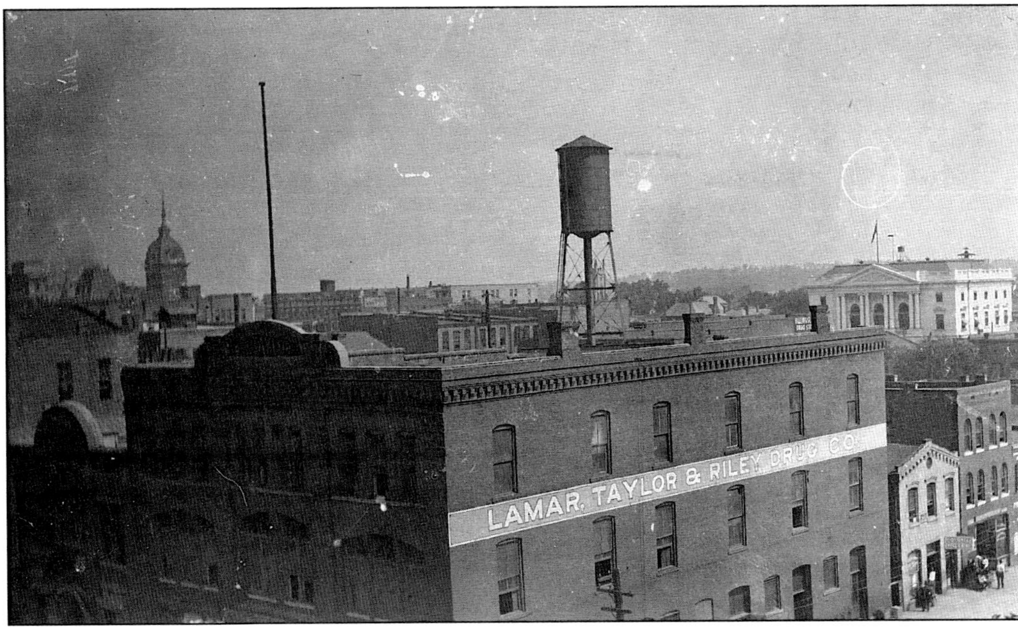

Lamar, Taylor, & Riley Drug Company, located on Cherry Street, was a drug wholesaler. Just beyond this building, you can see the Federal courthouse and post office building to the right. (Real photograph, *c.* 1918, B/W.)

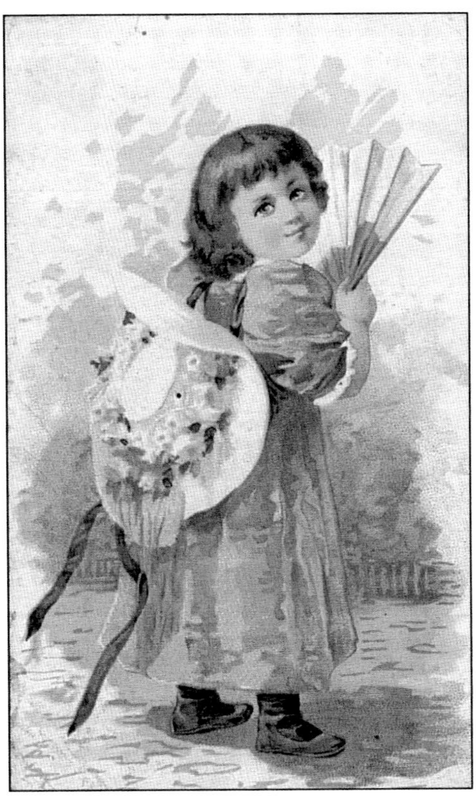

Lamar, Taylor, & Riley Drug Company advertised some of their products using premium cards such as the one shown. On the front of the card is a beautiful lithographic print of a young girl with flower, hat, and fan. The back of the card, shown here, advertises Lamar's Lemon Laxative, the very best medicine for constipation and all liver and stomach troubles. (Trade card, *c.* 1910, color.)

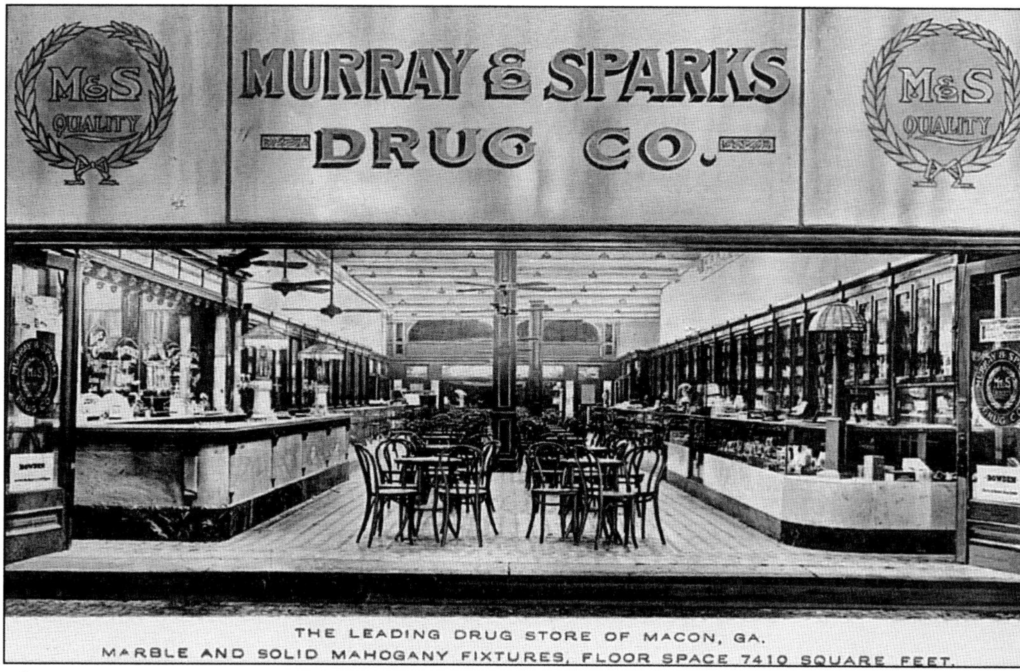

This interior view shows the soda fountain and drug counter of the Murray & Sparks Drug Company. The store contained 7,410 square feet with marble and mahogany fixtures. (Albertype, *c.* 1910, sepia.)

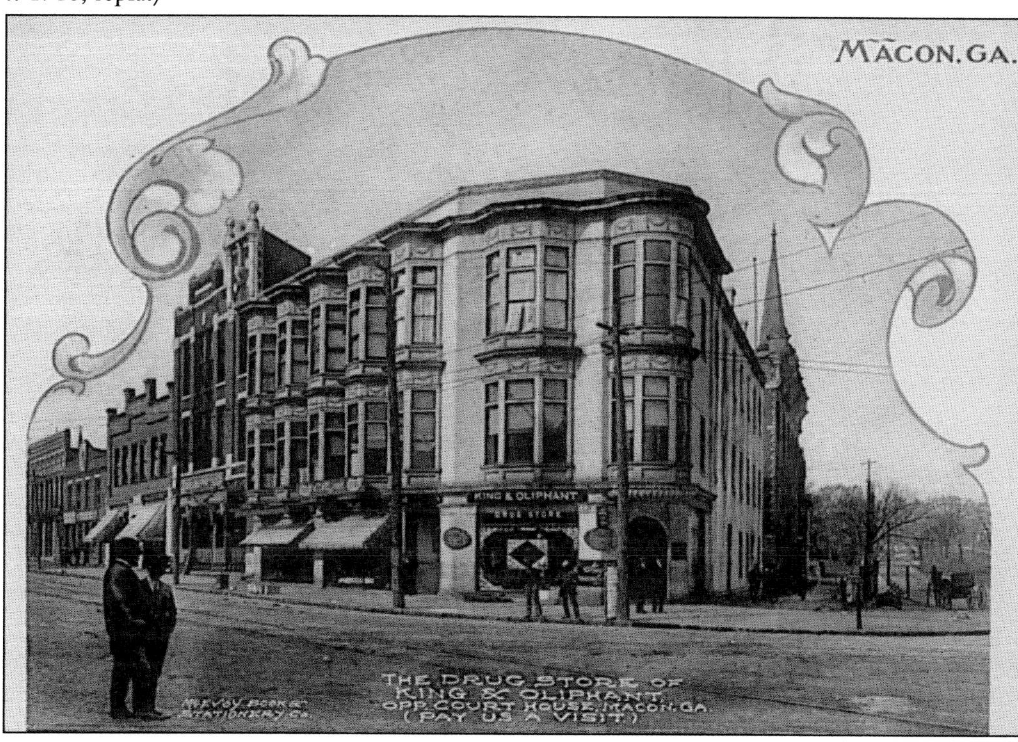

The drug store of King & Oliphant is one of the most beautiful buildings in Macon, located on Cotton Avenue opposite the courthouse. (McEvoy Book & Stationary, *c.* 1905, B/W.)

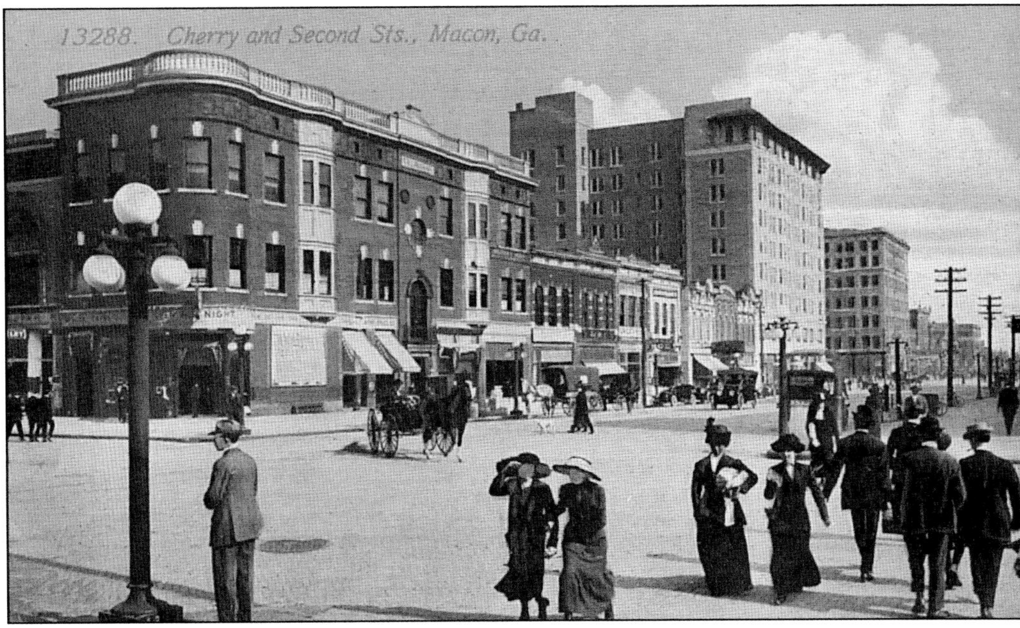

This busy downtown street scene at Cherry and Second Streets shows the Taylor-Bayne Drug Store. The drug store advertised, "Open All Night." (Powers Curiosity #13288, postmarked 1914, color.)

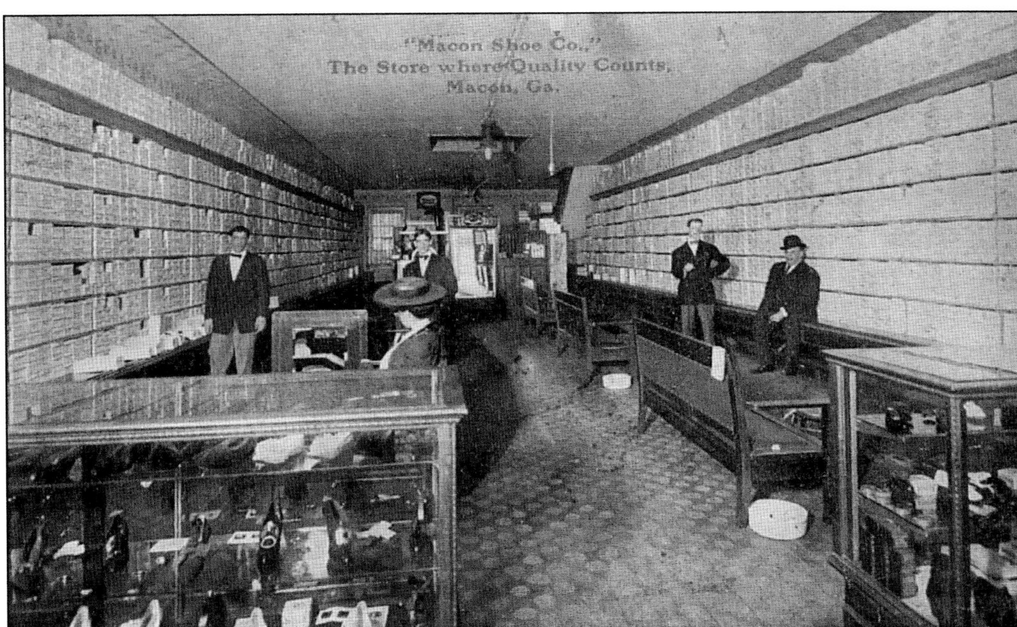

This interior view shows the Macon Shoe Company on Third Avenue. It was known as "The store were quality counts." On back of card is an advertisement for the "pump of gold bronze, a new note in spring footwear, $5.00." (Kropp Co., postmarked 1909, B/W.)

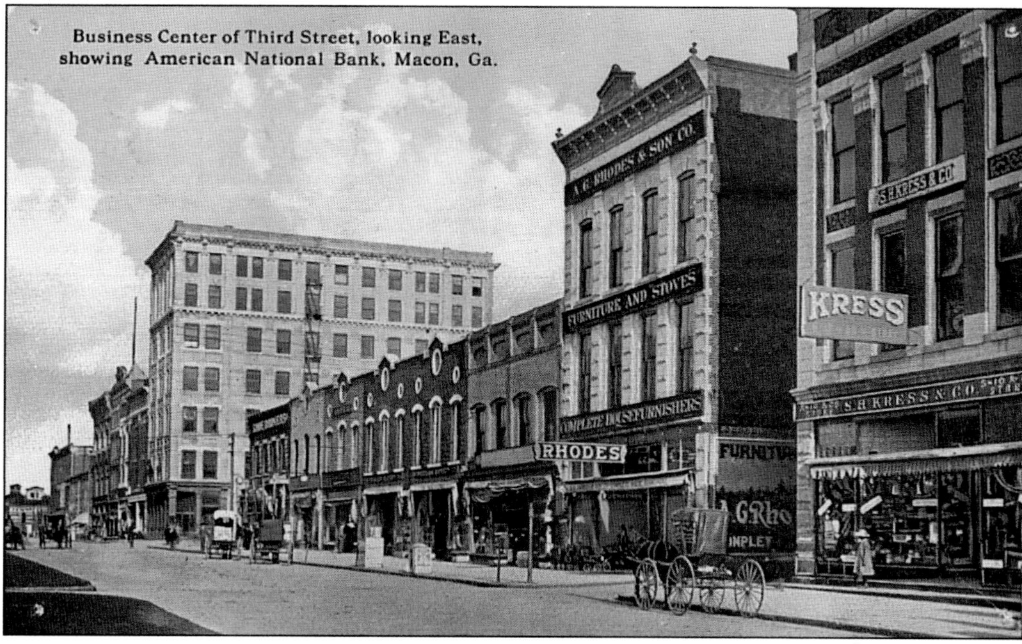

This image of the Third Street's business center looking east shows the American National Bank, S.H. Kress 5–10 & 25 Store, and Rhodes Furniture. The S.H. Kress Store ordered and sold thousands of postcard views of Macon. (S.H. Kress, Curt-Teich #A-27002, postmarked 1913, color.)

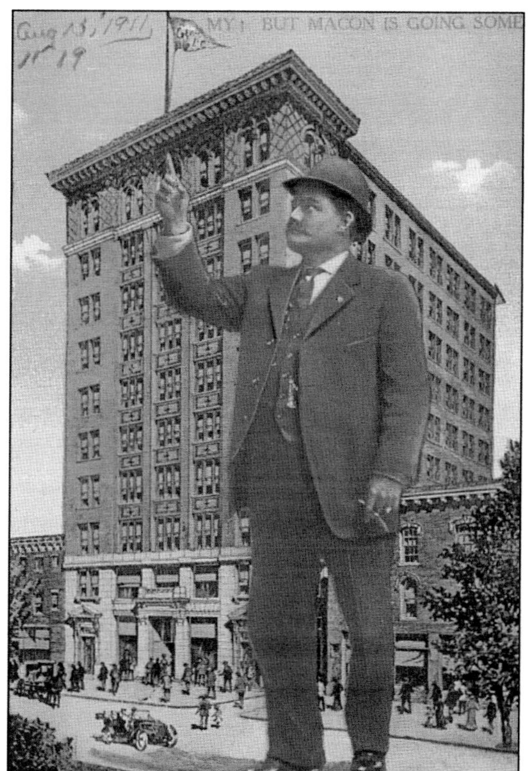

"My! But Macon is going some," says a giant man standing in front of the Georgia Life Insurance Building (Georgia Casualty Building). Trick photography was popular on postcards for making exaggerated images powerful. The Georgia Casualty Building was located on Mulberry Street, two doors down from the Plaza Hotel and across the street from the Hotel Lanier. (Power's Curiosity #540-19, *c.* 1911, color.)

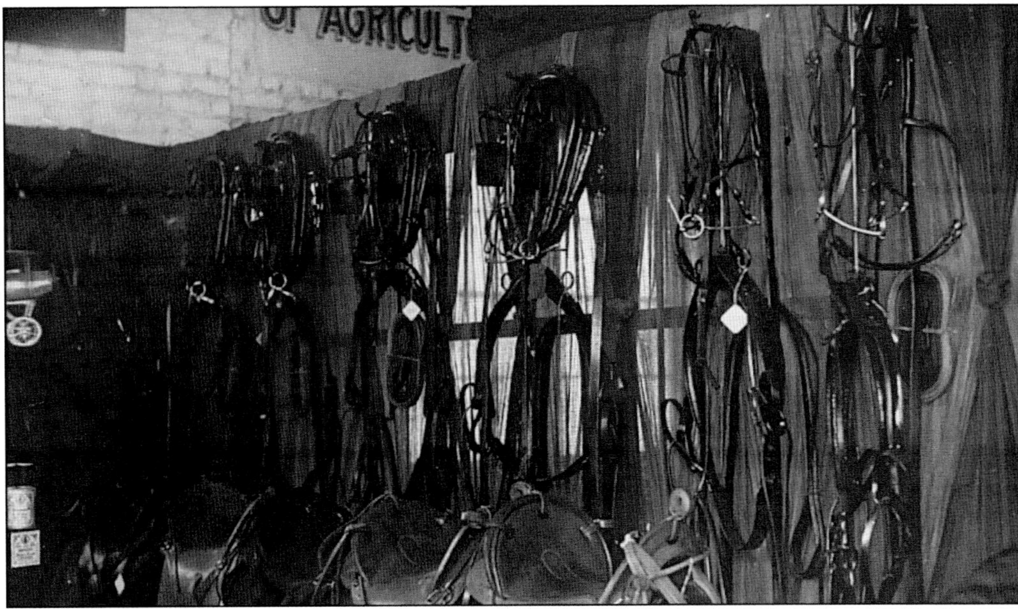

As transportation by horse and horse-drawn conveyances were still the primary means of transport at the turn of the century, the G. Bernd & Co. was an important business within downtown Macon. This display of saddles and harnesses, at the Georgia State Fair, was made by Bernd. (Real photograph, *c.* 1920, B/W.)

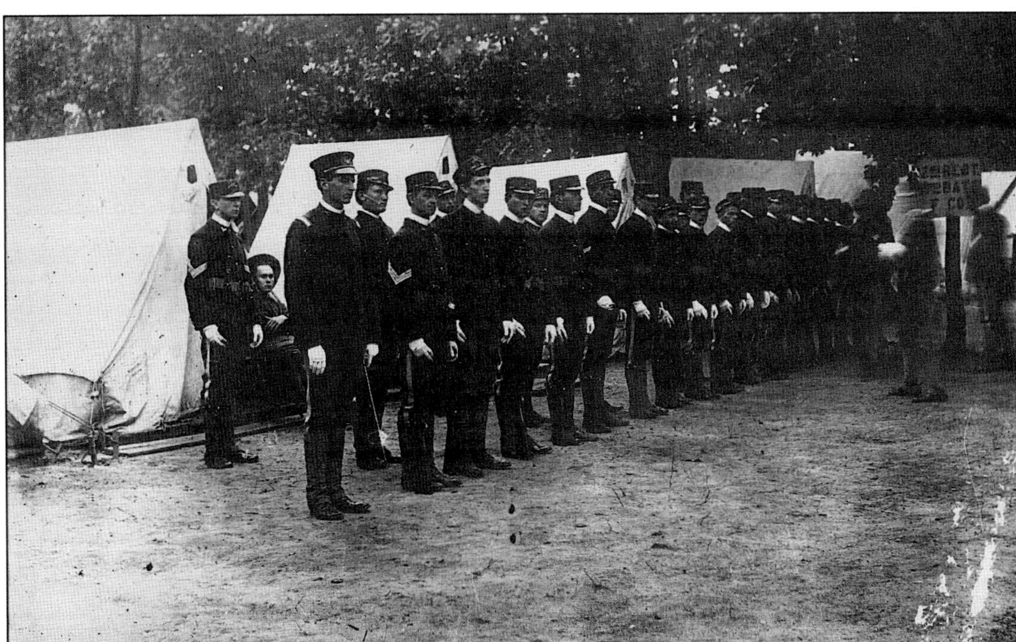

Macon's Historic Military Company can be seen in camp, *c.* 1906. Mr. Bernd, of the G. Bernd & Co., was a member of this organization. (Real photograph, *c.* 1906, B/W.)

Located at Fourth and Cherry Streets, G. Bernd & Co. was a manufacturer and dealer in harnesses and saddlery; the company was established in 1865. An early advertisement reads, "Our specialties: heavy saw mill and turpentine harness, collars and saddles, track, coach and coupe harness, and fine saddles of every description. We manufacture all the above articles and will meet all competition. Whips, robes and turf goods, leather and shoe findings. Send for prices." (McEvoy Book & Stationary, *c.* 1905, B/W.)

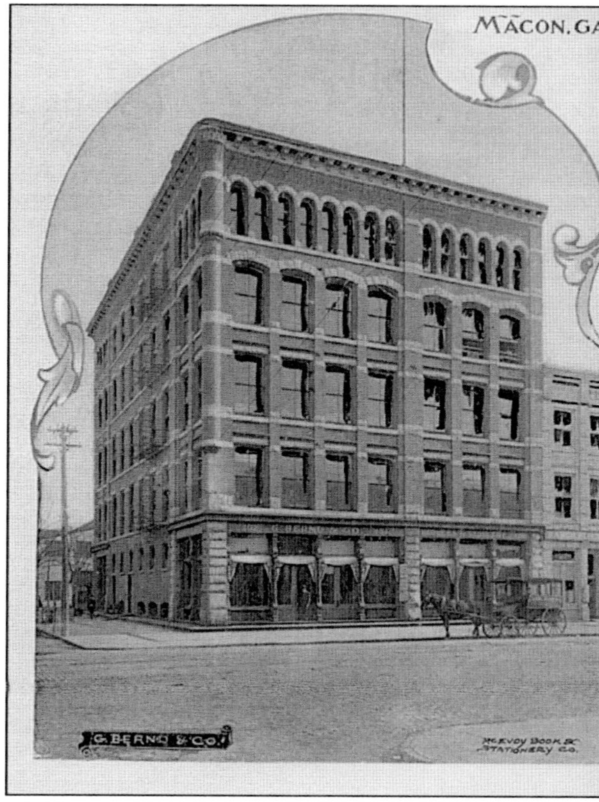

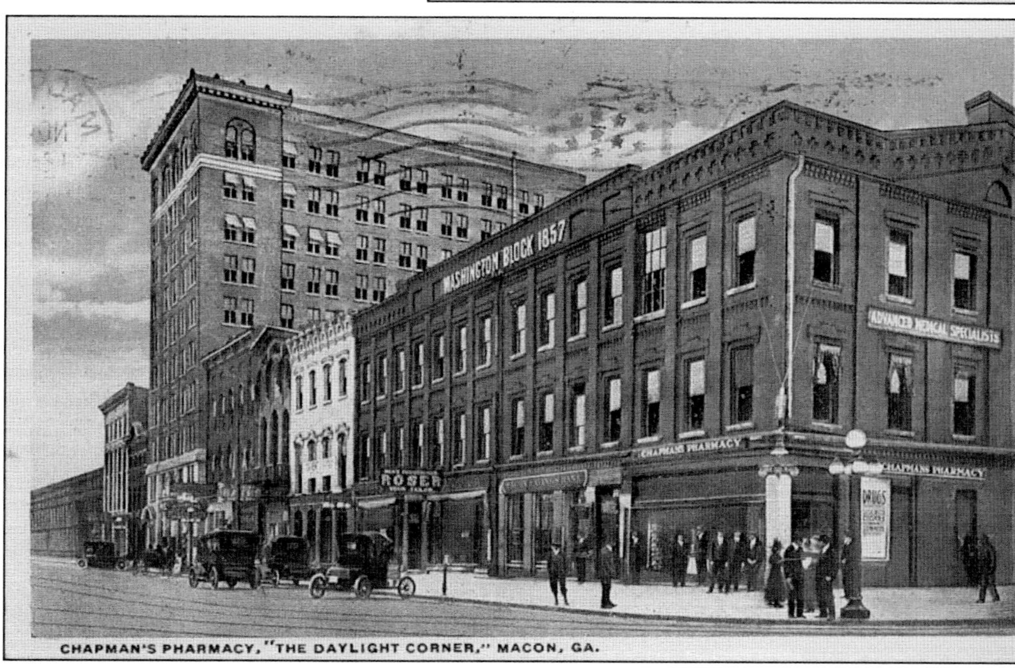

Chapman's Pharmacy was located at Second and Mulberry Streets, which was known as the "The Daylight Corner" in this Washington Block 1857 building. (Curt-Teich # R-58609, postmarked 1912, color.)

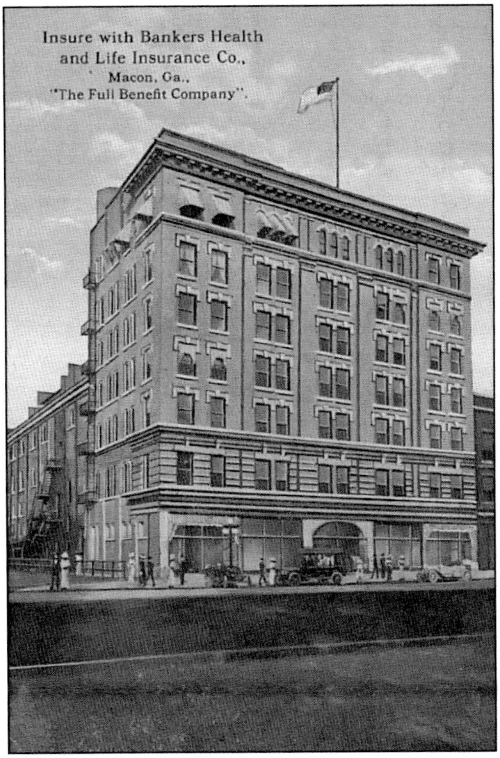

This picture shows the Grand Building that was constructed with commercial office space in front of the theater. One tenant was the Banker's Health and Life Insurance Company, "The Full Benefit Company." In 1940, the Banker's Health and Life Company built Macon's first skyscraper, a 14-story building on Cherry Street. (American Advertising Co., Curt-Teich # R42308, *c.* 1908, color.)

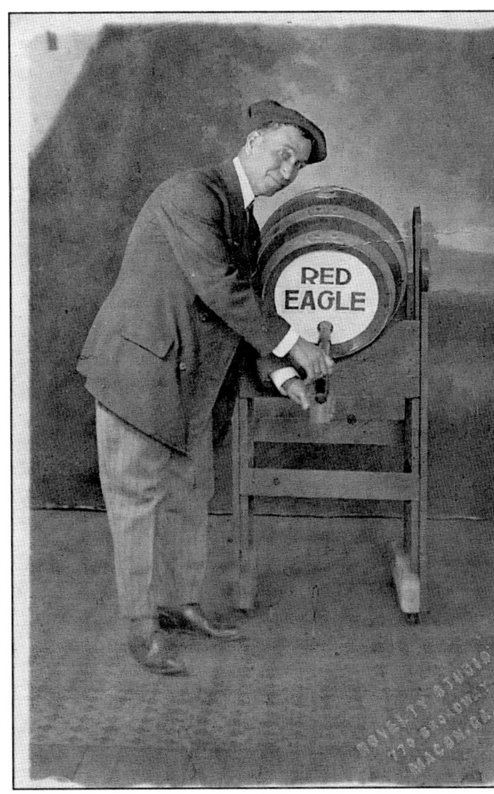

This picture, a fun, studio novelty card, was taken at the Novelty Studio on Broadway. Staged photographs such as this were popular during the early 1900s. People would have their pictures made on postcard backed paper and send them to friends and relatives. (AZO real photograph postcard, *c.* 1910, B/W photograph.)

Ten

PUBLIC PLACES

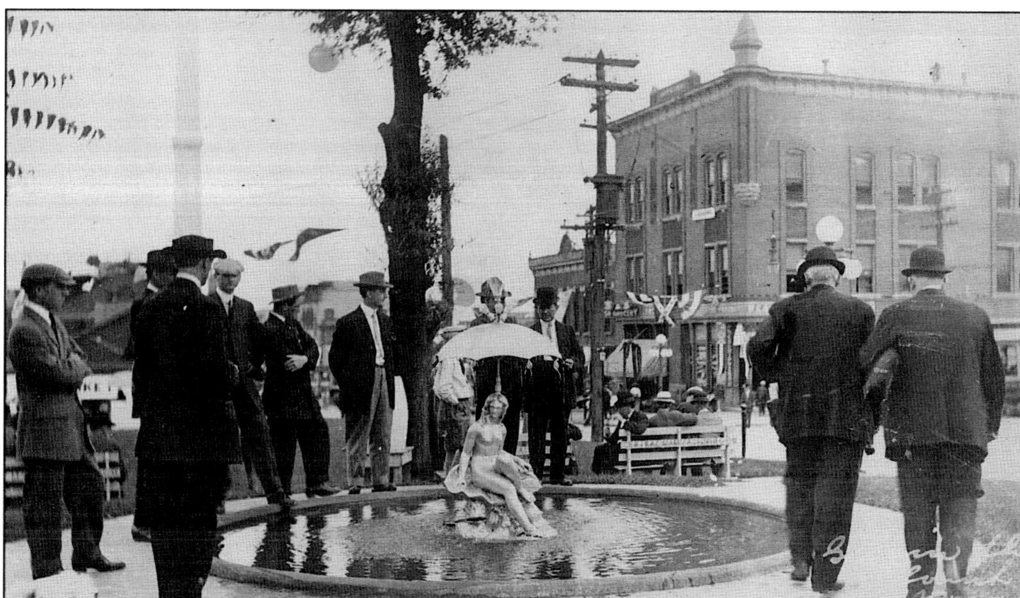

As with most cities' public affairs, Macon was not without her controversies. Shown here are a group of Confederate Veteran Reunion visitors admiring the "Girl in the Fountain" in front of the city hall. This nude statue was originally located in the courtyard of the Brown House Hotel. After being placed in front of the city hall, the statue sparked heated protests by some of the women of the city. In 1918, it was quietly removed and replaced with a flower garden. (real photograph, *c.* 1912, B/W.)

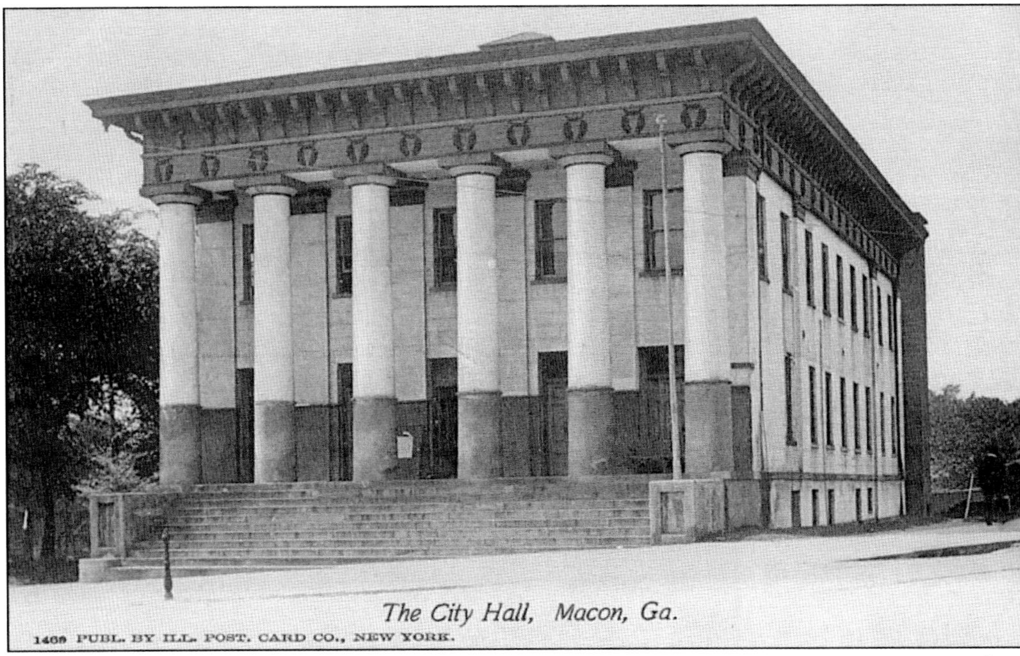

The city hall building was first built as headquarters for the Monroe Railroad & Banking Company. The company went bankrupt in the panic of 1837 and was sold to Jerry Crowles, who used it for a fireproof cotton warehouse. (Illustrated Postcard Co. #1469, *c.* 1900, B/W.)

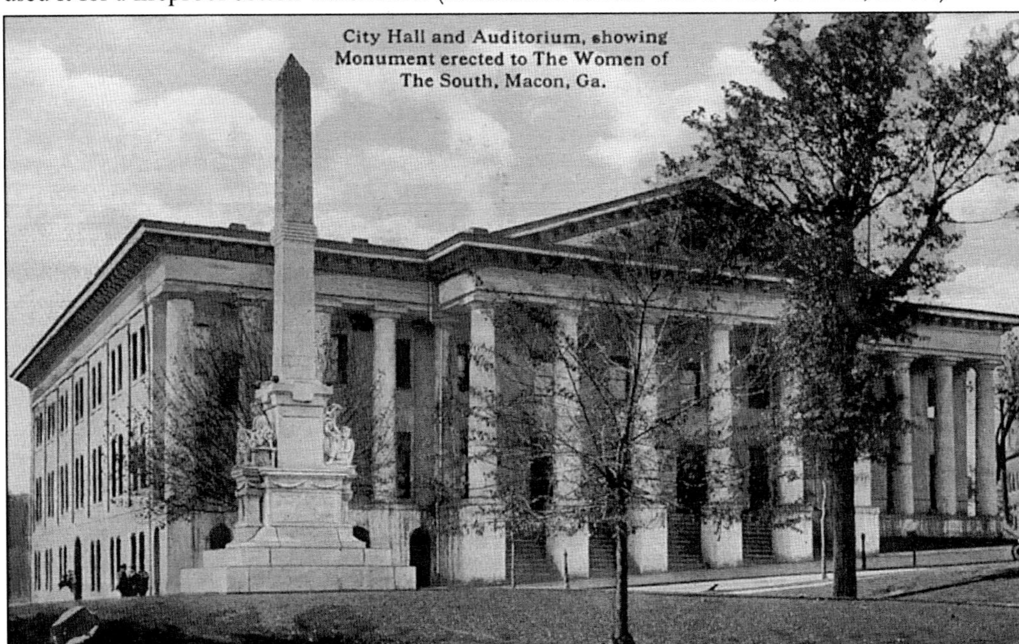

The city hall and auditorium building can be seen here after the wings and pediment were added to the front in 1905. In the foreground is the monument erected to the Women of the Confederacy, which was unveiled June 3, 1911. The monument is a 20-foot granite shaft depicting a southern woman with child and spinning wheel on one side; a woman helps a wounded soldier on the other side. (Power's Curiosity Store, Curt-Teich # A-27000, postmarked 1912, color.)

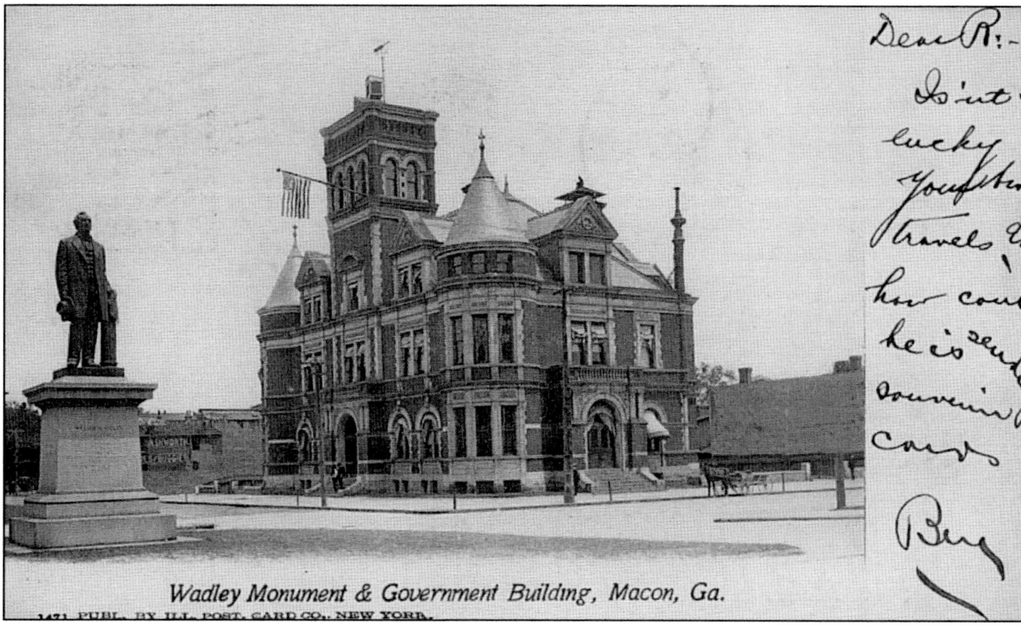

The original post office, a beautiful brick building, was located on the corner of Mulberry and Third Streets. Also seen in this picture is the Wadley Monument, honoring William M. Wadley, who came to Macon shortly after the Civil War. Wadley fought for the growth of the Central of Georgia Railroad. Upon his death, it was written, "Every bar of iron nailed upon the breast of Georgia is a monument to his foresight and industry." (Illustrated Postcard #1471, postmarked 1905, B/W.)

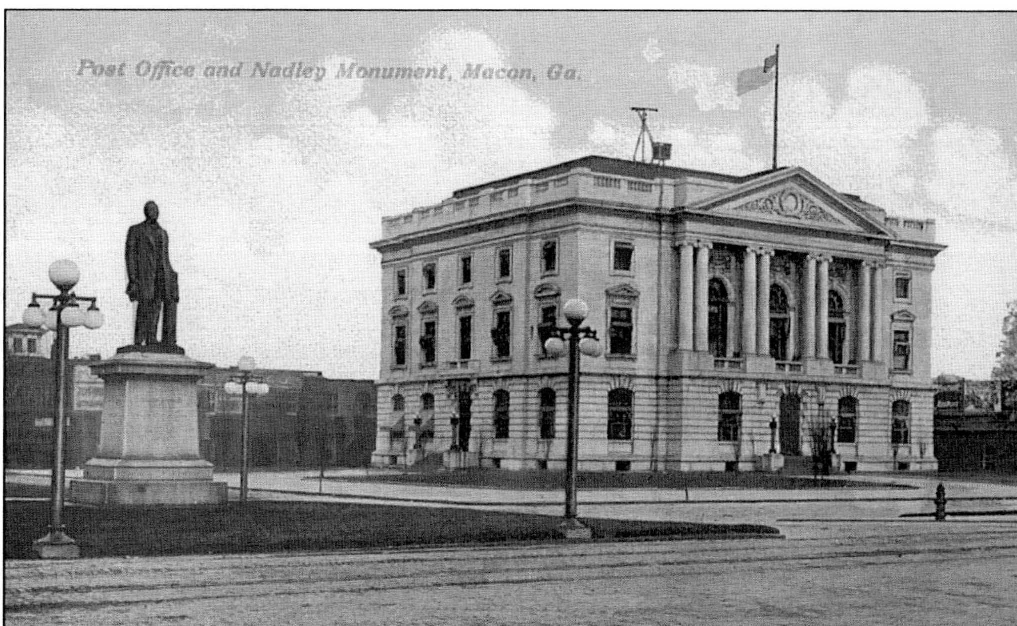

The original post office was torn down *c.* 1905, and a new marble structure was built in its place. The building houses both the Federal courthouse and the post office. In 1934, the building was enlarged. (S.H. Kress, Sexichrome #34258, *c.* 1910, color.)

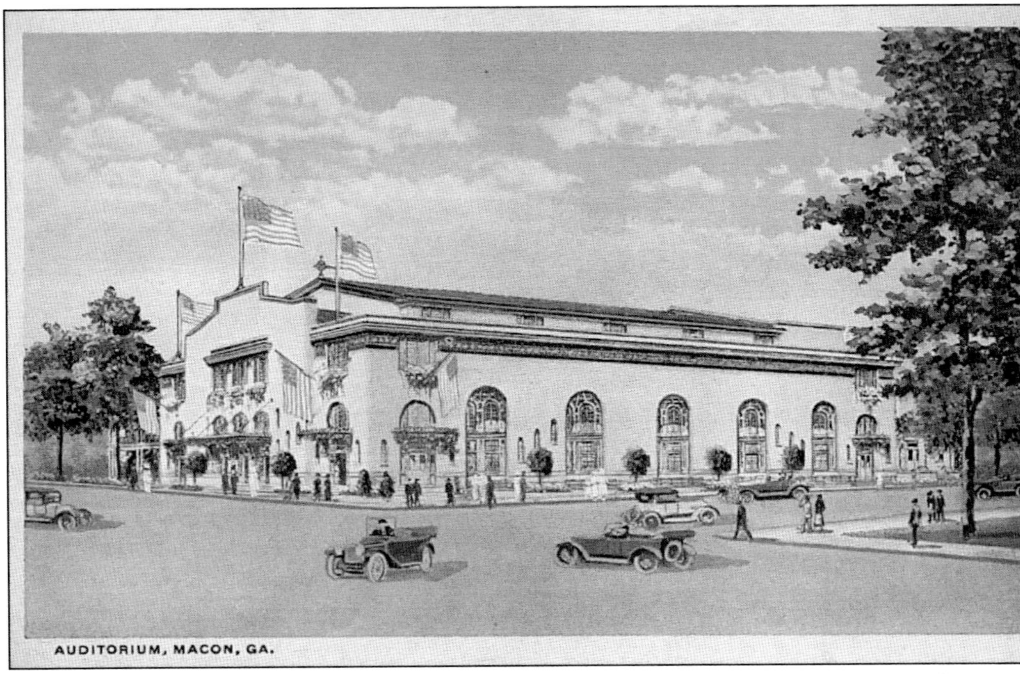

Originally, the city hall building was remodeled in order to fulfill the need for an auditorium. Then, a mammoth musical festival, the Chautauqua of the South, was lured to Macon with the promise of this new auditorium. Despite considerable political debate in 1917, the municipal auditorium shown here was constructed. Seven years later, in 1924, this building was razed. (Curt-Teich # A-62795, *c.* 1920, color.)

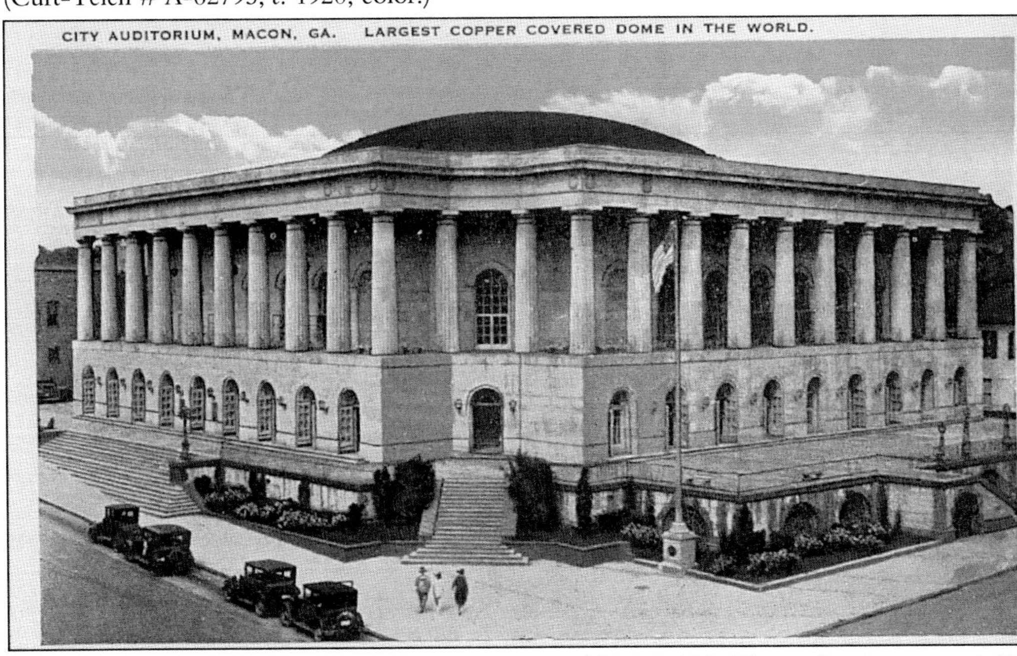

In 1925, a new city auditorium was built at a cost of $1,250,000. The auditorium seats 4,500 people and boasts the largest copper-covered dome in the world. (Tichnor Quality Views #129443, *c.* 1930, color.)

The original 1829 courthouse was located in the square at the center of Mulberry and Fifth Streets. In 1872, this lovely new courthouse was built on the corner of Mulberry and Second Streets. The Confederate Monument, shown here, was unveiled in 1879. This courthouse was torn down in 1922. (Peacock Series #8718, *c.* 1910, color.)

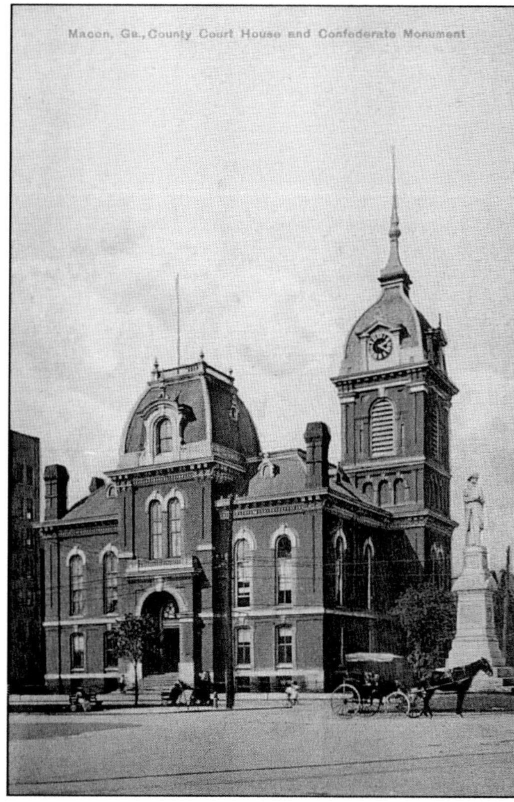

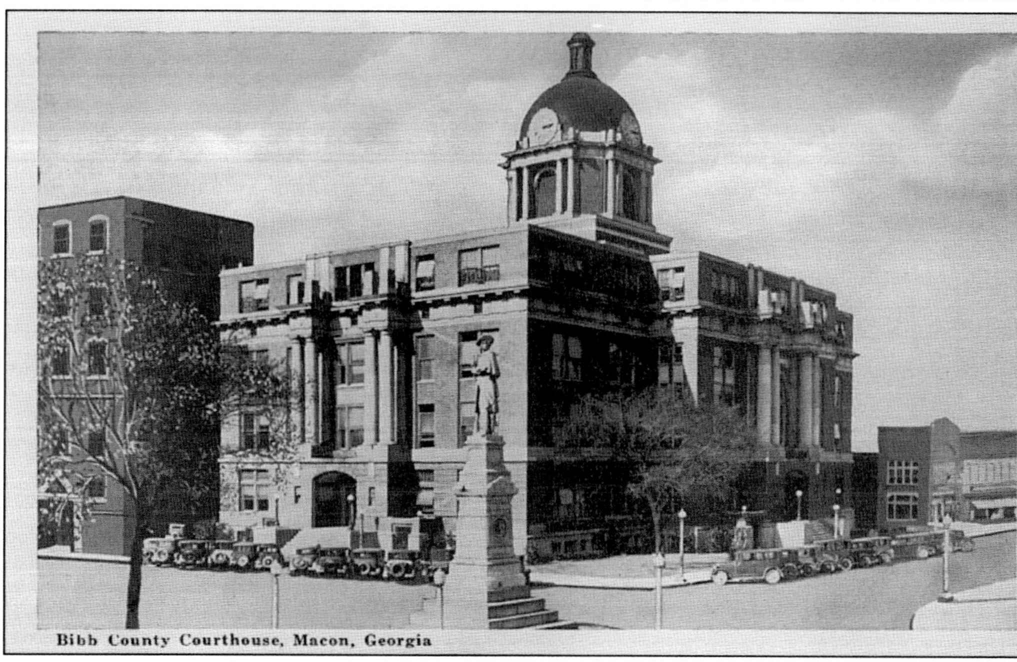

After the 1872 courthouse was razed in 1922, Bibb County's third courthouse was built. This newest courthouse is shown here along with the Confederate Monument in the foreground, which still stands proud. (Graycraft Card Co. # M-229, *c.* 1925, B/W.)

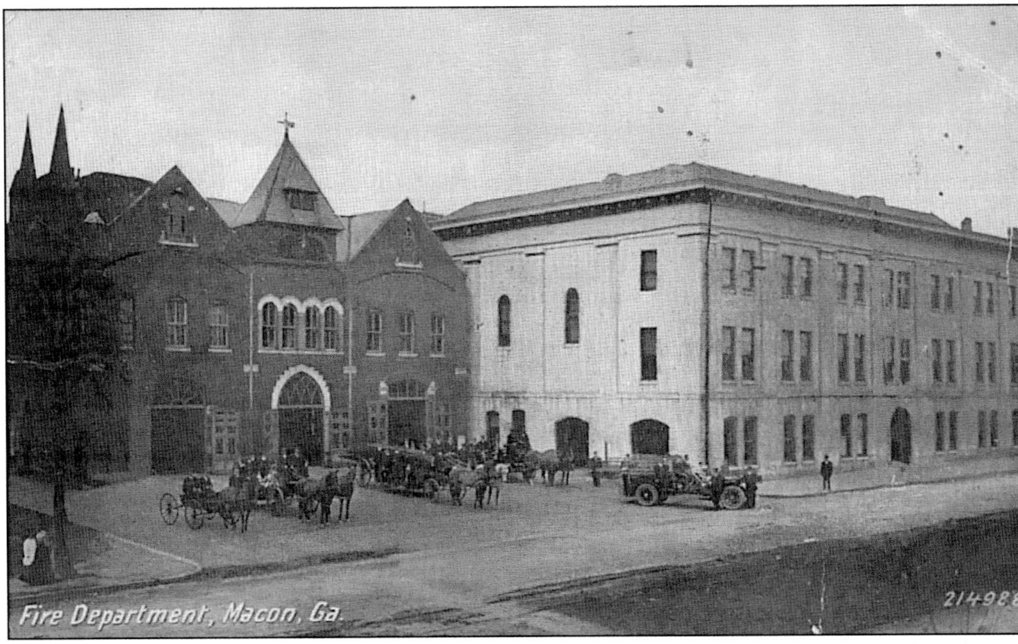

This view of the fire department shows horse-drawn fire equipment still in use, with only one motorized vehicle in the picture. (Leighton & Valentine Co. #214988, *c.* 1910, color.)

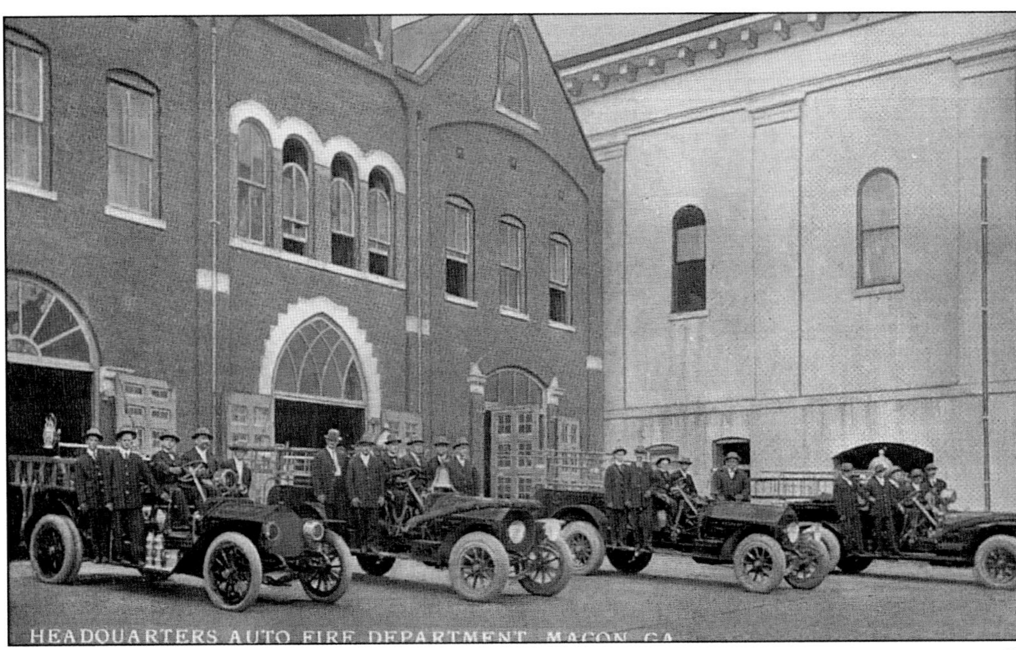

The fire department shows off Macon's all new automotive fire equipment as the firemen proudly pose for this picture. (Powers Curiosity, Curt-Teich #R-22322, *c.* 1911, color.)

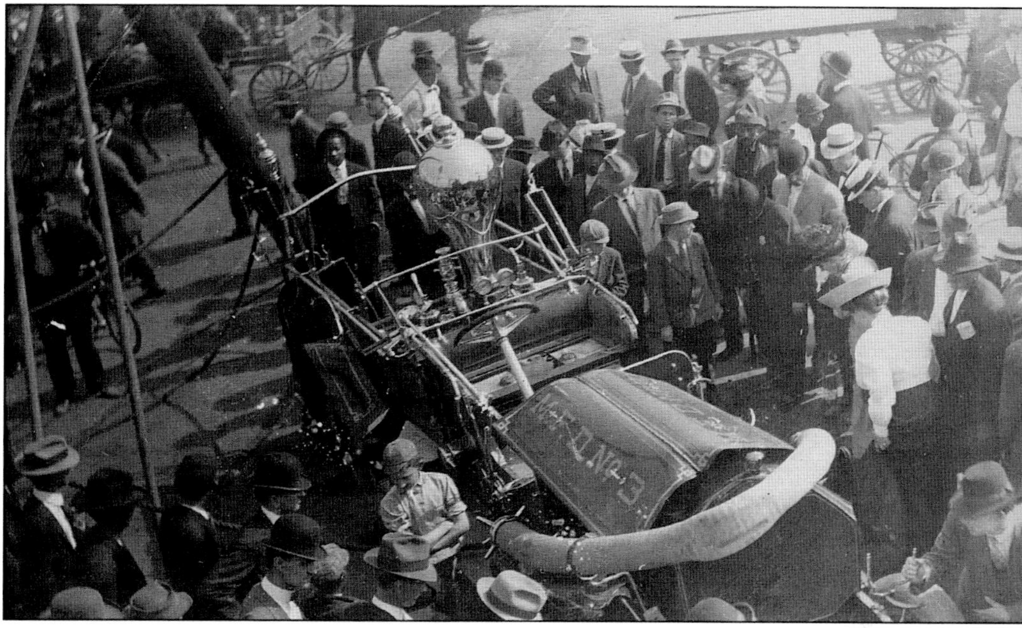

"Halley's comet was streaking through the early morning skies, leaving a tail of fire behind it; Kind Edward VII was on his death bed; horses were snorting at the horse-less carriages that threw off an unpleasant smell of gasoline and women were wearing high buttoned shoes when Macon's first motorized unit for fire fighting made its initial run down Cherry Street May 6, 1911." (Real photograph, *c.* 1911, B/W.)

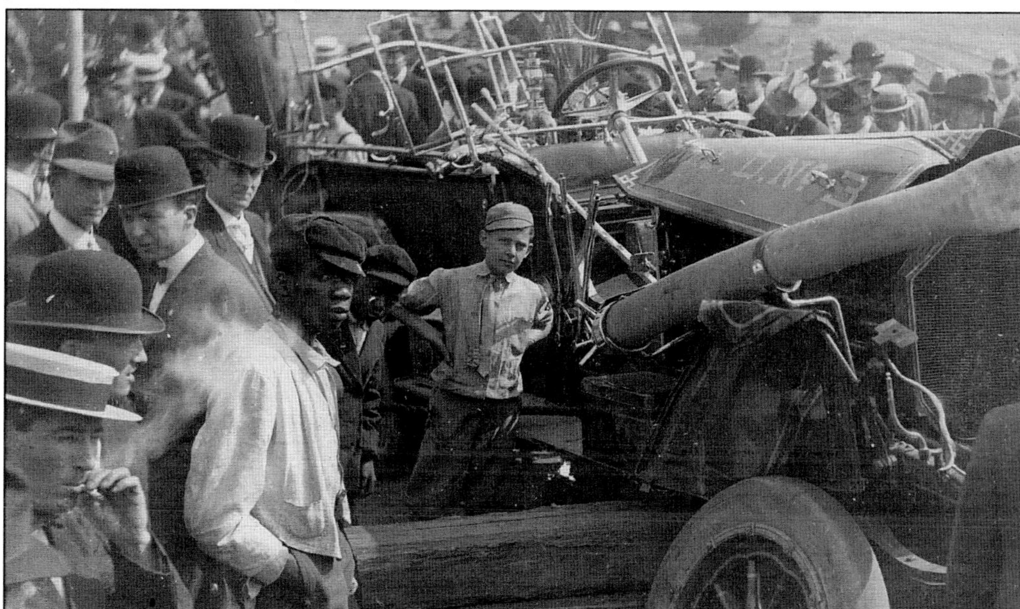

"The heavy truck hit a protruding curb at Fifth Street, swerved, blew a tire and hit a telephone post. Three firemen were killed and four more seriously injured," according to a historical sketch published. The disaster did not stop the progress of the fire department; later that year, Macon proudly boasted she was the first city in the world to have a completely motorized fired department. (Real photograph, *c.* 1911, B/W.)

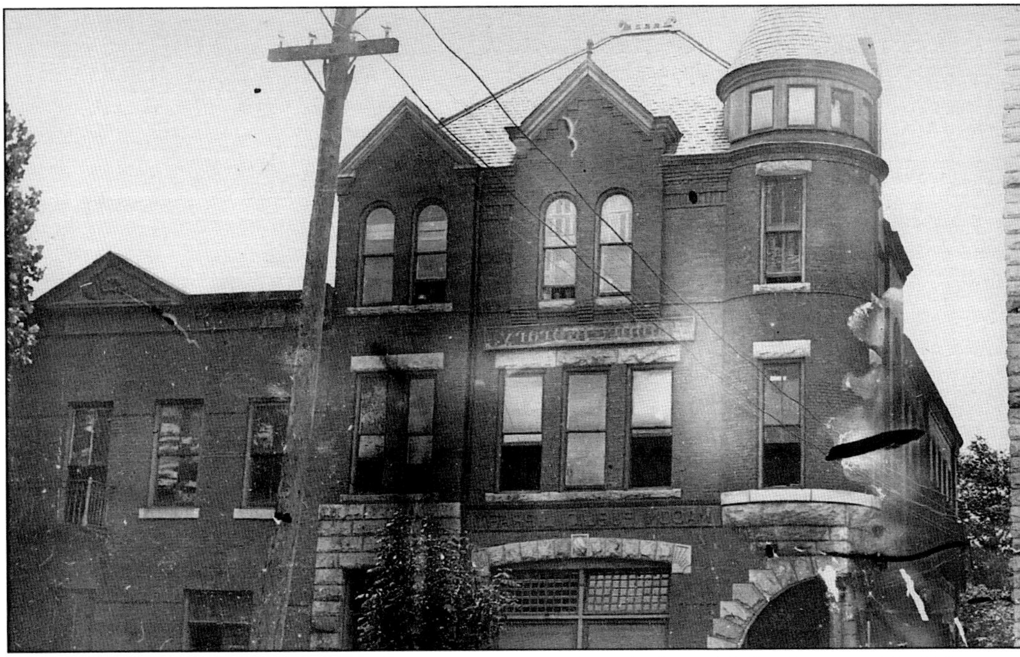

In 1876, the public library and historical society was founded. In 1889, this grand building was completed. The library was housed on the second floor, while the ground floor was leased commercially. The library was described as having every convenience, including a reading room, ladies' parlor, and toilet rooms with boudoir attached. (Real photograph, *c.* 1905, B/W.)

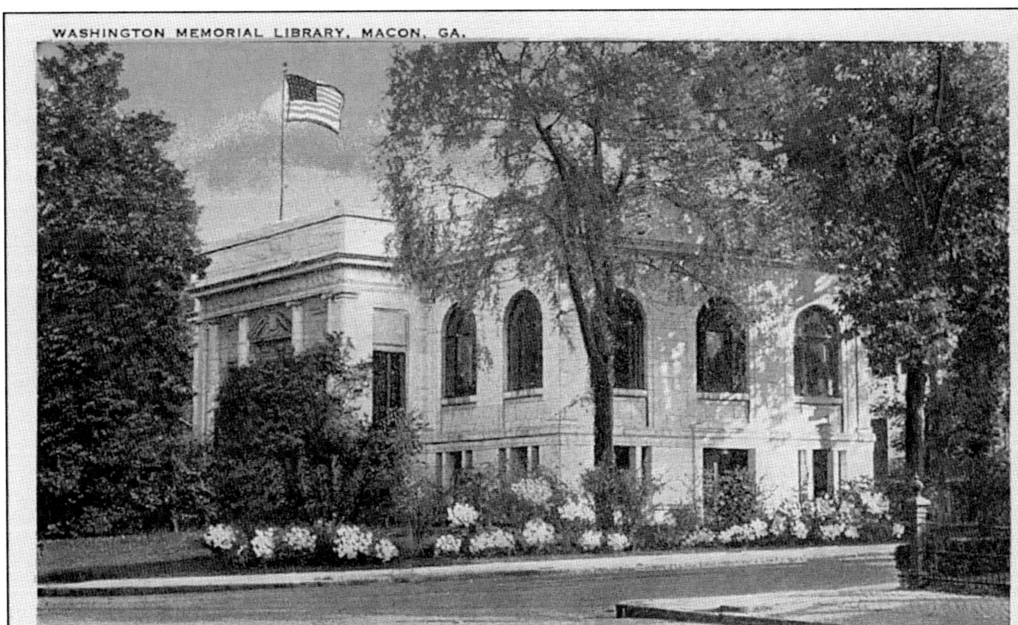

In the early 1920s, the library was moved to Washington Avenue. Mrs. Ellen Washington Bellamy made a gift of the property and $50,000 with which to build a new library in memory of her brother, Hugh Vernon Washington. In 1924, the building was equipped by the Macon Junior Chamber of Commerce. (Tichnor #1221395 , *c.* 1925, color.)

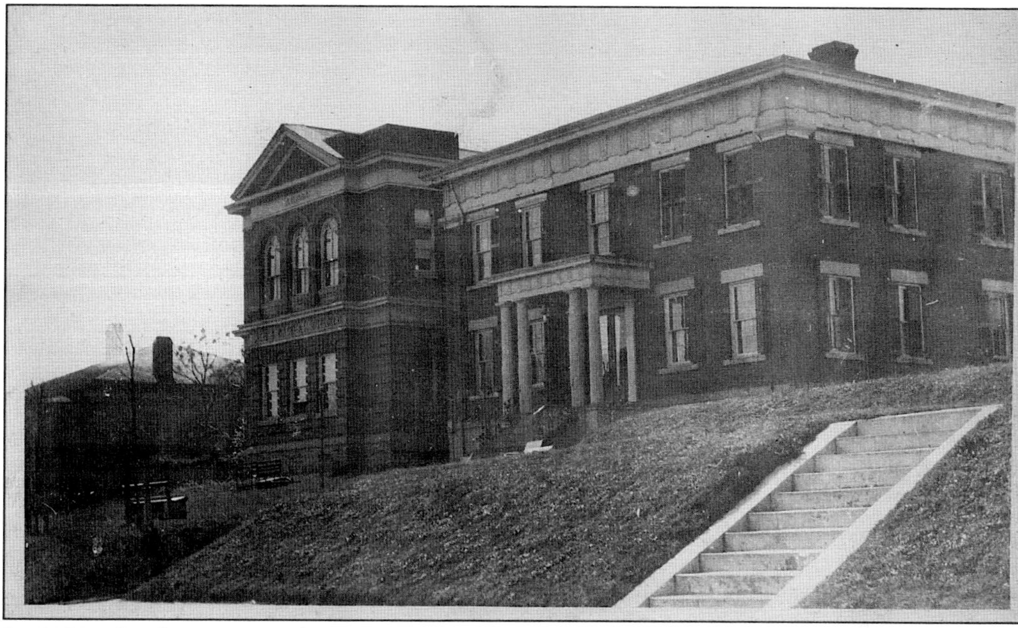

In 1895, the "Kings Daughters" raised funds to open the Macon Hospital in the old James Callaway residence on Pine Street. The city took over the hospital in 1915 when it had only 4 private rooms and 16 ward beds. (Real photograph , *c.* 1910, B/W.)

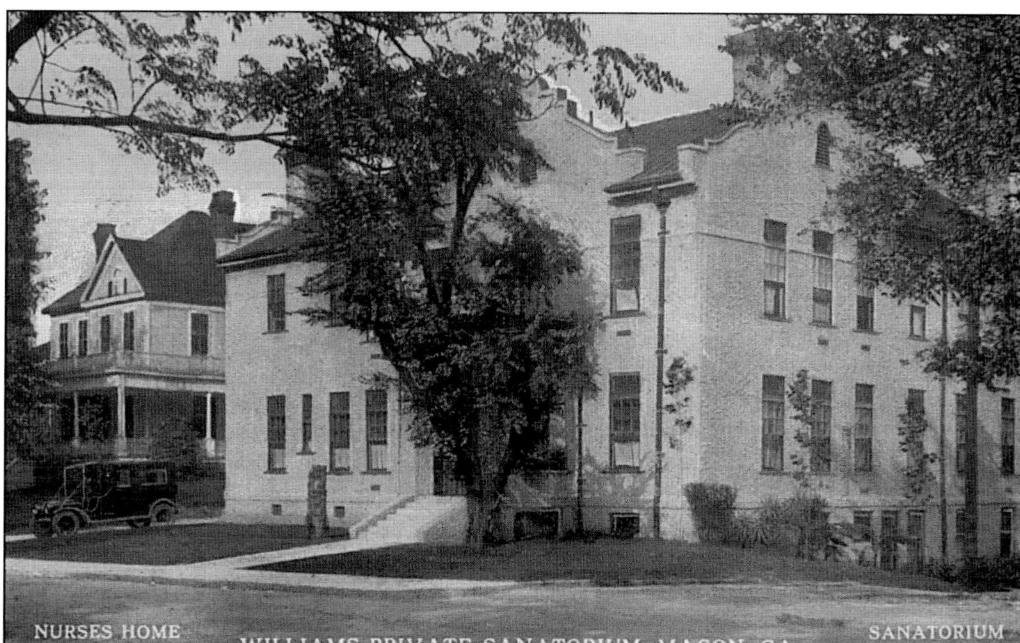

The Middle Georgia Hospital opened in 1911 as "Williams Private Sanitarium," so named after its founder, Dr. Howard Williams. This facility was the first privately owned hospital in Macon. After Dr. Williams's death in 1918, the hospital was purchased by a group of doctors. This picture shows the sanitarium building and the nurses' home. (Power's Curiosity Shop, Curt-Teich # R-32680, postmarked 1912, color.)

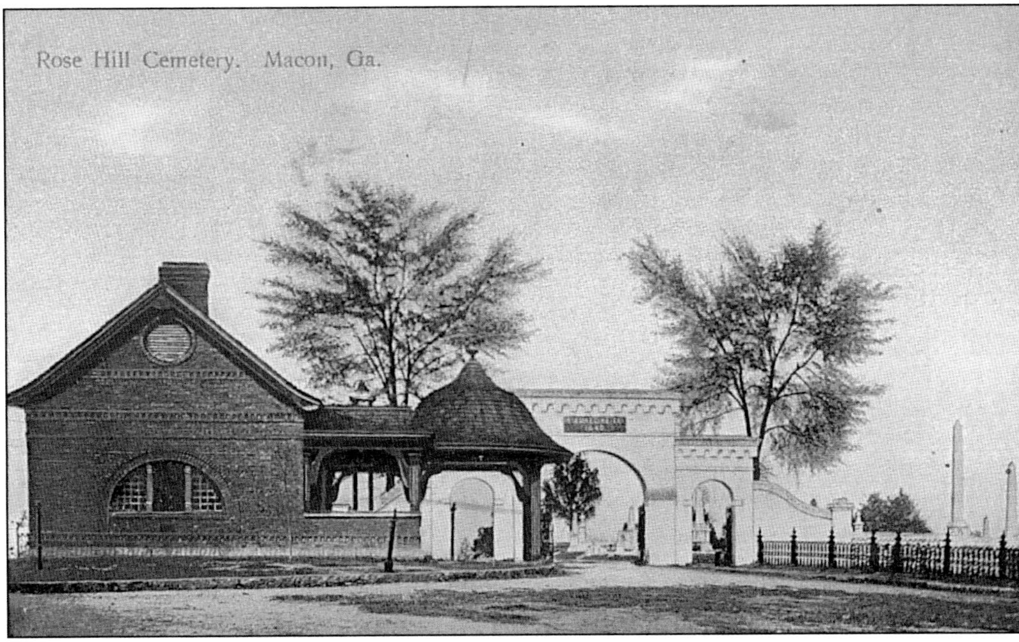

Semri Rose moved to Macon in 1818 and started a newspaper called the *Georgia Messenger*. He loved flowers and helped establish many of the city's parks. In 1840, he submitted plans for a new city cemetery, located high on the bluffs along the river. The appreciative city council then gave it Rose's name. Rose Hill Cemetery is now listed on the National Trust for Historic Places. (International Postcard Co. #723, *c.* 1910, color.)

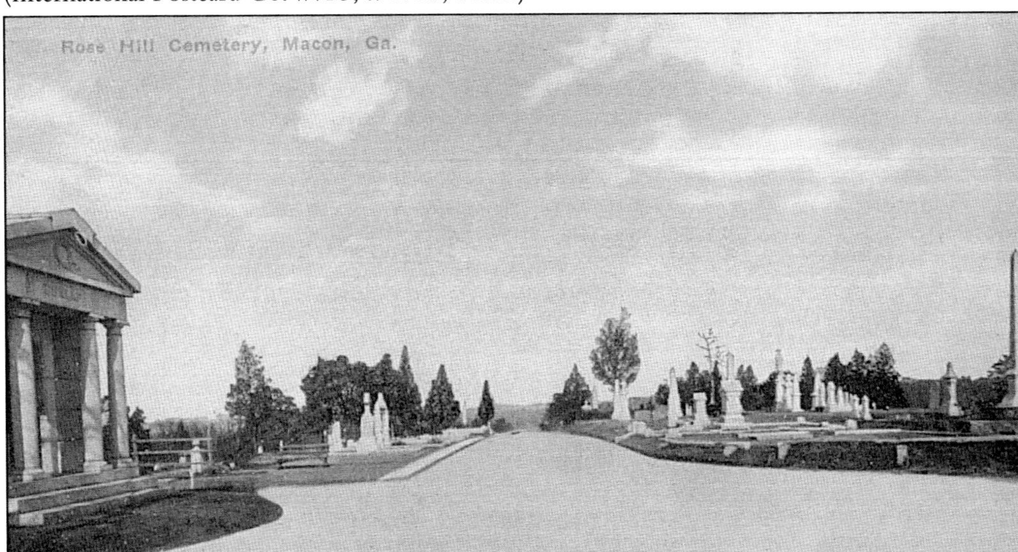

In the late 1860s, the Ladies of the Memorial Society (which later evolved into the United Daughters of the Confederacy) universally decorated the graves of all those who died in the Civil War, both the Confederate soldiers and the Federal prisoners who died while at Central City Park's prison. One of the society's first labors, during the 1870s, was removing the bones of soldiers from the old abandoned cemetery and placing them alongside their comrades in Rose Hill Cemetery. (Unidentified publisher #60206, *c.* 1910, color.)

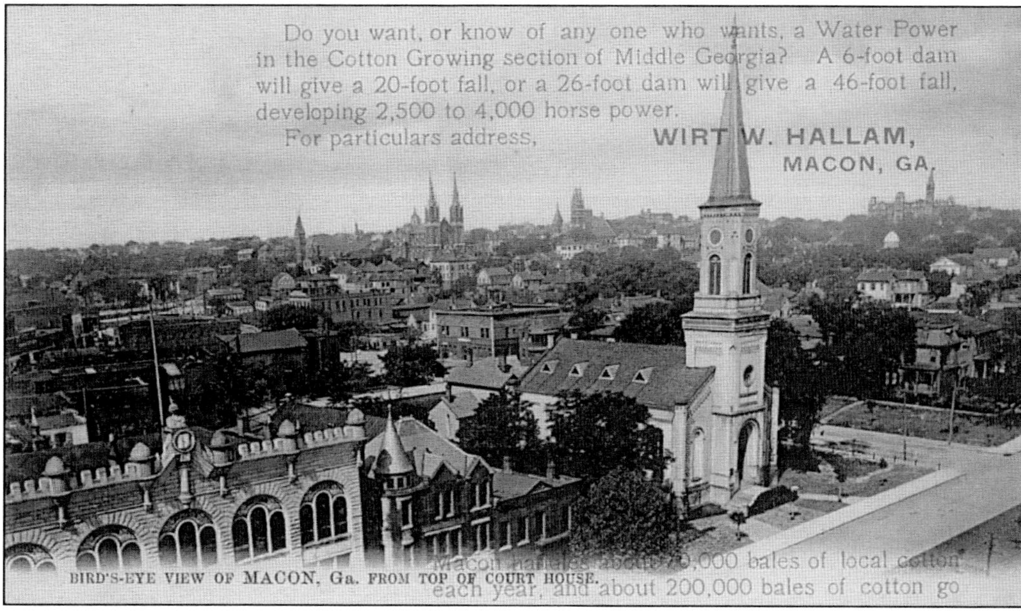

This bird's-eye view of Macon was taken from the top of the courthouse. This postcard was used by Wirt H. Hallam to promote the building of a dam in Middle Georgia. "Macon handles about 70,000 bales of local cotton each year and about 200,000 bales of cotton go through Macon compresses." (Raphael Tuck #1022, *c.* 1905, B/W.)

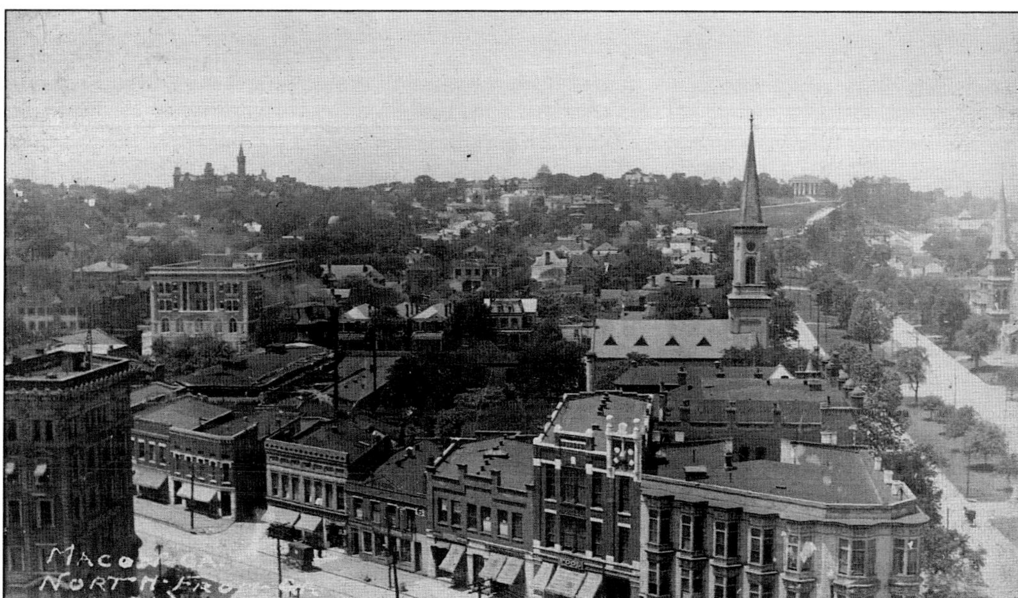

This Macon scene looks north from the Georgia Life Building. In the top right corner of the picture, one can see Coleman Hill. Wesleyan College can be seen in the top left corner. The Commercial Bank Building and the Drug Store of King Oliphant can be seen in the foreground. (Real photograph, *c.* 1921, B/W.)

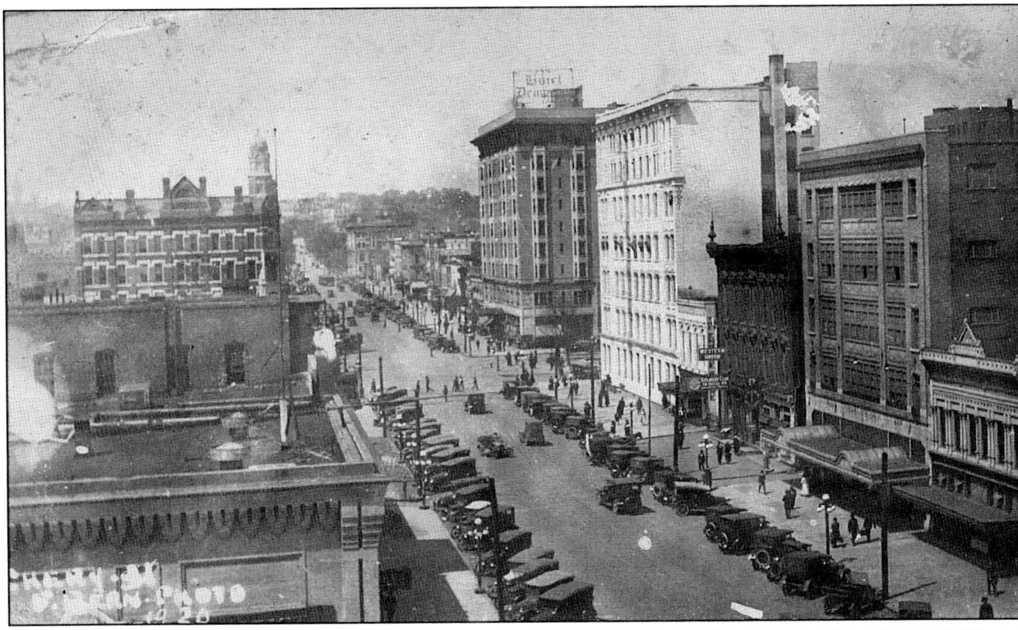

By the early 1920s, automobiles lined the streets of Macon, as can be seen in this view of Cherry Street. (Real photograph, *c.* 1920, B/W.)

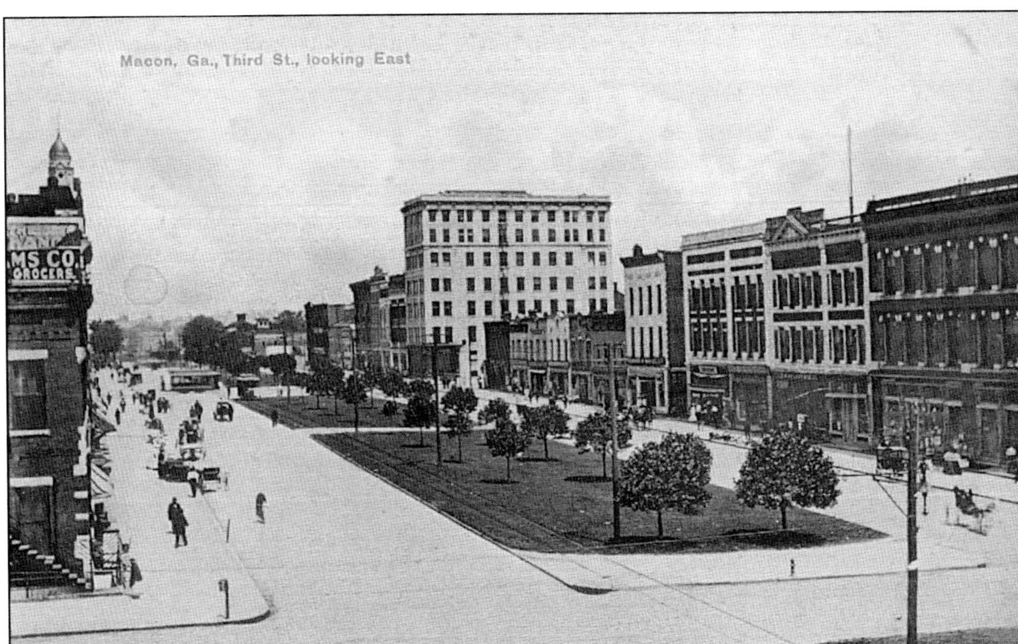

This view of Third Street is a great example of just how wide Macon's streets are. Visitors were always writing home about the streets. One person wrote, "Streets here are the widest I ever saw. 250 feet wide. Some fine flower gardens in the middle of the streets." Another person wrote, "I know you will notice the wideness of this street, but they are all like it, Macon being noted for such." (Peacock Series #8715, *c.* 1910, color.)

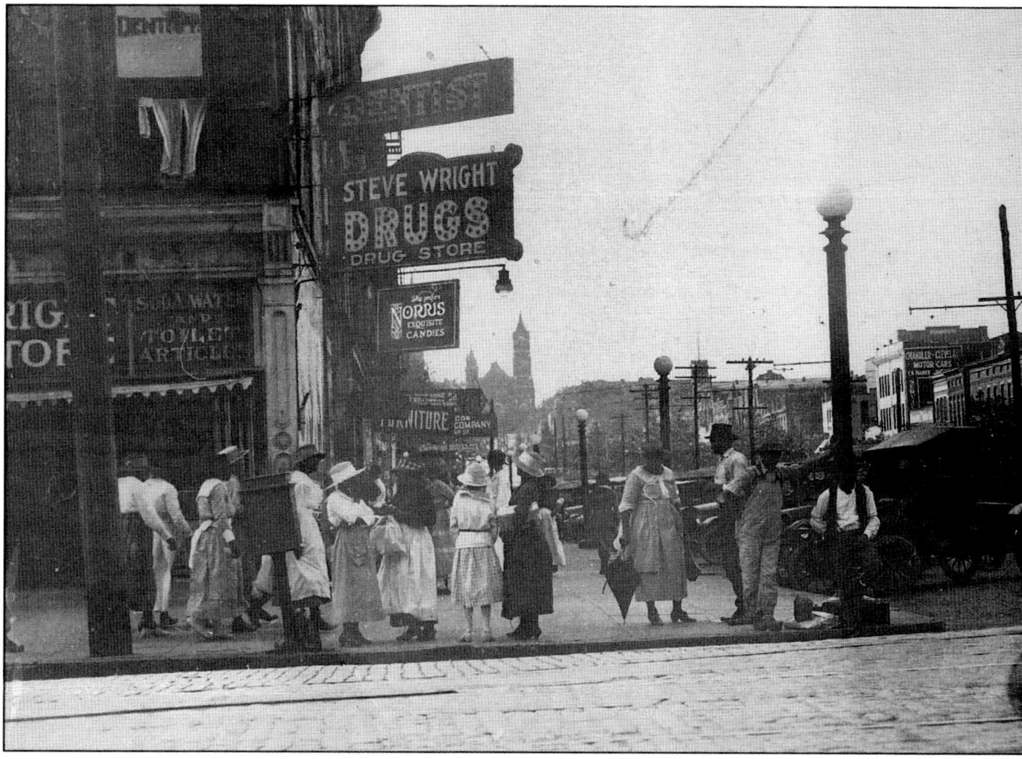

Shown here is a busy corner on Poplar Street in front of the Steve Wright Drug Store. Note the brick paved street. While Macon used the standard brick paving for many streets, in 1896, she was the first to use a new innovative technique called "shell concrete paving" on First Street. (Real photograph postcard, *c.* 1921, B/W.)

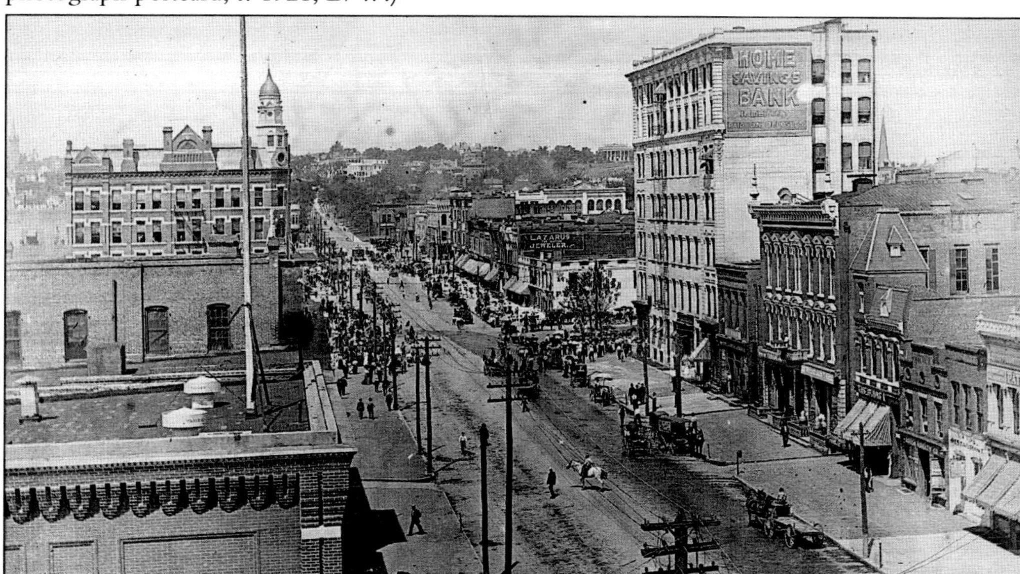

This photograph shows a dirt Cherry Street before the age of automobiles. Within just a few years, most city streets in Macon had been paved using either bricks or the new shell concrete method. (Real photograph, *c.* 1902, B/W.)

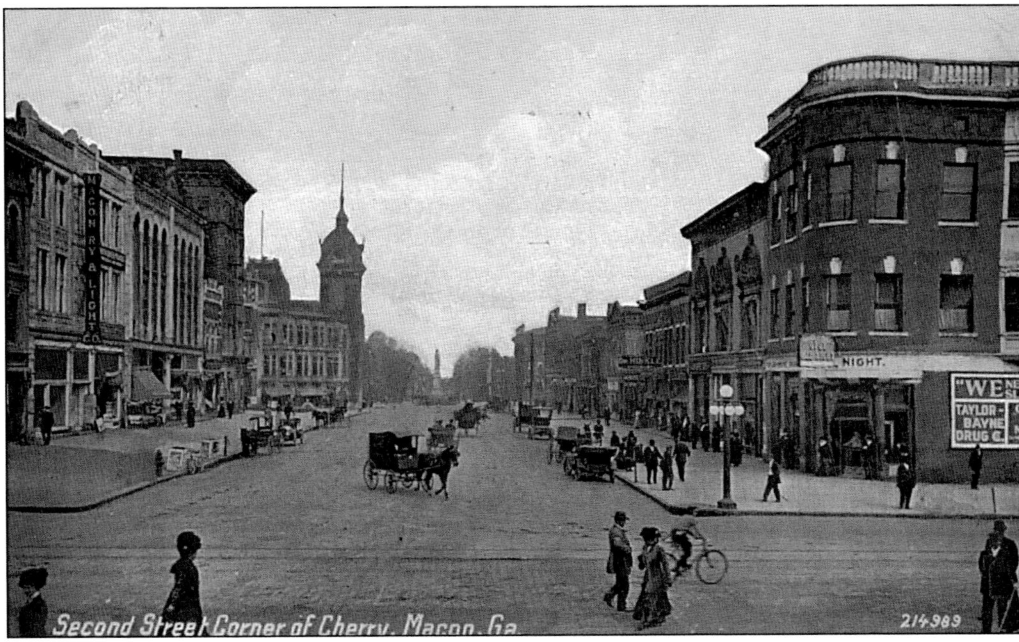

This view of the corner of Second and Cherry Streets reveals Macon's streets at the city's peak of transition. Note the streetcar rails, horse-drawn buggy, automobile, bicycle, and pedestrians, all on the recently brick-paved street. Macon was then, as now, changing with the times. (Leighton & Valentine Co. #214989, postmarked 1914, color.)

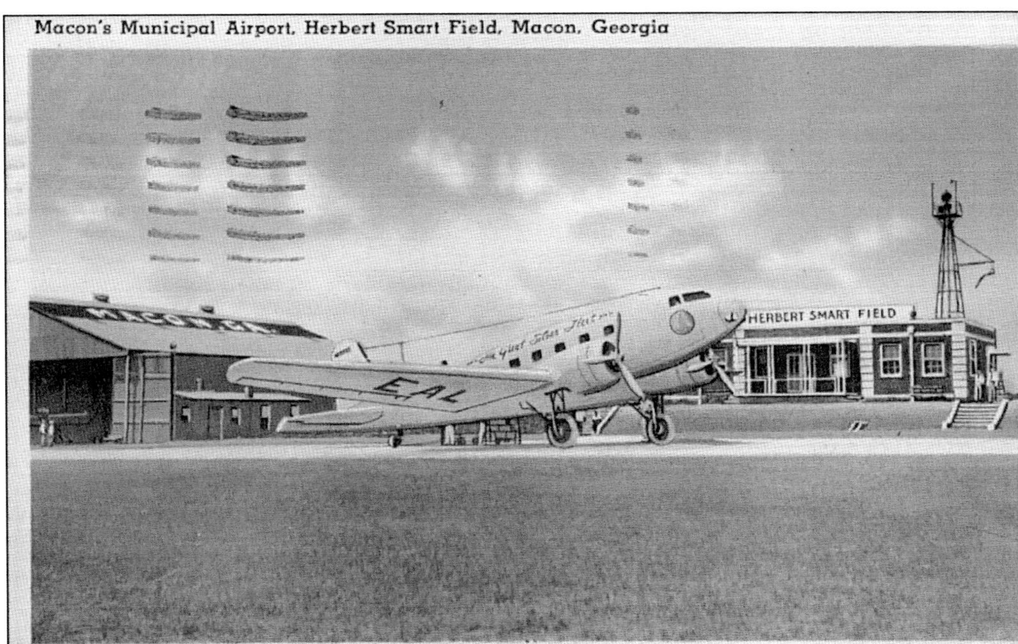

In keeping with her propensity for change and modernization, Macon built a municipal airport at Herbert Smart Field. Eastern Airline's Great Silver Fleet airliner, shown here, made regular stops and carried mail, passengers, and express. (Tichnor Quality Views #65055, postmarked 1943, color.)

Index

Academy of Music 72
Alexander Schools 55
Alexander, Elam 55
American National Bank 104, 109
Animals 36, 37, 126
Auditorium, Municipal 116
Automobiles 38, 124
Aviation 39, 40, 126
Bacon, A.O. 66, 76
Bacon's Field Park 76
Ballard Normal School 52
Banker's Health & Life Insurance Co. 112
Bartram, William 7
Bibb, William Wyatt 8
Block, A. 81
Bridges 28, 30, 31
Brown House Hotel 92, 93, 113
Burden Smith & Co. 105
Callaway, James 121
Camp Joycliff 74
Central City Park 39, 40, 64, 65, 122
Central of Georgia RR 27, 30, 31, 115
Chapman's Pharmacy 111
Cherokee Club 70
Cherry Street 18, 69, 108, 124, 125
Christ Church 59
Christian Church 60
Citizens National Bank 104
City Hall 24, 90, 113, 114, 116
Cobb, Major John A. 26
Coleman, S.T. 78
College Inn 98
Commercial Bank Building 26, 105, 123
Confederate 15, 80, 122
Confederate Cannons 7, 14, 16, 24
Confederate Monument 21, 66, 117
Confederate Veterans Reunion 15-24, 113
Cook, Captain Phil 7
Cook, Martha Pearson 7
Cotton 25, 64, 99, 100, 101, 102, 114, 123
County Courthouse 92, 117
Creek Indians 7
Crowles-Bond-O'Neil 23
Crump's Park 73
Daughters of the American Revolution 14
Davis, Jefferson 14, 23, 90
De Soto 7
Drug Store of King & Oliphant 107, 123
Ellisonian Apartments 87
Exchange Bank 103
Federal Courthouse 115
Fire Department 118, 119
First Baptist Church 59
First Presbyterian Church 24
Fort Hawkins 7, 14
G. Bernd & Co. 68, 110, 111
Gate 22, 67
Georgia - Alabama Business College 51
Georgia Academy for the Blind 47
Georgia Avenue 88
Georgia Casualty Building 109, 123
Georgia Life Insurance 109, 123
Georgia State Fair 15, 19, 23, 65, 67, 68, 110
Girl in the Fountain 113
Grand Opera House, Grand Building 72, 92, 112
Gresham High School 48
Harris & Co. Shoe Store 18
Hawkins, Benjamin 7, 14
Hay House 80
Heard's Warehouse 99
Herbert Smart Field - Municipal Airport 126
Hotel Arcadia 92
Hotel Dempsey 97
Hotel Dinkler 95
Hotel Lanier 89, 90, 91
Hotel Macon 94
Hotel Southland 96
Hotel Williams 96
John G. Gordon Camp 16
Johnson, Col. William B. 80
Johnson, J. Marsh 20, 23, 85
Johnson, William McEwin 85
Jordan, R.G. 83
Junior Chamber of Commerce 120
Katherine Court 84
Kelly, Dr. A.R. 9
Kennedy, J. Russell 8
Knights of Pythas 52
L. McManus Co. 102
Ladies of the Memorial Society 7, 21, 122
Lakeside Park 74, 75
Lamar, Taylor, & Riley Drug Co. 69, 106
Lanier High School 49
Lanier, Sidney, 79
Log Cabin Club 70

Macon Hospital 121
Macon Railway & Light Company 73
Macon Shoe Company 108
Macon, Nathaniel 8, 14
Masonic Home 66
Masse, W.J.78
Mercer University 23, 44-46
Merchants & Mechanics Savings Bank 103
Middle Georgia Hospital 121
Miller High School 49
Monroe Railroad & Banking 8, 27, 114
Moseley, Warren A. 16
Mount De Sales 53
Mulberry Presbyterian Church 61
Mulberry Street 66, 82, 84
Mulberry Street Methodist Church 62
Murray & Sparks Drug 107
Nancy Hanks 30
Navarro Apartments 87
Newtown 8
Nisbet School 56
North Carolina, The 8
Novelty Studio 112
Ocmulgee Indian Mounds, 7, 9-14
Ocmulgee River 7, 25 ,26, 28, 30, 31, 123
Ocmulgee, The 8
Orange Street 88
Parades 18, 63, 66, 67, 69
Park Hotel 16
Parker Brooks Construction Co. 29
Perry 83
Poplar Street 37, 102, 125
Post Office 115
Public Library & Historical Society 120
Queen of the Reunion 20, 21
Racetrack 18, 68
Rhodes Furniture 109
Riverboat 25, 26
Riverboat Bell 26
Rose Hill Cemetery 122
Rose, Simri 122
S.H. Kress Store 109
Second Street 100, 108, 126
Second Street School 56
Shriner's 66
Smithsonian Institute 9, 11
Southern Railroad 28, 33
Southern Railroad Depot 34
Speer, Judge 79
St. Joseph's Roman Catholic Church 58, 60
St. Paul's Episcopal Church 60
St. Peter's Claver 54
St. Stanislaus College 50
Stanley's Business College 52
Steve Wright Drug Store 125
Stevens, William P. 80
Stewart A.M. Episcopal Church 57
Stratford Academy 23
Synagogue 61
Taft, President William Howard 63, 64
Taylor - Bayne Drug Store 108
Tent City 16, 18
Terminal Hotel 98
Terminal Station 35, 98
Third Street 36, 109, 125
Train Wrecks 32, 33
Treaty of Indian Springs7
Tremont-Temple Baptist Church 57
Union Station 92
Union, Federalist 21, 22, 122
United Daughters of the Confederacy 122
Volunteer's Armory 22
Wadley, William M. 115
War of 1812 7, 11
Washington Block Building 111
Washington Library 120
Washington Park 76
Wesleyan College 41-43, 123
White City Amusement Park 73
Whittle School 54
William's Private Sanitarium 121
Willingham, E.J. 82
Willingham's Warehouse 63, 64, 100, 101
Wilson, General 23
Women of the South - Monument 114
YMCA 16, 71
YWCA 74